*Culture and
Customs of
Jamaica*

Culture and Customs of Jamaica

∽◦∾

Martin Mordecai
and
Pamela Mordecai

Culture and Customs of Latin America
and the Caribbean
Peter Standish, Series Editor

GREENWOOD PRESS
Westport, Connecticut • London

Library of Congress Cataloging-in-Publication Data

Mordecai, Martin.
    Culture and customs of Jamaica / Martin Mordecai and Pamela Mordecai.
      p.   cm.—(Culture and customs of Latin America and the Caribbean, ISSN 1521–8856)
    Includes bibliographical references (p. –) and index.
    ISBN 0–313–30534–X (alk. paper)
    1. Jamaica—Civilization.   2. Jamaica—Social life and customs.   3. Popular
culture—Jamaica.   I. Mordecai, Pamela.   II. Title.   III. Series.
    F1874.M67   2001
    972.92—dc21   00–035340

British Library Cataloguing in Publication Data is available.

Library of Congress Catalog Card Number: 00–035340
ISBN: 978-0-313-36059-6 (pbk.)
ISSN: 1521–8856

First published in 2001

Greenwood Press, 88 Post Road West, Westport, CT 06881
An imprint of Greenwood Publishing Group, Inc.
www.greenwood.com

Printed in the United States of America

The paper used in this book complies with the
Permanent Paper Standard issued by the National
Information Standards Organization (Z39.48–1984).

P

In order to keep this title in print and available to the academic community, this edition
was produced using digital reprint technology in a relatively short print run. This would
not have been attainable using traditional methods. Although the cover has been changed
from its original appearance, the text remains the same and all materials and methods
used still conform to the highest book-making standards.

Copyright Acknowledgments

The authors and publisher gratefully acknowledge permission for the use of the following material:

Extract from DE MAN is used by permission of Pamela Mordecai and Sister Vision Press.

Edward Baugh's poem "People Poem (The Leader Speaks)" from A TALE FROM THE RAINFOREST, Kingston: Sandberry Press, 1988 is used by permission of Sandberry Press.

Dennis Scott's poem "Birdwalk" from DREADWALK, London and Port of Spain: New Beacon Press, 1982 is used by permission of Joy R. Scott, Executor, Estate of Dennis C. Scott.

Mervyn Morris's poem "Windscreen" from EXAMINATION CENTRE, London and Port of Spain: New Beacon Press, 1993 is used by permission of New Beacon Press.

Extract from Louise Bennett's poem "Back to Africa" is used by permission of the poet.

All photographs appear by courtesy of Martin Mordecai.

Contents

A photo essay follows p. 84

Series Foreword

"CULTURE" is a problematic word. In everyday language we tend to use it in at least two senses. On the one hand we speak of cultured people and places full of culture, uses that imply a knowledge or presence of certain forms of behavior or of artistic expression that are socially prestigious. In this sense large cities and prosperous people tend to be seen as the most cultured. On the other hand, there is an interpretation of "culture" that is broader and more anthropological; culture in this broader sense refers to whatever traditions, beliefs, customs, and creative activities characterize a given community—in short, it refers to what makes that community different from others. In this second sense, everyone has culture; indeed, it is impossible to be without culture.

The problems associated with the idea of culture have been exacerbated in recent years by two trends: less respectful use of language and a greater blurring of cultural differences. Nowadays, "culture" often means little more than behavior, attitude, or atmosphere. We hear about the culture of the boardroom, of the football team, of the marketplace; there are books with titles like *The Culture of War* by Richard Gabriel (Greenwood, 1990) and *The Culture of Narcissism* by Christopher Lasch (1979). In fact, as Christopher Clausen points out in an article published in the *American Scholar* (Summer 1996), we have gotten ourselves into trouble by using the term so sloppily.

People who study culture generally assume that culture (in the anthropological sense) is learned, not genetically determined. Another general assumption made in these days of multiculturalism has been that cultural differences should be respected rather than put under pressure to change. But these assumptions, too, have sometimes proved to be problematic. For instance, multiculturalism is a fine ideal, but in practice it is not always easy to reconcile with the beliefs of the very people who advocate it: for example, is female circumcision an issue of human rights or just a different cultural practice?

The blurring of cultural differences is a process that began with the steamship, increased with radio, and is now racing ahead with the Internet. We are becoming globally homogenized. Since the English-speaking world (and the United States in particular) is the dominant force behind this process of homogenization, it behooves us to make efforts to understand the sensibilities of members of other cultures.

This series of books, a contribution toward that greater understanding, deals with the neighbors of the United States, with people who have just as much right to call themselves Americans. What are the historical, institutional, religious, and artistic features that make up the modern culture of such peoples as the Haitians, the Chileans, the Jamaicans, and the Guatemalans? How are their habits and assumptions different from our own? What can we learn from them? As we familiarize ourselves with the ways of other countries, we come to see our own from a new perspective.

Each volume in the series focuses on a single country. With slight variations to accommodate national differences, each begins by outlining the historical, political, ethnic, geographical, and linguistic context, as well as the religious and social customs, and then proceeds to a discussion of a variety of artistic activities, including the press, the media, the cinema, music, literature, and the visual and performing arts. The authors are all intimately acquainted with the countries concerned: some were born or brought up in them, and each has a professional commitment to enhancing the understanding of the culture in question.

We are inclined to suppose that our ways of thinking and behaving are normal. And so they are . . . for us. We all need to realize that ours is only one culture among many, and that it is hard to establish by any rational criteria that ours as a whole is any better (or worse) than any other. As individual members of our immediate community, we know that we must learn to respect our differences from each other. Respect for differences between cultures is no less vital. This is particularly true of the United States, a nation of immigrants that sometimes seems to be bent on destroying variety at home, and, worse still, on having others follow suit. By learning about other people's cultures, we come to understand and respect them; we earn their respect for us; and, not least, we see ourselves in a new light.

Peter Standish
East Carolina University

Acknowledgments

WE WOULD LIKE to acknowledge the generous assistance of the following persons who made valuable inputs into the creation of this book: Mervyn Alleyne, Edward Baugh, Lawrence Carrington, Barry Chevannes, Arthur Dayfoot, Gloria Escoffery, Barbara Gloudon, Ruby King, Olive Lewin, Irina Leyva, Daniel Mordecai, Rachel Mordecai, Mervyn Morris, Sandra Minott Phillips, Michael Ramsey, Barbara Requa, Olive Senior, Robert Stewart, Eugene Williams, Karin Wilson, Betty Wilson, and Donald Wilson.

We also acknowledge the invaluable participation of Peter Standish, the series editor, and of Wendi Schnaufer and Rebecca Ardwin of Greenwood, whose patient encouragement kept the project under sail, through occasionally rough waters, to final harbor.

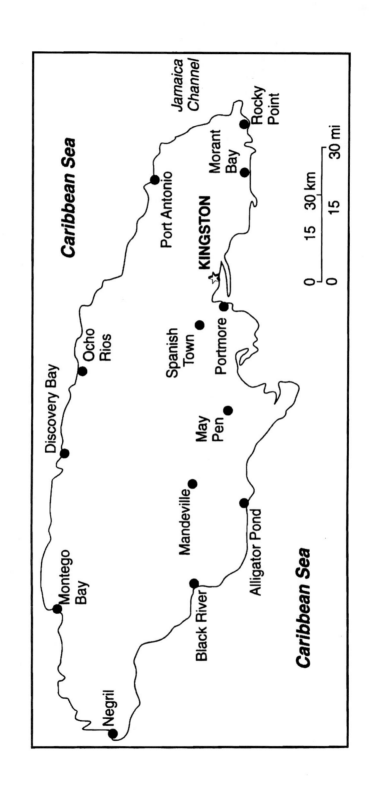

Introduction

THIS BOOK is an introduction to the customs and culture of Jamaica. We have taken a generally historical approach, not only in the plainly historical first section but in most of the other sections thereafter. This approach may seem to lead to a certain amount of repetitiveness. But the advantage, which we choose to emphasize, is that across chapters and topics the reader can have an idea of the wider society at a given point in time. Thus, for example, in pointing to the things that black nationalist Marcus Garvey did, in respect to the theater, politics, education, and so forth, the reader will get an idea not only of the breadth of Garvey's interests and vision, but of his impact on his society in several areas. And in placing Garvey within a historical narrative, one can see how the Jamaica of today evolved out of what went before, just as Garvey's work built on what went before him.

At the same time, space and format do not permit more than a cursory treatment of Garvey's *ideas*, or of his personality. This is also true of the treatment of many other individuals and Jamaican customs and cultural facets. Regrettably, important things and persons, of necessity, have been omitted from this narrative altogether. As for the structure, we felt that a narrative best suited not only our personal view of our country but the country's view of itself, as a society still in the process of creating itself.

We have tried to provide as comprehensive a bibliography as possible, and arranged it according to the chapters, so that readers and those wishing to go deeper into a particular topic can find a way. We would also like to acknowledge a few texts that were consulted across chapters, several times on numberless topics.

- *The Dictionary of Caribbean English Usage*, by Richard Allsopp, published in 1996 by Oxford University Press;
- *Jamaica Talk: Three Hundred Years of the English Language*, by Frederic G. Cassidy, published in 1961 by Macmillan and the Institute of Jamaica;
- *The A–Z of Jamaican Heritage*, by Olive Senior, published in 1983 by Heinemann and The Gleaner Company. An expanded edition of this important work is in preparation.

Finally, we must also cite two journals, *Jamaica Journal* (Institute of Jamaica) and *Caribbean Quarterly* (University of the West Indies), in which the student will find a compendium of scholarly but accessible writing on every facet of Jamaican life and thought. These journals may not be found in every library but are indexed in the Hispanic American Periodicals Index (HAPI) and available on microfilm.

Despite using these authoritative sources as carefully as we could, we take full responsibility for any and all errors in the text.

Chronology

Circa A.D. 600	The Taino (Arawaks) begin establishing settlements
1492	Christopher Columbus arrives at Discovery Bay, St. Ann, on his second voyage to the 'new world'
1509	Spain takes formal possession of Jamaica
1510	Sevilla la Nueva (New Seville) founded; abandoned in 1534, capital moved to Villa de la Vega (later, Spanish Town)
1611	Census shows 523 Spanish, 558 slaves, 107 free blacks, 74 Taino, and 75 'newcomers'
1655	English army captures Jamaica; Spanish retreat; rogue soldiers and freed slaves (maroons) wage guerrilla war until 1660
1670	Jamaica ceded to England in Treaty of Madrid
1692	Earthquake destroys Port Royal
1738	Peace treaty with Maroons signed
1760	First large-scale slave rebellion, in northeastern parish of St. Mary, put down by militia and troops
1764	Population estimated at 166,454, of which 140,454 are slaves

1795–1796	Second Maroon War, in Trelawny; defeated Maroons transported to Canada, and eventually Sierra Leone
1808	Abolition of the slave trade to British colonies; there are about 320,000 slaves in Jamaica
1815	Simon Bolivar, the Liberator, spends several months in Jamaica; writes his "Letter from Jamaica"
1830	Slave rebellion in western parishes
1831–1832	Final, and biggest, slave rebellion, led by Deacon Sam Sharpe
1834	Abolition of slavery; system of apprenticeship instituted, for six years; 313,000 slaves in Jamaica
1838	Full emancipation from slavery
1841	Arrival of first indentured Africans, to provide labor on sugar estates
1845	First indentured workers from India arrive
1848	Policy of free trade adopted by British government, removing preferential treatment for colonial exports, including sugar
1865	Morant Bay uprising; Paul Bogle and George William Gordon hanged
1866	Jamaican Assembly dissolves itself; Crown Colony government, meaning direct rule from Britain, begins
1872	Capital moved from Spanish Town to Kingston
1879	Institute of Jamaica established "for the encouragement of literature, science and art."
1892	Free elementary education instituted
1907	Major earthquake, followed by fire, destroys much of downtown Kingston
1914	Marcus Garvey founds the United Negro Improvement Association (UNIA) in Jamaica
1938	Labor unrest; Bustamante Industrial Trades Union, and People's National Party formed

1944	First general election under universal adult sufferage won by Jamaica Labour Party, formed previous year; new constitution proclaimed, giving more power to local elected officials
1955	People's National Party wins office for first time
1957	Internal self government established
1958	West Indies Federation comes into being
1961	Jamaica elects to leave Federation, leading to its demise the following year
1962	Jamaica achieves full political independence under the leadership of Alexander Bustamante
1964	Remains of Marcus Mosiah Garvey (d. 1940, London), first national hero, returned to Jamaica and reburied
1966	State visit of His Imperial Majesty Haile Selassie I, Emperor of Ethiopia
1967	Jamaica Labour Party returned to office in first post-independence general election; new prime minister, Donald Sangster, dies one month later of brain hemorrhage; Hugh Shearer appointed prime minister
1969	Currency changeover to dollars and cents
1972	People's National Party elected to office; Michael Manley appointed prime minister
1974	Higher royalties for bauxite imposed on foreign companies mining in Jamaica, after breakdown of negotiations
1976	People's National Party returned to office with increased majority in enlarged Parliament
1980	Jamaica Labour Party returned to office with largest majority in country's history
1983	Jamaica Labour Party calls snap election; People's National Party boycotts the polls, resulting in the first single-party Parliament in the country's history
1989	People's National Party returned to office under Michael Manley

1

Context

LOCATION

JAMAICA is the third largest of a chain of four islands (Cuba, Hispaniola, Jamaica, and Puerto Rico) known as the Greater Antilles which form the northern boundary of the Caribbean Sea. At its longest axis, roughly east to west, the island measures 146 miles (235 km); it varies in width from 22 miles (35 km) to 51 miles (82 km); its total area is 4,411 square miles (11,244 sq km).

Jamaica is very mountainous and is itself the tip of a submerged mountain. It is part of a range that also created Hispaniola, Puerto Rico, and the string of smaller islands running south to Trinidad, and the Venezuelan mountains bracketing the Gulf of Paria. The highest point in Jamaica, Blue Mountain Peak, rises to 7,404 feet (2,225 m) in the northeastern part of the island. The island presents all the common geophysical features (high mountains, flat plains, gorges, sloping valleys, waterfalls, marshland, and tropical rain forest) as well as a few unusual features of its own (the cockpit country, patches of temperate rain forest) in a relatively small area, making for a splendid variety of scenery and micro-climates. Its first European visitor, Christopher Columbus, was reported as describing it as "the fairest isle that eyes have beheld," an opinion approved by millions of visitors since then.

Jamaicans have a deep love for the landscape of their native country, never mind that they do not always treat the land with the deserved respect. Also, they are very conscious of their country being part of the archipelago of islands that is the Caribbean, and they acknowledge their Caribbean-ness.

But they are aware, too—history has prepared them—of being a small unit in the geographic and cultural shadow of much larger entities.

GEOLOGY

About two-thirds of the island is covered with sedimentary rock, primarily white limestone, up to 8,202 feet (2,500 m) deep in some places, and a smaller amount of yellow. In some of the limestone hills bauxite, the ore from which aluminum is made, is found in large quantities. At one time Jamaica was the largest exporter of the ore in the world, and it remains the foundation of the island's modern economy. The limestone also provides the main ingredient for cement, which, because of the threat from earthquakes and hurricanes, is extensively used in building. Large sedimentary deposits created several distinct alluvial plains on which the major agricultural and settlement areas share increasingly precious space.

The two main geological features of the island also infuse the main currents of its history and socioeconomic development. The plains have been and continue to be the site of large-scale agriculture: cattle-rearing in the Spanish period, then sugar, the foundation for the slave economy and society. The hills were the redoubt of the Maroons, symbols of freedom in that period; immediately after Emancipation (1838) the ex-slaves left the plantations by the thousands to clear small holdings in the hills where they planted coffee, bananas, and subsistence crops and raised small livestock for their own needs and to trade at market.

Smaller areas of igneous, or volcanic, and metamorphic rocks, formed in the early eons of the island's geologic life, are to be found in the higher mountain ranges, especially to the east. These have yielded, over the years, small quantities of iron ore, copper, lead, zinc, and gold; new explorations have renewed interest in gold in two areas of the country.

CLIMATE

The island displays a warm, tropical maritime climate all year round. The popular portrayal of Jamaica (and indeed the other Caribbean islands) as being "the land of sea and sun" is absolutely correct. The sea is never very far away, and influences most aspects of physical life in the island. Coastal regions receive an average of eight hours of sunshine every day; inland, where afternoon showers and cloudiness are more common, the average is six hours of sunshine daily. Average temperatures throughout the year are between 60°F (16°C) and 90°F (31°C); more often they are at the higher end of the scale. During the course of a day, however, the temperature may vary as much as 10°C.

The price paid for being located in these balmy latitudes can be a high one. Hurricanes, tropical cyclones that produce intense and prolonged rainfall, strong winds, and ocean waves or storm surges, are the natural scourge of the Caribbean islands. Hurricanes usually form in the Atlantic Ocean, moving into the Caribbean or the Gulf of Mexico, or staying their course through the Atlantic, and Jamaica is vulnerable from all three directions. Only a small number of those that form actually hit the island (meaning that the center or 'eye' of the storm system passes over land), but wind and rain from a proximate system can cause tremendous damage and dislocate the national economy. Fifteen hurricanes have hit Jamaica directly over the past century, but the island has been threatened and damaged by countless others.

Earthquakes are another hazard as the island is located near the northern edge of the Caribbean Plate. Movement between this plate and the North American Plate can release enormous energy. Earthquakes occur more frequently than hurricanes, with at least one noticeable tremor each year. Cataclysmic occurrences are much more rare, however. Two in the late seventeenth century destroyed Port Royal, across the harbor from Kingston, the capital, and one in the late nineteenth century devastated Montego Bay. In 1907, along with the fire that followed immediately, a quake leveled much of the city of Kingston. The inevitability of another such occurrence at some unknowable point in future time accords a special menace to this natural phenomenon.

DEMOGRAPHICS AND ADMINISTRATION

Demographics

As a consequence of its history and its geographical position, Jamaica has been a meeting place for almost all nations and races. Its motto, adopted upon independence in 1962, is: "Out of many one people." Many of today's Jamaicans are descendants of persons who arrived after the English capture in 1655. By then the native Taino had disappeared into the African and European populations; and while many Jamaicans today carry Spanish surnames, these derive from more recent migrations, mainly from Cuba over the past century. The antecedents of today's Jamaicans came mainly from Africa, and in smaller numbers from Europe, India, China, and the Mediterranean; the last three areas became important sources of population after 1850.

Table 1.1
Demographic Makeup of Jamaican Population

Ethnic group	% of total population
Negro/Black	90.4
East Indian	1.3
Chinese	0.2
White	0.2
Mixed/Negro	7.3
Other races	0.1
Not stated	0.5
ALL RACES	100

The official figures from the Statistical Institute of Jamaica (Table 1.1), with projections based on the 1991 Census, tell one sort of story. The story 'on the ground,' so to speak, is that in the crucible of a small island in one of the most traversed regions of the world, the average Jamaican has a complex ethnicity that defies the simplistic labels often employed by other societies. No Jamaican whose family has been there for more than three generations could honestly claim a pure ethnicity: the family tree has too many roots.

Officially, the population reached 2.5 million people in 1995, with a growth rate at that time of 1.1 percent. There were 1 percent more women than men. According to the 1991 census figures, more than 40 percent of the population was nineteen years old or younger. For complex historical and cultural reasons, formalized marriage is not the universal norm that it is in some societies. The last census records fewer than 20 percent of the adult population as being married. The census-takers do not apparently have a category for unformalized arrangements, often called common-law marriages, which are sometimes more stable and longer lasting than those made by church or civil authorities. Indeed, it was only in the 1970s that the law, for purposes of inheritance and related issues, abolished distinctions between 'legitimate' and 'illegitimate' children.

Administration

Jamaica's 2.5 million people live in an administrative entity divided into three counties—Cornwall, Middlesex, and Surrey—which are further di-

Table 1.2
Division of Jamaica by County and Parish (*with Parish Capitals*)

Cornwall	Middlesex	Surrey
St. Elizabeth (*Black River*)	St. Catherine (*Spanish Town*)	Kingston and St. Andrew (*Kingston*)
Trelawny (*Falmouth*)	Clarendon (*May Pen*)	St. Thomas (*Morant Bay*)
St. James (*Montego Bay*)	St. Ann (*St. Ann's Bay*)	Portland (*Port Antonio*)
Hanover (*Lucea*)	St. Mary (*Port Maria*)	
Westmoreland (*Savanna-la-Mar*)	Manchester (*Mandeville*)	

vided into fourteen parishes (Table 1.2). The number of parishes has not always been the same: when they were established in 1664 there were only seven; in the 1840s there were as many as twenty-two. In 1867 the parishes were reduced to the fourteen that exist today. But in administrative terms there are really thirteen units, as Kingston and St. Andrew are effectively one, known as the Corporate Area, or simply Kingston, which is also the name of the country's capital city.

The parish council meets to supervise the running of the parish. All things are relative, and parish councils today do not enjoy the authority and power that they did, say, before World War II. But they are still sources of patronage, such as road contracts, licenses for certain kinds of business, and development approvals.

Like other modern societies, Jamaica has seen its population, especially its young people, increasingly drift from the rural areas into the urban centers. Within one generation, market towns have been transformed into small cities. The capital, Kingston, is now in reality the nucleus of a conurbation stretching across three parishes and containing over 1 million people, with thousands more traveling in from outlying towns and villages for daily employment. The attendant infrastructural problems—roads, water and sewerage, schools, hospitals—are persistent challenges for national and sectoral planners; competing demands on limited resources make the political decision-making arena the locus of far-reaching power.

HISTORY

Pre-Columbian

Jamaica, like most of the Caribbean islands, had been occupied for several centuries before the arrival of Christopher Columbus. In fact some of the islands have been continuously occupied since the Stone Age. The people whom Columbus found in the Caribbean had come from the south, from the northeastern shoulder of the South American continent where their kinsmen and women (called Amerindians in Guyana) still live.

The first Jamaicans came to be known as Arawaks, a word thought to mean 'eaters of meal'—manioc, or cassava (a tuber), as it is known in Jamaica. Nowadays, they are more often called by the name they apparently gave themselves, Taino. They arrived in the seventh or eighth century A.D., having settled most of the islands from Trinidad through the Windward and Leeward Islands, and established large settlements in the four islands of the Greater Antilles. Haiti was their name for the island that the Spaniards renamed *La Isla Española*, and it was the major population center of the islands. The island where Columbus first stopped in May 1494 and called Santiago, or St. Jago (St. James), was first known by its inhabitants and their neighbors as Xaymaca.

The Taino were agriculturists of small stature who raised cassava, maize, and sweet potato, and caught fish, shellfish, and manatees (sea cows). They also hunted and ate birds, yellow snakes, conies (a small rodent now extinct), and the iguana, regarded as a great delicacy. In their villages, which were to be found in most parts of the island, they slept in *hamacs* (hammocks) and smoked *cohiba* (tobacco), which was cultivated on a large scale, in *tabacos* (pipes) or in tightly rolled tubes of the *cohiba* leaves, which looked like modern cigars. These practices were new to the Europeans and were quickly adopted.

Although their implements were of stone, the Taino built impressive dugout canoes from the trunks of cedar and silk cotton trees. They were of varying sizes; Columbus saw one that was 96 feet (29 m) long and 8 feet (2.5 m) wide. The art is dying now (and suitable trees are far less numerous in any case), but to this day Jamaican fishermen continue to build dugout canoes from the trunks of suitable trees.

The Taino had a religion complete with creation myths, male and female supreme beings, and a large number of spirits called *zemes*, which were embodied in wooden carvings, bones, skulls, and anything else believed to possess magical powers. Taino religion also ascribed to man a soul that went after death to *coyaba*, a place free from the tribulations of the world but full of pleasures like dancing and *batos*, a favorite ball game.

The Encounter

A veritable *coyaba*, or paradise, is how Jamaica seemed to Columbus at his first sighting in 1494—"the fairest island that eyes have beheld . . . the land seems to touch the sky" (Black 1983: 20). He named the place where he first dropped anchor Santa Gloria "on account of [its] beauty"; today it is known as St. Ann's Bay, and the parish of St. Ann is 'the Garden Parish' to Jamaicans. The Taino reaction to the arrival of Europeans was initially hostile. But eventually, as one historian put it, they "showed the Spaniards more kindness than they deserved" (Black 1983: 12), and, it should be said, more kindness than was returned.

Jamaica was used mainly to provide supplies (beef, hides, some cotton cloth) to Cuba and Hispaniola, and for expeditions to explore and occupy the potentially more valuable areas of South and Central America. After that important work was accomplished, Jamaica diminished even further in importance, and the settlers were largely left to their own devices to exist as best they could.

The Spaniards' first established settlement was in New Seville in St. Ann, founded in 1510. The site chosen was close to swamps and, therefore, unhealthy, and fourteen years later *Sevilla la Nueva* was abandoned. The settlers moved south over the central mountain ridge to the site that became the *Villa de la Vega*, or *St. Jago de la Vega*, later Spanish Town, which remained the capital of the island (under British rule as well) until 1872. From there the colonists spread out to establish settlements in most parts of the island, from Bluefields in the west to Morant Bay in the east.

The Taino provided the backbreaking labor to clear the land that the settlers claimed, to build their houses, plant their crops, rear and slaughter their animals, and hunt the other food that they wanted. It was work such as the Indians had never known before, and the European diseases, especially smallpox, decimated those who did not die from sheer cruelty and overwork. It is reported that thousands committed suicide by hanging themselves or drinking poisonous cassava juice; parents murdered their children to spare them this inheritance of oppression. When English soldiers arrived in the island in 1655, the Taino presence had ceased to be distinct, and survived only in the mingled blood of the living and the adopted cultural practices of the dead.

English Conquest and Consolidation

The English captured the island in order, as Jamaicans would say, to "wipe shame out dem yeye" (to save face). A large, rag-tag force of soldiers, sailors, and ships had been marshaled in England and the Caribbean and sent against the Spanish capital city of Santo Domingo in Hispaniola, then the administrative and maritime center of the Spanish presence in the region. This was the so-called Western Design of Oliver Cromwell, Protector of England: to contain Spain in Europe by attacking the routes by which ships carrying wealth (primarily silver and some gold) and supplies traveled from the Americas. The assault on Santo Domingo was a disaster for the English. Rather than return empty-handed, the expedition's leaders turned their sights on a target more congruent with their troops' powers of execution.

Jamaica at the time was occupied by only 1,500 or so Spaniards; a third of that population could bear arms. They were accustomed to raids from English and French privateers, conducted with the blessing of distant, hostile governments, who hoped to gain bounty from their citizens' predatory adventures. But these English soldiers stayed, and the Spanish withdrew from the capital, and eventually from the northern coast of the island itself, to Cuba and Hispaniola. They burned much of the city themselves and freed their slaves, thereby setting up for the English a military problem that stymied their best efforts at full conquest for almost a century. War with the Maroons, whose descendants harried the early settlers from impregnable mountain settlements, did not entirely cease until a treaty in 1739 gave them autonomy in the areas they controlled in return for cooperation in hunting down runaway slaves.

Under military governors, the prize was secured gradually, by a combination of compulsion and an appeal to greed. Garrisoned soldiers who survived—and hundreds did not—were turned into settlers by land grants and the ever-present threat of starvation. But the soldiers-turned-farmers could not work the land by themselves, and labor could not be brought there from England in sufficient numbers, either by inducement or force. Heat and disease took a heavy toll on those who did come.

On the other hand, Jamaica's size and topography held the promise of sustainability: its alluvial plains were suitable for large-scale cultivation of several crops, and for grazing; its mountains could support coffee and many European fruits and vegetables. The problem was labor. The solution to these problems lay all around them: sugar and slavery, both already entrenched in the Caribbean by the 1660s.

Slavery and Its Aftermath

Climate, topography, and soil were all new to the settlers in the Caribbean. Nevertheless, Spaniards flocked to Hispaniola and Cuba, Portuguese to what is now Brazil, and the English to Barbados, the first island intensively settled by them. In the 1630s, they went there in greater numbers than they did to Virginia. The lure was twofold: to escape from England, by then drifting toward civil war, and to cultivate tropical crops for profitable sale in European markets: tobacco, indigo dye, cotton, cocoa, ginger. These were crops which could be cultivated by the settlers themselves, with modest outlays for equipment and labor, whether hired or bought. Markets for these products proved unstable, rendering sustainable settlement uncertain.

Meanwhile, the colonists of other nationalities were successfully growing cane—the crop introduced (from the Pacific islands via India and Madeira) by Columbus on his second voyage, according to some reports—for sugar to supply the growing European market. English colonists on Barbados began to cultivate the crop on a large scale for export in 1640. With a land-size twenty-five times that of Barbados, Jamaica offered England the best prospect for becoming an exporter of sugar from its own plantations, to the mother country and the rest of the world. Beginning in 1664 with the first government-encouraged estates, fifty-seven plantations were established by 1673, and more than 400 by the centennial of English occupation, 1755. Sugar was the instrument that made Jamaica, for a period in the eighteenth century, the star in the British imperial crown: during that century, she became the world's leading producer of sugar.

By early in the eighteenth century the colonies became what they were to remain for another 200 years: monocultural, devoted to the cultivation of a single crop. This was true not only in Jamaica, but in the other English colonies like Barbados and St. Christopher (today St. Kitts) and the other European sugar-growing colonies: French-owned Martinique, Guadeloupe, and St. Domingue (today Haiti); Santo Domingo and Puerto Rico in Spanish hands; and the Guianas—Dutch (Suriname), English (Guyana), and French (Cayenne). These colonies produced other crops for export—among them coffee, timber, dyes, and cocoa—but none matched the importance of sugar until well into the nineteenth century.

The basis of sugar production and export, and of the immeasurable wealth created (mostly in the metropoles), was slavery. Slavery and sugar affected every aspect of life in the settler colonies and transformed them into colonies wherein the majority of people existed in a cycle of exploitation. The master and the slave both exploited the land in a relationship that had as its *raison d'être* the enrichment of factors in the homeland, and only incidentally in the colonies themselves. Economic activity was mainly directed at the fulfillment of this objective, and the political structure—a governor appointed from London, an elected assembly dominated by planters—ensured the primacy of those whose investment furthered its achievement (Knight 1990: 76).

Within twenty years of capturing Jamaica, the English whites found themselves a numerical minority, thus compromising one of the pillars of settler society. At the beginning of the eighteenth century there were already over 40,000 slaves in Jamaica; by the middle of the century, 130,000; and by 1800, double that number. At that point there were about 15,000 whites, a ratio of 1:20. Slaves were bought and brought from trading posts on the African coast, from today's Sierra Leone to Angola, though some slaves came from deeper in the continent. Jamaica was a major entrepôt and slave market for the Caribbean and the American colonies; but large numbers of those who came were bought locally.

The disparity in numbers and the brutality of the slave regime were threads of the same weave. The fear of rebellion, of being literally overwhelmed, was the organizing impetus of white society, in law and custom. And with good reason. The prospect of rebellion was real throughout the 170 years of slavery in Jamaica. Rebellions occurred with unsettling frequency, though only the last one, in 1831, threatened to become the islandwide uprising the whites dreaded.

In between large and small conflagrations there was the steady leakage of slaves away from estates into the hills to Maroon villages or to scavenge for themselves. Whites were surrounded by blacks: in the fields that the whites owned but the slaves worked, and in their houses that the blacks kept comfortable and functional. The whole island ran on the forced labor of people whose basic humanity was denied.

For many whites the odds were too great for comfort. In any case the real wealth in sugar was made in England. That was where credit was given—all estates ran on credit, ultimately—and where profits were realized after sale of the crop. A well-known accolade of the time "rich as a West Indian planter," derived from the lifestyle of 'planters' living in Europe rather than those in the colonies. Absentee proprietors were a standard feature of the sugar culture, as time passed becoming more numerous than estate owners who lived *in situ*. Their estates were handled by factotums called attorneys, though they were not usually lawyers. The sole interest of these professional managers lay in making a profit for themselves; they had no wider interest in either the land or the chattel on it, and were often harsher slave-masters than the owners.

It seemed to many whites in such colonies that theirs was a cruel fate: they were compelled to live in a situation of extreme hostility—from the climate and the slaves—to enrich persons living in the cultured cities of Europe on the profit from the colonials' dangerous labors. For such persons, validation—economic, social, cultural—was to be found elsewhere, in the metropole to which almost all, even those born in the colonies, hoped to return.

The spiritual focus of the slaves lay elsewhere, too. They also dreamt of returning to their mother country, and the large number of suicides during the notorious 'middle passage' between Africa and the Caribbean, and in their early days in the colonies, was less an escape from the rigors of bondage than an escape—so went the belief—back to the land of Africa. Despite sustained efforts at deculturation by the owners, backed by law, the attachment to Africa remained strong.

The proximity of blacks and whites led inevitably to intimacy, and to children who carried in them the blood of both races and embodied the dichotomies and deadly absurdities of slave society. They were born slaves, and some remained so all their lives, discounted, or with their very humanity denied, by their fathers, and distrusted by the blacks for their hated bloodline. In time, however, a class of brown Jamaicans, usually referred to as free colored, emerged. Significant in size—outnumbering whites two to one by the end of the eighteenth century—and often very wealthy, they were distrusted by both whites and blacks. Theirs was a highly circumscribed legal status, without many of the accepted attributes of citizenship of those times and with no vote, therefore having no representation in the local or national assemblies before 1830.

This frangible social order rested on the foundation of an overwhelming mass of 'nonpeople', the slaves. It is easy, given the uniformity of treatment, to view the slaves *as* mass. In fact there were many categories and divisions among them, based on origin and function. The identity of "African" is one that was forged by the middle passage, the brutal voyage between the west coast of that continent and the so-called New World. The slaves came from many parts of western and central Africa: from modern-day Senegal and Guinea through the Gulf of Guinea south to the coast of the modern Republic of Congo. They were (in Jamaica) predominantly Kromanti, Mandingo, and Ibo, but they were from several other peoples as well, even including Madagascars from east Africa. Each group had its own identity:

language, religion, cuisine, and so on. Some of them would have been torn from states that at the time were as large and as well-organized as were states in Europe.

Once in the new world, they were reculturated according to the primary needs of the slave society: submission and labor. The major actors in this process were other slaves, those who had already been adapted to the local situation or, after a time, born into it. They taught the new arrivals the necessary survival strategies in language, work, and social relations. Work in the house was less onerous than work in the field and, therefore, to be pre-ferred. But there was a price: house slaves were regarded with some suspicion by field slaves, as likely to be sympathetic to the interests of the masters and therefore untrustworthy; the epithet "house slave" is still a pejorative in the Caribbean. Ironically, house slaves were often prominent in rebellions, using their privileged position to gather information.

Thus the slave community was splintered into micro-cultures, which were under pressure to become as featureless as possible. Numerically it was in a state of constant, rapid evolution, with a very high turnover rate due to deaths, sales between plantations, and new arrivals. Labor defined life: rou-tinely twelve hours in the fields per day, longer in crop season; as well, the slaves were expected to provide most of their own food from provision grounds on the nonsugar lands of the plantation. (Root crops such as yams and eddoes are still called 'ground provisions' in Jamaica.)

Nevertheless, in this crucible of dysfunctional relationships, a society *was* created by the people who lived there, a creole society. The word *creole* has multiple meanings in the new world. In Spanish America it refers to people born in a colony "but not ancestrally indigenous to it" (Brathwaite 2000: xv). In the state of Louisiana it applies variously to the white francophone population and mulattos. In Brazil it was used to denote black slaves born there, and that is how it was used in Jamaica and some other colonies (though in Trinidad it is still used to describe white families of largely French and Portuguese extraction). Its roots are various; it may even have been a word first used by blacks themselves, those born in the colony, to distinguish themselves from those born in Africa (Allsopp 1996). The latter, on arrival, went through a period of 'seasoning' at the hands of creole slaves who had grown up within the system and place, and who inducted them into the exigencies of their new life: a process of *creolization*. With whites setting the operational parameters of the society, part of that process for the slaves meant learning aspects of the dominant culture.

On the other hand, the labor of slaves was the infrastructure on which every aspect of white life functioned. The black presence in white lives was ubiquitous; its influence inevitable. Cultural syncretism worked both ways: in dress, in music, in entertainment, and in language. Planters who visited Europe from the colonies often, to their chagrin, found themselves outsiders by virtue of their 'creolization.' Extensive documentation shows that the language spoken by creolized slaves *and* masters had become, by the middle of the eighteenth century, in essence the language that is still spoken by Jamaicans today. The issues of identity and race, of language as index of social class, continue to play themselves out in the culture and in the socio-political arena.

Slavery's End

It is difficult to know how many Africans were brought into Jamaica as slaves during the 170 or so years of English slavery there. Kingston, with a large protected harbor, was a busy transshipment port to other English colonies in the other islands and North America. In 1807, the year that the slave trade was abolished in the British Empire, there were about 350,000 slaves on the island. As opposition to the trade grew in England, the trading companies increased their activities, the result being a tremendous infusion of Africans into the colonies. In Jamaica alone 35 percent or so of the slaves in 1807 were African-born. The significance of this factor is to be seen in the important role played in all Jamaican slave rebellions by African-born slaves, especially the Akan (Schuler 1991).

The first decades of the nineteenth century were a troubled, tension-filled time. The planters watched helplessly as their fortunes and their support in Britain dwindled. There, they were under siege from two sides: the abolitionists, who, encouraged by the trade's banning, set their sights on destroying slavery itself; and the free traders, who wanted to dismantle protective barriers and give English consumers access to cheaper sugar from other producers like Brazil, Cuba, and Mauritius.

The English abolitionists had allies in Jamaica: nonconformist clergymen from Britain and the United States—some of these former slaves themselves—who established churches off the estates, taught those slaves who were prepared to take the risk (or could get their owners' permission, as some did) to learn to read and write. These men attracted a very special hostility from the planters and the chaplains of the established Anglican church, which had accommodated itself to the institutional structure of the island and made little effort to 'christianize' the slaves.

The slaves themselves were increasingly restive, some of them—primed by their religious reading and teaching—coming to believe by the end of the

1820s that the British parliament had already granted their liberty and that it was being willfully withheld by the Jamaican Assembly, whose members stated in a resolution in 1823 that the island's slaves were "as happy and comfortable, in every respect, as the laboring class in any part of the world."

The slaves kept abreast of measures taken on their behalf in London and of the actions of their masters in response. Their own response was rebellious, with uprisings in 1830 and 1831, the latter regarded as the final nail in slavery's coffin. It started at Christmas on an estate in western Jamaica. Christmas was the most important holiday for the slaves, when they were given extra rations and several days off work; normally, Sunday was the only rest day. At the end of the Christmas break, the slaves on this plantation, led by a Native Baptist deacon, Samuel Sharpe, refused to go back to work, initiating what was arguably the first strike in Caribbean history. Slaves on several other estates took heart, and in a matter of days the biggest rebellion in Jamaica's troublesome history was underway. In several parishes across the island, estate houses, factories, and fields were burnt. It was four months before order was fully restored on the last plantation. Fourteen whites, including soldiers, were killed. Retribution by the civil authorities was widespread and terrible: 580 slaves, including Sharpe, were hanged, and hundreds more were publicly and brutally flogged. Nonconformist missionaries were arrested and charged with inciting rebellion, though the charges could not be made to stick.

In August 1833 a bill providing for the abolition of slavery was passed in the British parliament, to be implemented across the Empire on August 1, 1834. But it was not the emancipation that the slaves had anticipated. Slavery as a legal construct was abolished, but the former slaves were required to give their former masters a stipulated number of hours of work (40½) without wages, while the masters were required to provide lodging, food, clothing, and medical attention. For the former slaves it was slavery without the name, while the former owners had none of the legal safeguards and bastions that had been their birthright.

Both sides resented the system of apprenticeship, as it was called. Thousands of blacks simply walked away from the plantations, striking out on their own. The former owners were delinquent in fulfilling their responsibilities. A system that the British parliament set for twelve years was abandoned after four. Emancipation, "Full Free" in the parlance of the ex-slaves, was proclaimed on August 1, 1838. The anniversary has remained an important Jamaican celebration.

Post-Emancipation

Emancipation removed the legal infrastructure of slavery, but it also re-moved the systems of support for both the plantation owners and the ex-slaves. The former slave was free not to work for his former owner, or indeed for anyone but himself. But he was not free to make use of the provision grounds on the estate or of the estate 'hospital,' or to receive the periodic handouts of clothing and imported food that were part of the routine of estate life under the unlamented institution.

Liberation of the slaves reduced the estate owner's assets, for which he was generously compensated by the British parliament—Jamaican planters re-ceiving almost one-third of the total reparations paid out across the Empire. It also sent up his costs, since labor now had to be paid for. These two factors, combined with the lower costs for sugar production to other (slave) producers around the world, resulted in a wage being offered to the former slaves by the planters that was derisory, and did as much as Emancipation itself to promote the establishment of an independent Jamaican peasantry.

After Emancipation in 1838 thousands of blacks withdrew their labor from the plantations and settled on Crown lands as peasants or small farmers. Some, with savings built up over years from the sale of foodstuffs from their provision grounds, and assisted by missionaries, were able to buy small plots for themselves. By 1840, according to one source, there were more than 7,800 such freeholders. As many as 200 'free villages,' as they were known, had been established by the early 1840s, many with church-organized finan-cial assistance from supporters abroad.

The Jamaican sugar industry had been in decline for some years before the end of slavery. In 1846 the British parliament passed a Free Trade Bill, under which the protective duties that had long favored British West Indian sugar exports were abolished. Many planters lost their holdings to the British merchants to whom they had been in debt for some time. Hundreds of planters and their families, and other whites, left the island during the mid- to late nineteenth century.

Economic and social factors were not the only ones at play. Throughout slavery and for much of the nineteenth century, mortality rates were high for all races on the island. In 1850 an epidemic of Asian cholera killed about 40,000 people—about 10 percent of the population. Two years later small-pox took a smaller but still significant number. Despite inflows of indentured African and Indian labor for the plantations—a scheme promoted by planters and funded by the British government—the population of Jamaica experi-enced a low rate of growth during the 1840s and 1850s. The 1860s started badly, with the American Civil War sending up the price of basic foodstuffs like cornmeal and flour.

The economic deterioration of the colony, in particular the desperate economic plight of the majority of the black population, marked by rising prices and droughts, and the long-standing resentment of white domination as a palpable factor in this deprivation, were the general reasons underlying the genesis of the Morant Bay Rebellion of 1865. As the Secretary of the Baptist Mission, Dr. Underhill, wrote to the British government after a visit to Jamaica: "the simple fact is, there is not sufficient employment for the people; there is neither work for them nor capital to employ them" (Gordon 1983: 20). The poor people of St. Ann's parish sent an appeal for help—in vain—to Queen Victoria in England. A group of peasants from Stony Gut in St. Thomas, led by Paul Bogle, a Native Baptist deacon, walked to Spanish Town to see the governor. Edward Eyre refused to see them. They returned to St. Thomas in an angry mood. A series of clashes between the Stony Gut men and the militia resulted in the torching of the Morant Bay Courthouse with members of the vestry, headed by the Custos, inside. Fifteen people including the Custos were killed as they tried to escape the flames.

The disorder spread, fed by long-standing resentment, and the whole county of Surrey, with the exception of Kingston itself, was put under martial law. Two warships with troops were quickly sent from Kingston to Morant Bay. One of them carried a prisoner, George William Gordon, member of the assembly for St. Thomas-in-the-East, who had vociferously pleaded the case of the poor for many years in and out of the assembly and was an outspoken critic of Governor Eyre in particular.

Bogle was eventually captured by Maroons and handed over to the authorities, who hanged him. Gordon too was hanged. (They are both now national heroes, and the parliament building is named after Gordon.) Up to 500 men and women were shot or hanged, a greater number were flogged, and more than 1,000 dwellings in that part of the island were destroyed in retribution. The ferocity of the action caused an outcry in Britain; an official inquiry led to Eyre's recall and dismissal from the colonial service.

Before that, Eyre, playing upon the racist fears of the whites that one day the blacks and the coloreds would take over the assembly and the government, had persuaded the assembly to abolish itself. A period of direct rule from London, Crown Colony Government, was instituted in 1866, bringing to an end 200 years of representative government.

Modern Jamaica

Jamaica's political progression from Crown Colony—the lowest rung on the colonial ladder of governance—to independence can be conveniently divided into three periods: 1866 to 1944, when universal adult suffrage was established; 1944 to full independence in 1962; and the postindependence era, up to the present. It is the story of the journey of ex-slaves through the thickets of prejudice and inequality to the present reality of a complex, anxious independence.

Crown Colony to Adult Suffrage

In the period following the proclamation of crown colony rule, "the official position of the colonial government was that racial distinctions between Her Majesty's subjects should not be made" (Bryan 1991: 87). But in a society already established on the direct relationship between skin color, wealth, and power, the distinctions were there. They were built into every aspect of a system of governance that taxed plantation land and its owners less heavily than small holdings and their owners; that levied heavier duties on imported foodstuffs, including those which centuries of habit had made into staples for the families of the poor, than on equipment and goods needed by the white upper class. These levies paid for the upkeep of the crown's civil bureaucracy in Jamaica and its global imperial defense, both of which protected the very distinctions it affected to disdain.

Distinctions were built into the franchise, the ultimate cocoon of white privilege. The Crown Colony constitution of 1866 gave the governor the basis for an autocratic exercise of power: at the national level Legislative and Privy Councils, and Parochial Boards for the parishes (reduced in number to the fourteen that still exist), all appointed by the governor. Adjustments in 1884, widening the eligibility for voting, also allowed for the election of some members of the Legislative Council, but within a structure that left the governor with decisive power. That power relationship was not disturbed by changes in the first decades of the twentieth century, until universal adult suffrage in 1944.

Before 1944, the franchise was dictated by property qualifications, both as to the vote and eligibility for election. This meant, in 1887, just over 42,000 voters existed in a population of half a million. Five years later, this small number was cut in half by withdrawing the assistance previously given to illiterate voters to cast their ballots. The last decade of the century brought economic hard times, which removed another 25 percent of persons from the list because of their inability to pay their taxes. Property qualifications for candidacy meant that there were never more than a couple hundred persons who could even stand for office. The first black member of the Legislative Council was not elected until 1899.

Little changed in the fundamentals of social structure and dynamics for 100 years after emancipation. The government saw its role as 'regulating' relations between the two major groups in the society, the ex-slaves and the ex-masters. But no one in the government, either in London or in Jamaica, would have seen this task as involving any disturbance of the social order prevailing immediately after emancipation. To have undertaken such a mandate would have required the authorities to do violence to the 'natural' order of things, thereby kicking away the underpinnings of privilege of their Jamaican fellow whites, and of themselves. All men were free, now, but all men were not equal, except within the narrow technicalities of the law. The law was administered by white men anyway: the Jamaica Constabulary—established two years after the Morant Bay riots—had white officers, and the courts, while reorganized, were staffed by white and (a few) colored judges.

The power relationships between the different racial groups in the society were not changed by the change in the political relationship between colony and metropole. The oligarchic power of the local whites was indeed enhanced, given *de facto* support. The final third of the nineteenth century was, after all, the era of European imperialist expansion into Africa and Asia, of 'the white man's burden' of carrying 'civilization' to the 'darker' regions of the globe. For the British, Jamaica was just another outpost in this mission, albeit one somewhat more 'civilized' because of its long settlement by whites.

This paternalism did not sit comfortably with all members of what were routinely referred to throughout the empire as 'the subject races,' meaning nonwhites. Indeed, it was not always to the comfort of the whites. In Jamaica, by 1865, most of the senior administrative posts were being filled by Jamaican-born bureaucrats, whites and men of color. Following the establishment of Crown Colony government, most of these posts were reserved for Englishmen sent out from London, officers of the Colonial Service, and it was to be half a century and more before any but a few of the lightest-skinned Jamaicans were allowed back into the upper reaches of officialdom.

Nevertheless, the civil service was a favored professional option for the country's colored or brown population. It offered, as well as remuneration, high status and a sense of public service. But here, as in the society as a whole, the coloreds were as a group objects of suspicion from both ends of the racial continuum. By blacks they were seen as agents of the colonial masters and local white oligarchy; to the latter their loyalty was forever in doubt. As a class, and responding to the *realpolitik* of their situation, the values aspired to by the browns were the (often idealized) virtues of the dominant group, since the rewards of such acculturation were manifest and palpable.

A large part of the energies of the society as a whole centered on the question of pigmentation and the rewards given for its absence. First and foremost, being white in Jamaica—and the rest of the Caribbean—meant not being black (Bryan 1991: 67). Upon that still point, the whole world turned.

Being black was something that even some black people did not want to be: "Every johncrow t'ink 'im pickney white," is a saying of long standing among Jamaicans, the johncrow being a black bird of carrion, useful but despised. Being black meant that a minister of religion could be refused burial in a churchyard where he had once served. In churches with mixed congregations, blacks 'knew their place,' which was in the pews in the rear, so that, as one white planter said, "[white] lips may touch the [communion] wine cup . . . before it becomes blackened by Ethiopian lips" (Bryan 1991: 87). The church attended was indicative of social status or at least aspiration. Elaborate strategies were evolved to 'improve the color' of a son or daughter through the 'right' relationship: marriage, or 'faithful concubinage.' The values driving the society were synonymous with its political, economic, and social leaders, who were uniformly light skinned and Eurocentric until well into the twentieth century; and the values changed more slowly than the complexion of the leaders.

But the society was not entirely static. Within groups, possibilities for change existed, revolving around land and education. Neither was easy to come by. Most of the burden for educating the descendants of slaves was placed on the churches and a few private trusts; their resources were not equal to the task. Elementary education gave the fortunate the opportunity to acquire basic literacy and numeracy. Further education was offered in three teacher training institutions to those who wanted to be teachers.

Anyone aspiring to tertiary education as it is understood today had to go abroad, and few black families could afford that. Those sent were the favored offspring of the more affluent of the landed peasantry—cultivators of bananas and coffee, pen-keepers, landlords of parcels of land leased to others—or from successful artisans, shopkeepers, and tradespeople in the towns. Teaching itself paid barely a living wage. Many teachers were also, of necessity, farmers, shopkeepers, and traders. The same was true of pastors of the various churches that served the black population, including those in the Anglican church after it ceased receiving stipends from the state in 1870.

Out of that milieu of landed peasantry, teachers, preachers, artisans, and tradesmen grew the black middle class and intelligentsia who provided, both within the establishment and from outside, the loyal opposition to the white oligarchy. Despite comprising 50 percent of voters by the turn of the century, very few blacks were eligible to stand for election to the Legislative Council, where, in any case, "the opinions of elected persons were heard but need not be heeded" (W. Adolphe Roberts in Aarons 1983: 60). The first black member, Alexander Dixon, was elected in 1899. But a steady stream of alternative perspectives on the society could be found in letters written to the white-owned newspapers, in the columns of black-owned newspapers like the *Jamaica Advocate* of Dr. Robert Love (a member of a group called the People's Convention, of which Dixon was chairman), and in books like *The British Empire and Alliances, or Britain's Duty to Her Colonies and Subject Races*, by Rev. Dr. Theophilus Scholes in 1899.

On matters of government policy the tone of the writers was admonitory and frequently caustic, linking criticism of policies to the racism inherent in colonialism. But even the most scathing critique of British policy was usually careful not to raise questions of loyalty to the Crown and the Empire. Until the end of World War I, in which thousands of black colonials from around the world fought and died—and, in the case of the West India Regiment, mutinied in the face of blatant racism—the horizons of most people who were English-speaking and not American did not extend beyond that Empire on which the sun never set. Men like Rev. Scholes and Rev. C. A. Wilson (*Men of Backbone and Other Pleas for Progress*, 1913) had been given essentially an English education. Robert Love, an Anglican clergyman, while excoriating the authorities for the myriad injustices meted out to his fellow blacks, implored his readers to send their children, especially their girls, to school in England, in the belief that "the race rises as its women rise" and that "the elevation of women to equality with their white counterparts is the Condition *Sine Qua Non* of the elevation of the Negro race" (Bryan 1991: 233).

Censure, then, was directed more at the men (because there were no women in the colonial service at that point) who embodied and administered the system of inbred inequality that was colonial governance than at the system itself. More radical ideas were planted later, in the 1920s, by the actions and words of Mahatma Gandhi in South Africa and India and of one of Jamaica's own, Marcus Mosiah Garvey.

Garvey was born in 1887 in the parish of St. Ann. The son of a bricklayer and a housewife, he was, unusually for the time, kept in classes to the end of elementary school. He was also fortunate to have grown up in a family in which books were not exotic artifacts and in having a godfather who was a printer, the profession in which Garvey started his working life at the age of fourteen, and which, allied with journalism, provided him with both profession and pulpit for most of his adult life. By eighteen he was living in Kingston, and, while managing a printing works, encouraged the underpaid workers to strike against the owner. In his early twenties he sought work (as timekeeper on a banana estate, then as publisher of a newspaper) in Costa Rica and Panama. In 1912 he paid his first visit to England and Europe, returning to Jamaica in 1914. Within two weeks of his return he called the first meeting of the Universal Negro Improvement Association (UNIA), the purpose of which, *inter alia*, was "to promote a spirit of race, pride and love; to reclaim the fallen of the race; to administer and assist the needy; and to assist in civilizing the backward tribes of Africa" (Lewis 1988: 50). "One God! One Aim! One Destiny!" became the motto of the organization; even in its most radical phases, the UNIA never lost the Christian underpinnings of its mission.

By 1916 Garvey was in New York, establishing the UNIA there. He had been invited by Booker T. Washington, the founder of Tuskeegee Institute, but was not able to make the trip before Washington died. In Harlem, Garvey founded the *Negro World*, a newspaper that became an outlet for many of the writers who became part of the Harlem Renaissance of the 1920s, including Garvey's fellow Jamaican Claude McKay. It was a time of national and worldwide instability: the grueling world war, the communist revolution in Russia, and the aftermath of both. There were race riots in several U.S. cities in 1919, as men who fought abroad in the name of democracy returned to be reminded that it was denied them at home. Large numbers of blacks moved into the northern states from the south, and from the Caribbean, where there were riots after the war also.

The American reality transformed Garvey's thinking: the UNIA steadily became a more radical and political organization than it had been in its early days. Increasingly, he distanced himself from the burgeoning communist movement, whose internationalism was hostile to black nationalism, and from the conservative black American organizations like the National Association for the Advancement of Colored People, who sought a workable accommodation with the white mainstream. Garvey focused on two issues: race and self-reliance.

A charismatic speaker, Garvey galvanized his audiences of mostly working-class blacks, who were frustrated by decades of deferred dreams and rampant discrimination and who were hungry for hope and direction. "Up you mighty race, you can accomplish what you will!" he encouraged them (Clarke 1974: 17). The UNIA, with its philosophy of self-help and self-reliance, built on the institutions that black Americans had established for themselves to circumvent discrimination and became a formidable economic as well as social and political force.

Central to Garvey's vision was a return to Africa but now less "to assist in civilizing the backward tribes of Africa" than to "redeem our Motherland Africa from the hands of alien exploiters and found there a Government, a nation of our own, strong enough to lend protection to the members of our race scattered all over the world, and to compel the respect of the nations and races of the earth" (Bryan 1991: 22). "Africa for the Africans, those at home and abroad," became the battle cry of the movement. The mechanism for returning diasporic Africans to Africa would be the Black Star Line, founded by Garvey in 1919, a venture which had financial and technical problems from the start.

Over the next decade, the UNIA and its message of black solidarity, self-reliance, and redemption spread like the proverbial wildfire, first through hundreds of branches in the Americas (there were four in Mexico), and to Africa, and beyond—there was at least one branch in Australia. By 1926 there were branches in all but ten of the United States. The *Negro World* circulated throughout the world, by mail and carried by traveling seamen. The king of Swaziland told Mrs. Garvey many years later that he had known the names of only two black men in the west: Jack Johnson, the heavyweight boxing champion, and Marcus Garvey (Clarke 1974: 20).

But by 1926, Marcus Garvey was in a federal penitentiary, convicted of mail fraud: a martyr to the unscrupulous behavior of some of his followers, and to the machinations of the U.S. federal government. The following year he was deported to Jamaica. The great mass movement, which had discomforted both white America and black organizations like the NAACP, appeared to wither on the vine: UNIA branches closed, the Great Depression of the 1930s dissipated energies; the *Negro World* folded in 1935. But really, Garveyism went underground, into the subsoil of black culture around the world. The children of Garveyites were the leaders and foot soldiers of the Civil Rights movement forty years later. His name was invoked by the African independence generation of the 1950s and 1960s; the UNIA colors—black, red, and gold—and the Black Star adorn the flag of Ghana. A few UNIA branches never disbanded, and today there are more than there were twenty years ago.

The UNIA was very much alive in the Jamaica to which Garvey returned in 1927, and he received a hero's welcome. "Deafening cheers were raised," reported the *Daily Gleaner* of December 12, "and remarks heard on all sides in the huge crowd showed the high esteem in which he is held by the ordinary people of this country." But not by the *Gleaner* itself, which, speaking for the white elite and some in the colored middle class, editorialized: "It is with profound regret that we view the arrival of Marcus Garvey in Jamaica." He was a man, in the editorialist's opinion, "for whom the island as a whole, or the more intelligent section of it, has no use."

Garvey was not daunted. He traveled the country, encouraging his troops, reestablishing the UNIA as a public presence with speeches, mass meetings, concerts, and conventions. Eventually, in 1929, he formed the first modern political party in Jamaica, the People's Political Party (PPP), to contest local government elections in that year. Its platform was a mixture of current concerns and visionary objectives: protection of native labor; representation to the Imperial Parliament for a larger modicum of self-government for Jamaica; a minimum wage; a public health system for the entire island; land reform; a Jamaican university, polytechnic, and national opera house; a legal aid scheme; an islandwide public library system; and transforming a racecourse in the center of Kingston into a national park (Bryan 1991: 24–25). (Ironically, Garvey's remains came to their final rest in that place, renamed National Heroes Park, in 1964.)

Garvey himself won his seat but was prevented from taking it because he was in jail when the council met officially. This time it was for contempt of court, arising out of one of the PPP's platform promises to impeach dishonest judges. He ran again in the by-election and won. He contested a seat on the Legislative Council, but lost: the mass of Garvey's supporters did not have the vote.

Garvey left Jamaica for the final time in 1935, for London, beset by financial and personnel problems within the UNIA. He continued his work there, speaking, writing, and publishing, but with diminishing energy as his health declined. He died in near poverty of a heart attack in 1940. Twenty-four years later the government of an independent Jamaica—and not without opposition from many of the same quarters as Garvey had encountered in life—brought his remains back to his native land, declaring him the young nation's first national hero.

At that time Garvey was virtually unknown to younger Jamaicans, and still a figure of ridicule to many middle-class Jamaicans. But among working-class blacks, especially those who had been young in the turbulent 1920s and 1930s, his stature was still heroic, almost mythical; and these now had the vote. While routinely invoking his name and "legacy," successive governments, in thrall to the motto of modern Jamaica—"Out of Many, One People"—and perhaps in awe of this multi-faceted figure, have quietly kept Garvey and Garveyism on the sidelines of official philosophy and action. As in his own lifetime, however, and helped in no small measure by the popularity of Rastafarianism in modern Jamaica, affection for Garvey among the broad mass of his countrymen has been rising steadily.

By the time Garvey left Jamaica, the West Indian islands were on the road to turmoil. The Great Depression that gripped the world's major economies was being visited hardest upon the poor of their colonies and dependencies. The late 1920s and 1930s saw ongoing labor unrest—strikes, work stoppages, occasionally full-fledged riots—on plantations and on the wharves in island after island. Starting in the island of St. Kitts in January 1935, a wave of civil unrest—marches, riots, defiant clashes with police and in some cases the army—occurred in St. Vincent, St. Lucia, Barbados, Trinidad, Guyana, and Jamaica.

The labor unrest of the 1930s threw up some remarkable men and women who came to dominate public life in the region well into the 1960s. Their energy and political will created the short-lived West Indies Federation in the 1950s; when that experiment failed they became, individually, the leaders of their new countries. Their political heirs—and in a few cases their children—are the leaders of today's West Indian nations.

In Jamaica, these men were Alexander Bustamante and Norman Manley, who were cousins. Though both aspired to lead the black masses, neither man was black; Bustamante, the populist trade union leader, was the lighter-skinned of the two. Bustamante first 'materialized'—he was christened Alexander Clarke—in a series of letters to the *Gleaner* that began to appear in 1935. He was already fifty years old, having spent much of his life away from Jamaica.

Bustamante's letters challenged the oligarchy of government and plantocracy in language as direct and colorful as the voiceless people that he spoke for would have used. "The great Lord might have John the Devil closed up in some pen," he responded to an apologist for the large banana producers, "but He certainly has let loose a lot of devils in Jamaica, sewing the evil seeds of injustice for their own personal benefit and their friends', while the masses suffer more and more, too weak to fight for themselves, praying to Almighty God to liberate them from these angels of the Devil, some of whose writing make me feel that they could better occupy their time by becoming theatrical clowns" (Hill 1976: 62).

The letters were long and combative, and dealt with the full range of the public issues of the day. They were not without counterproposals to the prevailing policies, delivered in the same hectoring tone. Building on the efforts of early trade union organizers, Bustamante seized control of the sporadic street protests that were occurring in Kingston and elsewhere, and proved as effective an orator as he was a letter writer.

The flash-point came early in 1938. In March the governor decided to form a commission to enquire into wage rates and conditions of employment for the lowest paid field and day laborers. Those in Frome, a large sugar estate in the west, did not wait for the findings and struck in early May. Four workers were killed in clashes with police sent from Kingston and eighty-nine arrested; eighty acres of cane were set afire. The dock workers of Kingston struck two weeks later, and by May 21 a general strike was in effect, led by Bustamante and St. William Grant, a long-time unionist. Over the two weeks of the strike eight persons lost their lives, 171 were wounded, and over 700 arrested.

Bustamante—or simply 'Busta' as he was affectionately known for the rest of his long life—was arrested and held for four days, his release secured by a combination of popular pressure and the work of his cousin Norman Manley. Manley was in most respects the antithesis of his cousin, and as much a paradox. The son of a pen-keeper and a brilliant schoolboy athlete, he went to Oxford University as a Rhodes Scholar and volunteered for the ranks during World War I, resisting all efforts to make him an officer. Returning to Oxford he qualified as a lawyer and married his (and Busta's) cousin, Edna, a strong-willed woman and promising sculptor, before returning home with her. Manley and J.A.G. Smith—a voluble black member of the Legislative Council—were the outstanding barristers of the time, Manley specializing in complex cases that appealed to his formidable intellect and allowed ample room for its display. Manley's course for a successful (and highly profitable) career in the courts was diverted by what he saw as his responsibility to do something about the poverty and frustration around him. In 1937 he founded Jamaica Welfare Ltd., with funds negotiated from international banana companies, to enable "the cultural development of the island and its peasants" (Girvan 1993: 7). By mid-1938 he was mediating peace between his fiery cousin and a nervous colonial administration, and on September 3 of that year he took an irrevocable step into the political arena, accepting from a group of middle-class activists the presidency of the newly formed People's National Party (PNP).

The frustration and diffuse nationalism that had been growing among the black and colored professional class of Jamaicans for several generations found a natural home in the PNP, and a focus in its call for self-government for Jamaica. With its multihued membership and support base, race could not become an issue, certainly not of policy. Nationalism was the mantra of the day, nurtured politically by the intellectuals surrounding Manley and culturally by his wife, Edna.

Two months before the PNP was formed, Bustamante had established the

Bustamante Industrial Trades Union (BITU). He poured his energies into organizing workers and wresting decent wages and conditions from employers, leaving politicking to his cousin. By the end of 1938 a Royal Commission had been sent out to the British West Indies specifically to investigate and report on the conditions of the poor and the workers. The Moyne report was not published until 1945, sat upon by the wartime British government, which feared the propaganda value of it to the Nazis. The report was a scathing indictment of British imperialism, in essence finding that the various administrations and their supporters, through their myopic policies and prejudices, had brought the troubles upon themselves.

Writing in the year of the Jamaica troubles, a young St. Lucian economist W. Arthur Lewis (later the region's second Nobel Prize–winner) saw the upheavals in the West Indian islands as resulting in "nothing short of a revolution" because "the working classes have become organized politically, and their interests have been forced into the foreground." His succinct summary of the context for that revolution is worth quoting at length:

> Vested interests, in close alliance with governments, have held unchallenged sway in these islands for three hundred years, opposing . . . any measure which in raising the standard of the masses would react unfavorably (from their point of view) on the level of wages. . . . They are careful through the use of indirect taxation to keep the burden of taxation mainly on the masses, and they refuse to tax themselves sufficiently to provide decent educational, medical and other social services. Their power has lasted long, but its end is in sight. (Lewis 1991: 391)

Universal Adult Suffrage

The beginning of the end came in November 1944, with a new constitution that abolished Crown Colony government and created two chambers of the legislature: the elected House of Representatives and a nominated Legislative Council. An Executive Council of ten members, five from each chamber, was presided over by the governor. The elected members were known as ministers, a first step along the road to full responsibility.

The larger step had been taken with the adoption of universal adult suffrage (age 21 and older) for the election held under the new constitution; there were no conditionalities as to literacy or income or taxes paid. This resulted in a potential electorate of 700,000 persons, where before there had been fewer than 50,000.

The prospect of political power galvanized Bustamante, who, almost overnight in 1943, willed the Jamaica Labour Party (JLP) into being. With the backing of his labor stronghold, Bustamante's JLP won the first election in 1944. Norman Manley, the proselytizer of universal suffrage and self-government but a poor campaigner all his political life, did not even win the constituency in which he ran. For that he had to wait for the next election in 1949, though his People's National Party lost again to the JLP.

By then the shortcomings of the 1944 constitution were evident, at least to the Jamaican politicians on the front line: they had ostensible responsibility over the departments of governments in their 'portfolios,' but no executive authority. That rested with the Executive Council and, ultimately, with the governor. In 1953 there were changes to the constitution, giving elected ministers, increased to seven, a majority on the Executive Council and allowing the appointment of a chief minister, Bustamante, as head of the political arm of the government. Further changes in 1957 created a Council of Ministers, a cabinet of up to twelve ministers, three of them appointed by the governor but only on the advice of the chief minister. Except for defense, external relations, and the justice system, which remained in the hands of an appointed attorney general, Jamaica had achieved internal self-government.

By then Norman Manley was chief minister, having led his party to its first electoral victory in 1955. The PNP had loosened the BITU's grip on labor by encouraging the formation of the National Workers Union (NWU), which has, over the past fifty years, been as closely associated with the PNP as has the BITU with the JLP. The labor movement has provided three of the six prime ministers of independent Jamaica, in the persons of Bustamante (BITU, 1962–1967), Hugh Shearer (BITU, 1967–1972), and Michael Manley (NWU, 1972–1980; 1988–1991).

Within a few weeks of its own constitutional upgrade, Jamaica became part of the Federation of the West Indies, which came into being on January 3, 1958, and involved all the British possessions in the Caribbean except British Honduras (now Belize) and British Guyana (now Guyana). A federation of all the West Indian colonies was an idea beloved of British colonial administrators from the beginning of their settlement of the region. It had an organizational tidiness that appealed, especially from the distance of London. It appealed also to several West Indian intellectuals and popular leaders, like Marcus Garvey in his time, who promoted the idea. It received a boost across the whole region in the 1930s, an outcome of cooperation among labor leaders in building their national movements. Several of those unionists had formed parties to translate their popular appeal into political power. But, as island leaders became used to the realities and possibilities of their own local power, they became reluctant to surrender it to a center outside their island. Ambivalence was rife. Jamaicans, far away from their cousins on the other side of the Caribbean Sea, were the most ambivalent of all. Finally, after three and a half years of indecision, Manley called a referendum on the single question of remaining in the federation or not, and with Bustamante skillfully appealing to the insularity of uninformed voters, Jamaica opted for withdrawal in September 1961.

The result created a bitter divide between Jamaica and her West Indian cousins, traces of which linger still. Efforts were made for the Federation's continuance in the geographically tighter grouping of the Eastern Caribbean, but the commitment of Prime Minister Eric Williams of Trinidad and Tobago, the second largest entity in the grouping, waned after Manley's loss. Eric Williams's famous phrase "Ten minus one equals zero" signaled the end of the federal idea (Mordecai 1968: 426).

In Jamaica Manley, having been rebuffed by the electorate on the federal issue, declared an intention to go for full independence and felt obliged to take that issue to the people as well, though the PNP's term had two more years to run. In general elections in April 1962, they chose Bustamante, by a margin of twenty-six seats to nineteen, to become the first prime minister of a new nation.

The 1950s were a time of significant economic development for Jamaica. A concerted effort was made, with the support of the British government, to move the economy away from its historical dependence on primary agricultural products and a high level of imports. The manufacture of cement, utilizing the large limestone deposits in the hills east of Kingston, began in 1952. Tourism was becoming well established in Montego Bay, Port Antonio, Kingston, and Ocho Rios.

The most significant development of all, however, related to the exploitation of Jamaica's huge bauxite-bearing deposits in several areas, including St. Ann, Manchester, St. Elizabeth, and Clarendon. Identified earlier in the century, they became potentially very valuable after the war with the boom in consumer goods, automobiles, and aircraft, all of which used aluminum. Tens of millions of pounds sterling (the currency of Jamaica at the time) were invested by North American companies to establish the mining activities and the refining of the ore to the intermediate stage of alumina.

By the early 1960s Jamaica was the world's largest producer and exporter of bauxite and alumina; and although that position was eventually eclipsed, and the international market has suffered periodic recessions, mining, processing, and export of the mineral have remained mainstays of the Jamaican economy. Its importance rests not only in the employment it has provided and the revenue earned by government and other service providers, but also in the fact that the industry represents a considerable enterprise in the rural areas in which it operates, providing foci outside of the main city of Kingston and transforming previously small towns such as Mandeville and May Pen. It has also been responsible for training a large number of Jamaicans in skills they would not have otherwise been exposed to in their native land; indeed, the industry is now Jamaicanized to its highest levels.

The prospects for independence, then, seemed very good in 1962. The surge of nationalistic pride and optimism that most Jamaicans felt at midnight on August 6, 1962, when the British flag, the Union Jack, was lowered for the last time and Jamaica's new flag went up the flagpole at the spanking new National Stadium, seemed fully justified.

Independence to the Present

In an opinion poll done in May and June of 1998, after thirty-six years of independence, a representative sample of Jamaicans was asked to respond to various questions about the experience of independence for them. To the question: "How do you personally feel as a Jamaican, knowing that Jamaica is politically independent?" a majority, 62.1 percent, felt "a sense of pride." To 30.7 percent of respondents, independence did "not really matter." Asked whether Jamaicans as a whole had "benefited" from independence, 51.9 percent felt they had, "a lot" or "somewhat." Of all the respondents, 23.6 percent felt there had been no real benefit from independence, and 24.5 percent, most of them born after 1962, were unsure (*The Daily Gleaner*, August 1–6, 1999).

The more interesting aspect of the figures was the breakdown of respondents between what the pollster called "upper income" and "lower income." In every case—several questions were asked—the former group had a more positive view of the experience of independence than the latter. A cynical view would be that nothing very much has changed in the lives of the Jamaican masses over the thirty-six years of independence. There is certainly a high level of cynicism abroad in the country, shared by all classes and interest groups.

But it was not always so. Jamaicans went into independence with a high level of optimism. They were setting off into the future in the hands of known and loved leaders, Bustamante and Manley, in a democracy that had shown its mettle by changing governments twice by election in a wider region— Latin America—where most countries changed them at the point of a gun. It had the goodwill of powerful countries in North America and Europe, who lent and gave funding for development projects. At the time Jamaica had a per capita income equal to that of Singapore, which came of age around

the same time. Now, the latter is counted among the most developed countries in the world, and Jamaica struggles to maintain its place in the lowest
ranks of middle-level countries. It is that kind of massively unfavorable com-
parison, translated on the ground into individual and communal hopes deferred, that has created the sense of anxiety that characterizes the country at
present.

Most Jamaicans would attribute the change in their country's fortunes,
and their own, to the incompetence and veniality of their political leaders.
They would be aware of other factors: an international economic climate
hostile to small primary-producing countries; a population growing faster
than available (or foreseeable) resources; a labor movement that, in the view
of managers and controllers of capital, bullies the government, a sentiment
shared by trade unionists about employers and capitalists; and so on. Not all
adverse factors should be laid at the door of government, either individually
or in the abstract. But Jamaican politicians have so assiduously concerned
themselves with the minutest details of everyday life in the country, somehow
managing to claim credit whenever things go right, that inevitably they are
blamed when things go wrong, even when it is not their fault.

A generous view of the intrusiveness of politicians—one that politicians
themselves routinely unleash at their critics—is that they are the voice of the
voiceless, the arm of the powerless, and the arbitrator between contending
forces in an arena of scarce resources. This, in a society without long
traditions of social welfare, equality, or justice, is as it should be. But it sounds
very like the self-regarding view of British colonialists about their role during
Crown Colony government. As often happens, in seeking to become part of
a solution, politicians become part of the problem.

The disillusion set in early. Bustamante was seventy-eight years old when
he became prime minister of the new nation. Before the end of his first term
of office in 1967, when he officially retired, he had effectively handed over
running of the government to his trusted political deputy, Donald Sangster.
Within a month of clinching his own electoral victory, Sangster was dead of
a brain hemorrhage. Busta's heir apparent in the labor union, Hugh Shearer,
newly elected to the House of Representatives, became prime minister. On
the opposition benches of parliament the other patriarch, Norman Manley,
defeated for the second consecutive time, grew weary of the fight without
his traditional sparring partner. In February 1969 he retired from politics;
he died in September. After a fierce intra-party fight, the younger of his two
sons, Michael, took over the leadership of the PNP. The incestuous relationship between labor and politics had reached its apogee: Michael, leader
of the opposition, was at the time chief organizer for the National Workers

Union, an affiliate of the PNP; Hugh Shearer had left the leadership of the BITU to become prime minister. A new generation had taken charge.

Although the persons were new, the policies of the government belonged to the past and were clearly not working. Despite increased expenditure on education, low-income housing, and other social areas and increases in gross national product and the other conventional indices of 'progress,' the quality of life was in manifest decline. As the decade progressed, the bloom faded from the economy. Large-scale investment in bauxite and alumina production was drying up, and Jamaica's position as the number one producer of the ore in the world was under threat. Tourism was growing, but expansion in light manufacturing, food processing, and chemicals had slowed by the end of the 1960s. Unemployment was rising; so was violent crime, fueled by economic hardship and facilitated by increasing numbers of illegal guns, first introduced in large numbers in the run-up to the 1967 elections and a plague on the country ever since.

The income gap within the country widened during the 1960s, creating social tensions. The ideas and tactics of the Civil Rights movement in the United States struck a responsive chord in Jamaica (some of the leaders of the movement had Caribbean roots), especially among the young. On the other hand, the new political leadership, at least on the government side, proved to be as conservative as the old—Bustamante having set the country's foreign policy in concrete with the 1962 statement "We are with the West"—banning literature from socialist countries, including Cuba, with which they nonetheless maintained consular relations despite the U.S. embargo.

In 1972, in a context of economic stasis and social unease, the electorate responded to Michael Manley's promise that "better must come" and voted the PNP into office with an outpouring of goodwill and hopefulness never seen before or since in Jamaica. That optimism notwithstanding, the most obvious difference between the new administration and the old in the first year or so was the energy level. The first sign of what was to come was the announcement by Manley in May of 1973—reportedly without consultation with his minister of education—of free education at all levels in Jamaica. There was a rapturous public reception but ongoing administrative and financial difficulties.

The watershed year that differentiates the 'old' Jamaica—of, say, the 1930s—from the new was 1974. Following a fourfold increase in oil prices by the Organization of Petroleum Exporting Countries (OPEC) in 1973–1974, Jamaica, like much of the developing world, found the cost of its energy imports, and the sudden effect on local goods and services, undermining its whole economy. In May of 1974, after negotiations broke down with the bauxite companies, all of them foreign-owned, the government imposed a levy on bauxite and alumina exports, along with a program of Jamaican participation in ownership of the industry to be phased in over several years.

Then, four months later, at its annual general conference, the PNP declared itself a 'democratic socialist' party. Later that year, the leadership of the Jamaica Labour Party changed: Edward Seaga, a senior minister in previous JLP governments, was elected to replace Hugh Shearer. Seaga was, and remains, something of an anomaly in Jamaican politics. A Jamaican of Syrian descent from a family of merchants, he was a graduate of Harvard University. While doing postgraduate field research on religious Revivalism, Seaga lived in the poorest section of the capital city, West Kingston; he ran for office in that constituency in 1959 and is still its representative in parliament. He was the first political leader of that generation with no direct links to the union movement. Seaga's elevation to leader of the JLP, a post he still holds, marked the end of an era for the JLP, taking it further away with each passing year from its roots in labor, though the icon of Bustamante, the fiery champion of the black masses, continues to be routinely invoked.

In the next six years, which older Jamaicans refer to simply as 'The Seventies'—the most tumultuous period in the island's post-slavery history—what had been a broad consensus between the two parties as to economic and social policy, and external relations, was transformed. Up to that point, in the view of one political scientist:

> It was assumed that Jamaica was aligned to western countries; that the private sector should be given full freedom to develop the economy in cooperation with the public sector and within the framework of government planning for development; that the role of government should involve the state using its economic resources to assist the poorer classes through employment, housing, general social services, agricultural credit, and by expanding educational opportunity; and that competitive party politics supported by freedom of speech and civil liberties would provide a liberal political environment that promoted social justice. (Stone 1982: 26)

Consensus was not so easily achieved after 1972. Michael Manley saw himself as "constantly in the presence of a personal, moral imperative: How to isolate a single, central thesis of belief from the welter of conflicting categories. . . . The more I have thought about the morality of politics, the more there has emerged for me a single touchstone of right and wrong; and the touchstone is to be found in the notion of equality" (Manley 1974: 17). Manley's persuasive salesmanship of the centerpiece idea of 'equality' within a 'morality of politics' galvanized a society increasingly aware of its historical inequalities. He did not discourage portrayal of himself as the Biblical prophet Joshua, assaulting the walls of injustice; 'democratic socialism' was his trumpet.

From its founding, PNP leaders had managed an uneasy fusion of left wing and centrist policies; and there had been, from the 1930s, self-confessed Marxists among its members. A traumatic purge of Marxists had taken place in 1949. Michael Manley, perceived throughout his early life as on the left wing of the party but not a Marxist, had publicly eschewed ideological "-isms" in his 1972 campaign and postvictory speeches and interviews. With the declaration of 'democratic socialism' in 1974, however, the left wing was perceived as having triumphed.

In the war for public opinion the party's opponents successfully separated the two words and tarred the government with the damning label of 'socialist,' managing to render it interchangeable with 'communist.' Jamaica was turned into a battleground for the ideological and physical forces contending in the larger world in that penultimate decade of the Cold War. A sweeping election win by the PNP in 1976 merely emboldened the activists on all sides—ranging from parties on the right fringe who wanted union with the United States to those on the far left who wanted a Maoist state—to work and fight harder for their goals. At times, it seemed that the needs of the 'ordinary Jamaican' were forgotten, and the people themselves become cannon fodder, in this war.

The 1970s were memorable in positive ways also. Legislation obliterated the difference in entitlements between children born in wedlock and the 70 percent born outside of it, a historical impediment to inheritance and status that had blighted many families. A Family Court was created, not least to give an arena for children and their mothers to assert their rights. Pregnant mothers were given three months paid maternity leave and protection from dismissal while on leave. A minimum wage act was passed, as well as legislation encouraging worker participation in ownership and management of some industries.

In external relations, where Jamaica had played an active but docile role, siding with the United States and western Europe on all major issues except apartheid, the country became outspoken and aggressive in articulation of a nonaligned agenda, in which a formal movement, the Group of 77, became a leading light. A close relationship developed between Jamaica and its nearest neighbor, Cuba, with whom it had been on discreetly cordial terms throughout the years of U.S. hostility. This new relationship, personalized in a friendship between Fidel Castro and Michael Manley but extending to Cuban doctors in Jamaican rural hospitals and Jamaican students studying in Cuba, poisoned relations with the United States and within Jamaica itself. Previously esoteric issues of world trade and finance—especially relating to the harsh economic prescriptions of the International Monetary Fund, which were a dominant feature of Jamaican economic life for twenty years after 1976—became poster campaigns and terms of abuse in an increasingly vitriolic public debate.

It was a time of paranoia, the most visible signs of which were the daily murders, mostly by the gun, the greater number of them political, including a junior minister of the government who was shot outside a police station in his own constituency. As noticeable, and related, was the phenomenon of outward migration: not only the historic pattern of the working class seeking better opportunities, but the middle class and the prosperous, seeking security and peace of mind, at any price, including that of abandoning substantial property and investment in the island.

"The mistakes of the 70s had much to do with naive views of the world, and with the construction of social relations which emphasized differences and conflict at the expense of similarities and consensus," said Ian Boxhill, a social scientist at the University of the West Indies. "Many of the ideas and policies of the period, especially on the left, seemed to have been motivated by our enduring 'search for recognition' as human beings" (Boxhill 1998: 4).

After a decisive change of government in October 1980 to the Jamaica Labour Party, now led by Edward Seaga, the 1980s brought a measure of social peace. The period was marked by two dominant features. There was massive borrowing from multilateral lending agencies, primarily the World Bank, the Inter-American Development Bank, and the International Monetary Fund, who between them virtually dictated the economic policy of the Jamaican government. The borrowing, said the government, was to restore economic stability and repair the depredations of the 1970s. It is arguable whether it did either. What it did do was to double Jamaica's national debt in less than a decade. Taking into account subsequent borrowings by later governments, less than half of Jamaicans' tax dollars—a flat rate for income of 25 percent and companies of 33⅓ percent, plus a 15 percent point-of-sale tax, at the end of the twentieth century—are available to spend on projects and recurrent costs within the country itself. It is a burden from which the country has little hope of extricating itself without widespread debt and interest payment forgiveness on the part of lending agencies and the countries that control them.

The second feature of the 1980s, in Jamaica and across the Caribbean, was the rooting out of ideological socialism, democratic or otherwise. With the eclipse of Manley in Jamaica (1980), the murder of Maurice Bishop in Grenada (1983), and the death of Forbes Burnham in Guyana (1985), Caribbean socialism was descried and discredited. The collapse of communism in Europe and the triumph of global capitalism in the 1990s appear to have cauterized it from the body politic.

But in small economies such as Jamaica's, there are limits to the distance a government can afford to maintain between itself and the unfettered workings of 'the market.' While in the 1970s the PNP gave the process an ideological patina that had been absent before, government has always been interventionist in the Jamaican economy, from colonial days. The 'commanding heights' of the economy, which the PNP attempted to scale, more often than not fell into their hands: the sugar industry that collapsed from slow production and low prices; banks and insurance companies that sold out to private Jamaicans and/or the government on very favorable terms; tourism properties that were nationalized to save jobs when original investors pulled out or invoked government letters-of-comfort. For the most part the policies were cobbled together to meet changing circumstances.

The divestiture of these industries in the late 1980s and 1990s—largely presided over, ironically, by a 'reformed' PNP, which came back to power in 1989 singing the virtues of an 'open' economy—did not effect any overall improvement in the economy and has been, in the event, disastrous to the personal fortunes of thousands of Jamaicans. After a decade of spectacular 'growth' after 1985, all but a handful of the leading financial institutions in the country—banks and insurance companies—are back in the hands of the government. Unwise expansion into areas about which they knew nothing, such as tourism, agriculture, and housing, left many of them bankrupt as economic conditions changed. The government has had to step in again, with billions of taxpayers' dollars. At the start of a new century, the cycle has begun again: consolidation and divestiture, with government underwriting of future eventualities.

Politically, the picture is, on paper at least, slightly more encouraging. Jamaica continues to hold regular democratic elections, based on the first-past-the-post method favored by former British colonies. Governments change through the ballot. Within the limits of the law, political parties and their agents operate unhindered. There are, at time of writing, three political parties, though only the two long-standing ones have seats in parliament or the municipal councils.

It is this fact that gives rise to concern among many people. While the range of opinions in public debate is wide, the options at the ballot box are narrow. Perhaps the most commonly expressed feeling about the political scene by the average Jamaican is a feeling of helplessness in the face of entrenched political interests. As elsewhere in the world, the practice of politics has become suspect in the eyes of nonpoliticians. Voter turnout for general elections has declined steadily since the 1970s. Technically, Jamaican governments since 1993 have been elected by far fewer than 50 percent of the registered electorate of 18 years and over.

The people of Jamaica look back with pride and look forward with some apprehension. At the end of a century that began with complete political powerlessness for the vast majority of people, Jamaicans are now fully in charge of their own destiny. Their members of parliament are the sons and daughters of laborers, shopkeepers, small businesspeople, teachers, and clergymen and are predominantly black. The citizenry take their democratic institutions—regular elections, a bicameral parliament, elected parish councils, an independent judiciary, an independent civil service that is ostensibly a meritocracy—for granted. But at the same time they wonder, in public and privately, whose interests these institutions serve.

The change in political representation is mirrored in the country's social dimension. There is no church now that would dare to expect its light- and dark-skinned congregants to sit separately. Clubs and hotels where, as recently as the early 1970s, the only dark faces would have belonged to service staff have adapted or gone out of business. Education is no longer the preserve only of the privileged or very talented—though it is not the 'free' entitlement that governments have been known to boast of. The widespread availability of primary and secondary education, though of very uneven quality and not yet universal, is perhaps the single greatest achievement of independent Jamaica. At the same time, the consistent outward migration of professionals, from accountants to zoologists, has been one of the greatest impediments to the fulfillment of the promise of independence.

At social gatherings, whether for business or pleasure, one would generally find a mixture of races, with no automatic connection between color, status, and wealth. The old—in fact, not so old—prejudices and social conventions are things of the past, at least as manifested in the public domain. Historically, many Jamaicans/West Indians have always rejected the blanket classifications of North America, wherein anyone who is not observably 'white' is 'black,' or some other thing. The range of skin color within many individual families is too great to allow such simplistic labeling.

That having been said, color remains a present concern, though more politically than socially. The ethnicity of the country's political leaders has come to play an increasingly important role, at the very least in the manipulation of popular perception. The towering personalities of founding fathers Bustamante and Norman Manley were such that comments about their color—Bustamante fair but not Caucasian, Manley brown, not black—would have been publicly uttered at the speaker's peril. By the 1970s, however, both men had passed from the political scene. In the 1976 general elections Edward Seaga, born of Middle Eastern parents in the United States but schooled and domiciled for most of his life in Jamaica, was pilloried for his birthplace. (It helped the agenda of the governing party's spinmeisters that by then the United States was becoming public enemy number one to many in the party fold.) It was a thinly disguised attack on his ethnicity by a party headed by a man more light-skinned than the vast majority of the Jamaicans he led.

A process of change that began in the 1950s has brought to the leadership of banks, insurance companies, the judiciary, and professional associations personalities whose skin color reflects that of the majority of their fellow citizens. As has been said, the same is true in the political arena, dominated by Percival J. Patterson, a black lawyer from rural Jamaica and prime minister since 1993. The 1990s have been described as 'Black man time.' But occasionally, an understandable racial pride has worn the masquerade of intolerance and even retribution.

Fuelling this feeling of pride, and deriving from it, has been a conscious effort to research and recover the past, to clear away the distortions of Eurocentric historiography and myth making and to arrive at a Jamaican evaluation of a people's place in history and their accomplishments.

2

Religion

POPULAR LORE has it that there are more churches per capita in Jamaica than anywhere else in the world. (Wits go on to say that next door to every church is a rum-shop, or bar.) A drive through the cities and towns and along the roads of rural Jamaica gives substance to this piece of folk wisdom: solid structures of brick and mortar, some 200 or more years old, some still being built, stand cheek by jowl with wooden lean-tos supporting zinc roofs, with signs, often hand-painted, declaring the names of the congregations. These range from denominations whose members span the globe to individual churches that exist only in that location. There are also places—certain trees, riverbanks, burial grounds—the religious importance of which is invisible to the non-believer.

There are now more than 130 churches or denominations registered in Jamaica, and new applications for registration are received every year. The large number in such a relatively small population is testimony to many things, as we shall discuss, but certainly to the importance of religion to Jamaica's national life, presently as in the past.

It would be difficult to overestimate that importance, but it might be just as difficult to describe it. History (again) gives the best clues. The outpost Caribbean (and American) colonies were less hidebound in their social and religious attitudes than Europe. For many people, the attraction of the colonies was the freedom to worship in ways that were unacceptable and sometimes illegal at home. Even in cases where the same strictures existed on the colonial law books, they were less rigidly applied: societies and social norms were still being formed.

In Jamaica, from the English capture onwards, religious tolerance and freedom to worship—except for slaves—were significant factors in the early development of the society, attracting nonconformist businessmen and traders, and people of other faiths, to complement the planters, who were largely Church of England. One of the earliest Jewish synagogues in the New World, for instance, was built in Jamaica in 1676.

On the other hand, there was stringent prohibition, legal and social, against the slaves' practice of their own African beliefs. This does not mean they were forgotten; quite the contrary. But religion became one more layer, perhaps the deepest and most significant, in a secret 'other' life hidden from the white world and even from some fellow slaves. In several respects it has remained so.

Jamaica presents itself as a largely Christian country, notwithstanding the presence, free from curtailment of any kind, of numbers of Jews, Muslims, and Hindus among the major world faiths, as well as members of smaller faiths such as the Bahá'i and Ananda Marga. One could divide the Christian denominations into three categories: those of European origin, those of North American origin, and those of Jamaican or African-derived origin (Chevannes 1998: 2). Table 2.1 measures the membership in the first two categories.

Denominations such as Baptist, Anglican, Roman Catholic, Methodist, and Moravian would belong to the first category; they were the first introduced into Jamaica *qua* denominations. Among the second category, introduced in the late nineteenth and early twentieth centuries, are Pentecostalism, Adventism, and Church of God; the category would include the African Methodist Episcopal (AME) churches, from the United States, though these are not mentioned as a separate denomination in the census. The churches in this category are the fastest growing denominations in the country. The third category is an ill-defined, or perhaps indefinable, group, represented within the census categories of "Other," "None," or "Not Stated," depending on how the individual chose to report his or her affiliation. Their numbers would also be concealed among the other two groups. Historically, a higher status has been accorded European and North American denominations than home-grown faiths; therefore, in religion as in other facets of life, many Jamaicans have reported themselves as one thing while being in fact another.

Among this third category of religions would be a spectrum of belief systems, from Kumina, a "living fragment of an African religion" (Brathwaite 1978: 46) through African-Christian Revival (itself divisible into different

Table 2.1
Percentage Distribution of the Population by Religion

Religion	Census 1970	Census 1982	Census 1991
Baptist	17.8	10.0	8.8
Church of God	17.0	18.4	21.2
Anglican	15.4	7.1	5.5
Roman Catholic	7.9	5.0	4.1
Seventh-Day Adventist	6.5	6.9	9.1
Methodist	6.0	3.1	2.7
Presbyterian/Congregationalist	5.2	*	2.8
Moravian	2.9	1.4	1.2
Pentecostal	3.2	5.2	7.6
Brethren	1.8	1.1	1.1
Jehovah's Witness	—	—	1.7
Other	16.3	12.9	8.6
None	—	17.7	24.1
Not stated	—	11.2	1.5
TOTAL	100.0	100.0	100.0

*Included in other.

Source: Pocketbook of Statistics Jamaica 1998.

cults) to Jamaican-derived Rastafarianism (herinafter Rastafari, as singular and plural noun, referring to the faith, people, and culture—see Chapter 4).

THE FOUNDATIONS

DEO GLORIA

ERECTED
BY EMANCIPATED SONS OF AFRICA
TO COMMEMORATE
THE BIRTH-DAY OF THEIR FREEDOM
AUGUST THE 1ST 1838.
HOPE

HAILS THE ABOLITION OF SLAVERY
THROUGHOUT THE BRITISH COLONIES
AS THE DAY-SPRING OF
UNIVERSAL LIBERTY
TO "ALL NATIONS OF MEN WHOM
GOD HATH MADE OF ONE BLOOD."

"ETHIOPIA shall soon stretch out her
hands onto GOD" LXVIII Psalm 31 verse

This famous tablet, erected in the Falmouth Baptist Church where a lead-ing antislavery activist, William Knibb, was pastor, expresses first the pious hope for universal abolition, directed at the United States[1] and the nearby Spanish colony of Cuba. The epitaph declares the more immediate desire: that the newly freed blacks would "stretch out [their] hands onto God."[2] This was a tacit acknowledgment by the white missionaries[3] that the Chris-tian message and ministry had hardly touched the vast majority of Jamaicans up to that point in time. In the eyes of even the most enlightened European missionary, that majority was still pagan. The more observant, however, rec-ognized the existence of a spiritual force at work among the ex-slaves and were aware of at least some of the rituals in which it manifested itself.

The African societies from which the slaves came, and whose spiritual dimensions they brought with them, were polytheistic. There was a supreme Creator Being and several lesser but powerful beings. "There is no dissocia-tion opposing sacred and secular, sacred and social, political or artistic do-mains" (Pradel 1998: 145). Every aspect of life was infused with the sacred. All elements of the temporal life were reflections of the spiritual. In its 'nat-ural' state the world was orderly, harmonious, good. Evil, therefore—in-cluding slavery, racism, and obeah—occurred as a result of disharmony between the spiritual and temporal worlds.[4] Harmony could only be re-established through beneficial contact with the spirit world after identifying the evil. The rituals of eradication and healing included drumming and danc-ing, leading to a trance-like state. The "plasticity" (Pradel 1998: 145) of such a belief system made it easily transportable, and suitable for creolization, which is what happened. It also placed the African in contradistinction to the white European world, with its fairly rigid distinctions between the spir-itual and material domains.

Official suppression of expressions of African spirituality, gathered under the label of 'obeah,' may have had an effect opposite to that intended. The policy of mixing ethnic groups across several plantations and regions did, for a time, engender a sense of isolation, which strikes at the essence of African religions, which is communal. But in the 1760s a pan-African 'society' called Myal appeared, "the first documented Jamaican religion cast in the 'classical' African mold" (Schuler 1979: 66). Interestingly, Myal was not included in the proscriptive laws of the late eighteenth century against obeah and its manifestations. Myal was indeed resolutely against obeah, which dealt with 'magic' and individual curses and cures, not with the community as a whole. For that reason, and from the fact that they adopted/adapted certain Christian beliefs being taught by the missionaries, Myalists were less unacceptable to the planters. Myal 'doctors,' experts at discerning the source of ailments in slaves, worked alongside medical doctors in some slave hospitals (Schuler 1979: 66–67). Myal is most succinctly described in the *Dictionary of Caribbean English Usage* as: "a folk religion in which the power of spirits of the dead is enlisted in order to cure ills or counteract evil (especially that of obeah); it involves the use of herbal medicines and baths, drumming and dancing to induce spirit possession, ritual sacrifice of fowls, and other ceremonial rites, some of which are performed under a silk-cotton tree" (Allsopp 1996: 395).

The relationship between Myalists and the Baptist churches was a complex one, as were the relationships among Baptists themselves. The faith was brought to Jamaica in the immediate aftermath of the American Revolution by black Americans who had supported the British cause and thus saw their hopes of freedom or a better life dashed. George Leile, who had been ordained in 1775 in Savannah, Georgia, was the first Baptist minister in Jamaica. Born a slave but freed by his owner, Leile came to Jamaica to escape the schemes of his former owner's relatives who reasserted ownership of him. Several others, slave and free, followed and worked in different parts of the island, teaching and converting slaves on plantations where owners permitted it. Not all slave owners were averse to their slaves acquiring literacy and Christian instruction, though none supported emancipation.

Two aspects of Baptist theology particularly appealed to the Africans: baptism by immersion as the primary channel to salvation, and the transporting power of the Holy Spirit.[5] These accorded with important elements of their own belief system—rivers being host to powerful spirits—and allowed them easy ingress into the Baptist fold. Many, however, were 'bow-down' Baptists, who attended services in the mission house and chapels but fully participated in Myal ceremonies also.[6] These came increasingly under suspicion from the Baptist missionaries of the British Baptist Missionary Society, who had been called upon for help by some of Liele's fellow ministers when the cost of running a mission overwhelmed their resources.

The Native Baptists found the supervision and superiority assumed over them by the foreign missionaries galling: they were men accustomed to running their own missions. The style of worship, lively by Anglican standards perhaps, but staid to Myalists, was restricting. Several 'leaders,' as the heads of individual groups were called—that naming itself a part of African religious culture, where charismatic individuals were acknowledged as prime intermediaries with the spirit world—went their own way, and their congregations followed.

There was a surge in membership immediately after Emancipation, when the missionaries, with help from benefactors in Britain, could offer practical help in establishing 'free villages' and other structures for coping with freedom, among them education. For a few years after 1838, the British government made available directly to the missionary societies a small grant for educating the ex-slaves. The ex-slaves attended services, for the 'word' (preaching) and the singing and the witnessing. But the missionaries did not endear themselves to their congregants in matters of social morality and behavior. They were against drumming and dancing, both religious and social. Regarding marriage and concubinage, some refused to baptize the children of illegitimate unions and were prepared to revoke membership of persons who broke the Sabbath or were frequently drunk. In these respects they were more strict than the Anglicans. The new Jamaicans generally resisted attempts to make them the quiescent, 'respectable' laborers for the colonial vineyard or plantation, which is what the planters expected of the clergy. From the mid-1840s and into the 1850s, membership in the missionary churches declined; with no figures kept for African sects, we cannot know if there was a general decline in spirituality. But flare-ups of Myalism in the 1840s that led to its legal proscription would suggest not.

The Great Revival, an outpouring of repentance, conversion, and general religious zeal[7] in all churches and across faiths in 1860, gladdened the hearts of even the most conservative clergy—at first. "Like a mountain stream, clear and transparent as it springs from the rock," wrote one Congregational minister later, "but which becomes foul and repulsive as impurities are mingled with it in its onward course, so with this extraordinary movement." The impurities were, of course, the "trances and dreams, 'prophesying,' spirit-seizure, wild dancing, flagellation, and mysterious sexual doings that were only hinted at in the missionary reports" to their home base (Curtin 1998: 171).

The Great Revival, which lasted until about 1863 or 1864, was a breath of life to the mainstream churches, increasing attendance and membership, however defined. But as it "turned African" it became an assertion of identity that diverted the onward march of conversion into unwelcome channels. And when, in 1865, a Native Baptist deacon, Paul Bogle, and his followers challenged the colonial powers in Morant Bay, the brutal reaction of the regime deepened the divide between mainstream churches—which increasingly came to include the Baptists and Wesleyans, as well as the Anglicans—and the Native churches.

Thereafter the words 'Myal' and 'Myalism' are superseded by 'Revival'—without definite article or qualifier—and 'Revivalism,' in reference to a distinct form of worship in which elements of denominational Christianity are present but which exist even outside the realms of the Native churches.

Revivalists believe in a high god who is the creator and ruler of the universe. He is God the Father. . . . [but he] does not leave his throne in the high heavens to attend a revivalist 'trumping'.[8] . . . Jesus Christ, who is God the Son, comes to the service, but he too never trumps. God, the Holy Spirit, however, not only comes to every service, but he is the chief spirit in the revival and he trumps.

The important trumpers at a revival service are Biblical characters—prophets, evangelists, archangels and apostles. . . . But they are not the only spirits that possess the revivalist worshipers. Important shepherds and shepherdesses of revivalist bands, who, on dying, enter the spirit world, also come to labor and trump. (Bisnauth 1989: 178)

This explanation conflates what are in fact two cults of Revivalism: Zion and Pukkumina. Zion 'bands,' the (always collective plural) name for each group in the cult, deal primarily with *heavenly spirits* (the Triune Christian God, archangels and saints) and, among *earth bound spirits*, biblical prophets and apostles, but not fallen angels. They do not deal with *ground spirits*, who, along with fallen angels, they regard as evil. Pukkumina bands deal primarily with ground spirits (the human dead, except those in the Bible) and fallen angels, regarding neither as evil (Seaga 1969: 10–11).

Revival 'bands' can still be found in the countryside and towns. More commonly, bands have formed Pentecostal churches, or have found homes in modern Pentecostal churches, especially those of AME Zion. Revival endures as more than a theological oddity or colorful footnote. It is the well-spring of a peculiarly Jamaican spirituality, presenting a unique view of man's place in the cosmos and his relationship with eternity. The influence of Revival on Jamaican culture also is significant: in the music, rhythms, and most of all a style of singing that can be found in churches of the fully Christian denominations; also in popular music, in the growing religious music sector, in reggae, and even in dancehall.

MODERN TRENDS

The black independent church tradition led in a wandering path from Revival through Bedwardism to Rastafari. Bedwardism is a colorful tributary to the broad historical river of Jamaican religious expression, but an important one. At its height, like Myalism in the Great Revival, it was a signal factor in the political life of the time.

Alexander Bedward was a laborer at a sugar estate in Kingston before, like thousands of Jamaicans before and after him, emigrating to Colon to work on the Panama Canal. While there he had a vision that brought him back to Jamaica and a church just outside Kingston, the Jamaica Native Baptist Church, which already existed and whose leader, popularly known as 'Shakespeare,' had prophesied the rise of a great leader from within that church.

Bedward began his ministry in 1891, at the age of 32. He became renowned for his eloquence as a preacher, but even more so as a healer. Miracle cures were attributed to his ministrations beside 'the healing stream'—a small river near to the church, described as "pure God water" by a witness at the time (Chevannes 1994). Thousands came from across Jamaica to be baptized in the river; the water was taken home in bottles.

Bedward preached the imminence of a black Jesus, and some of his followers even accorded him that persona. He was also vigorous in his denunciation of poverty, the 'black wall' surrounded by the 'white wall' of oppression. Bedward's services were attended by sufficiently large numbers of people to attract the attention of the authorities and the police, who arrested him in 1895 for sedition and tried to incarcerate him for insanity. On his release from prison he returned to August Town and continued his ministry, which grew larger as the years passed.

An announced 'millenium' on December 31, 1920, when Bedward himself would fly to heaven and for which thousands came from as far away as Panama, Costa Rica, and Cuba, did not happen. A year later he was arrested and charged once more with sedition, along with hundreds of his followers; they were on a march into Kingston "to do battle with his enemies." This time he was confined as insane, and died in the mental asylum in 1930 (Chevannes 1994: 39).

Bedward's name is still invoked as part of the folk history of Jamaica,[9] even though, without its charismatic shepherd, his church dissipated. His Revivalist African church was the most dynamic among the many functioning around the same time. His ability to organize and motivate large throngs of people gave courage to the plethora of small Revival churches across the country, which were joined to Bedward's in a loose alliance. Some Bedwardites found a secular home in the UNIA of Marcus Garvey in the 1920s, with its affirmative African-Jamaican identity. Others, in the 1930s, sought their Creator in the revelations of Rastafari.

Rastafari could be said to have begun as a religion with the coronation in November 1930 of Ras Tafari, the crown prince of Ethiopia, as His Imperial Majesty (H.I.M.) Haile Selassie I, King of Kings, Elect of God, Conquering Lion of Judah. The crowning was to many black people in Jamaica and elsewhere the fulfillment of several biblical prophesies, most importantly Psalm 68:31: "Princes shall come out of Egypt; Ethiopia shall soon stretch out her hands unto God."[10] Reports of the coronation and events surrounding it were read and followed eagerly in Jamaica. The attendance of several heads of state and members of European royalty, and their obeisance before the Emperor, were noted. Within a very few years there were men proclaiming, and other men believing in, the divinity of Haile Selassie.

The tenets of Rastafari are several, and not all of them are subscribed to by all who call themselves Rastafarians. The core set of beliefs, with which the largest number agree, is small:

- Rastafari believe in a supreme creator God, Jah.
- God is black (Jeremiah 8: 21). There is the fact of Haile Selassie's color to support this, despite efforts by 'propagandists' of the time to portray him as 'Semitic' rather than Negro/black/African. The throne of Abyssinia/ Ethiopia was founded by the son of Solomon and the Queen of Sheba (Abyssinia is an earlier name for Ethiopia), who was black.[11] Selassie is a direct descendant of the child of that union.
- H.I.M. is the Messiah, one in divinity with the Godhead. He is in fact— according to the informants of a Jesuit priest, Joseph Owens, who wrote one of the earliest and most comprehensive studies of Rastafari theology— the returned messiah. Jesus—who, significantly for Rastafari, is also in the Davidic line and was also black—is not the Jesus of Christianity, who is part of a 'dead' religion (though Jesus himself never died), his meaning deliberately 'confused' by white theologians (and their black co-conspirators). Jesus—called 'Jes-us' or 'Iyesus'—lived on within man, and is 'returned' in Haile Selassie. "Jesus *was*. Rastafari *is*" (Owens 1976: 104).
- The "God-ness" of Jah inheres in each person: man is divine. Individual Rastafari sometimes give their names simply as 'Rastafari,' not only because they reject the Babylonian name by which they were christened, but to emphasize their identification with Ras Tafari (H.I.M.'s name before his coronation), their one-ness with Jah.

- Rastafari is not a faith of converts, and there is no faith activity that resembles conversion activities in other churches. Truth, Jah, is within every man, and will in time 'manifest' Rastafari. There are elders, wise in the Word, but no priests.

- The Bible (King James Version) contains the word of God, but the true message has been distorted by white theology. Rastafari are extremely knowledgeable in certain books of the KJV Bible: the Psalms, the prophetic books of the Old Testament, certain chapters of the New Testament Epistles, and the Book of Revelation. They share these predelictions with most Native Baptist and Revival believers, though Rastafari see the Word fulfilled in H.I.M.

- Africans are Israelites, the real Jews (identification with the children of Israel is a recurring theme in Jamaican churches), banished from Israel/paradise/Ethiopia by sins against Jah. Rastafari shares with Myal and Revival the belief in a world unbalanced by evil: slavery, white racism, Babylonian oppression. Africans outside of Ethiopia are the Lost Tribe of Israel. Redemption lies in withdrawal from society governed by white values and, ultimately, in repatriation.

Repatriation, while central to belief, is not prominent in the *activities* of Rastafari. Nor is repatriation to Africa unique to Rastafari. It was a central tenet of Garveyism, and the longing for Africa, as we have seen, began with the very uprooting that was slavery.[12] Rastafari was not the first to give the return to Africa spiritual significance, and in that respect it connects with the earliest forms of spirituality and resistance. But they are the first to blend the two elements, so to speak, of repatriation, to place 'heaven' on earth, and to anticipate placement there in this life. The placement will be by divine action of Jah, not the earthly maneuvers of governments or even of Rastafari themselves; that is merely migration.

The sacramental use of the 'weed of wisdom'—marijuana or ganja—brought to Jamaica in the middle of the nineteenth century by indentured laborers from India, and the hairstyle—the dreadlocks—are not articles of faith. Ganja is not universally used by Rastafari, and dreadlocks did not become common until the 1960s. Both speak to the Rastafari view of itself as outcast, rejected by Babylon but itself in turn actively rejecting Babylon. The wearing of uncut, uncombed hair was a deliberately cultivated statement "representing a total symbolic break with society" (Chevannes 1998: 116). The word 'dread' as a prefix to locks, describes both the intent of and reaction to the appearance of 'locksmen.'

Organizationally, Rastafari's roots are diverse. The revelation of Haile Selassie's divinity was arrived at by at least two persons, Leonard Howell and Joseph Hibbert, apparently independently of each other, in the early 1930s, and at least five other preachers and teachers expounding similar ideas were active around that time. Different groups, camps, or houses continue, and there have recently been efforts by some Rastafari at umbrella-type organizations.[13] Rastafari treasure their freedom to act as they feel justified in the spirit: "Man free."

The reported death of Haile Selassie appears to be more of an issue for non-Rastafari than for believers. The confusion and mystery surrounding the Emperor's treatment and whereabouts after the military coup contribute to H.I.M.'s "current prolonged disappearance" from earth. Being divine, one with the Godhead, he cannot die (Wint 1998: 165).

Many scholars see Rastafari, like Myal and Revival before it, as a response of resistance to the prevailing civil and theological order. It goes beyond the earlier faiths in offering a "viable answer to the problem posed by white racism" (Chevannes 1998: 39), which became possible after Garvey. Rastafari remains a marginal faith in terms of its numbers. But as a worldview and a cultural movement its influence is far reaching, within Jamaica and the Caribbean, and beyond. Rastafari communities are to be found wherever in the world people from the Caribbean have settled, and the faith has 'manifested' in people from all racial groups, including whites.

MODERN REALITIES

Since independence, the mainstream churches in Jamaica, as elsewhere, have found themselves losing membership and influence to the newer Evangelical and Pentecostal churches, both home-grown denominations and those originating in the United States, which have been very active. The tremendous growth of the Pentecostals as a group, and of some of the evangelical churches such as the Adventists, can be attributed to missionary zeal supported by considerable financial resources, and to their comfortable fit with forms of worship and belief elements with deep roots in the Jamaican spirit. Further, an important aspect of the influence of the older churches, their schools, have largely been lost to them, partly through more active government involvement in education generally, but also because of diminishing church resources.

Census figures show the largest of all affiliations—21.2 percent in 1991, probably larger now—as Church of God. Several churches/denominations are in fact grouped under this heading. Church of God (Indiana), a holiness denomination, first came in 1907 by invitation of some Jamaicans, partly to offer service following the earthquake. The first chapel was built in 1913, and is still being used. A Bible School began in 1926 offering a four-year course in theology; a high school opened in the following year and is now regarded as one of the leading secondary institutions in the island. Church of God (Tennessee), a Pentecostal denomination, came during World War I and now operates in the Caribbean as New Testament Church of God. Divisions in the U.S. churches have been echoed abroad.

But even before that, in the second half of the nineteenth century, the older (British-based) evangelical faiths—the Methodists, the Moravians, and the Baptists—found themselves competing for converts with recently formed 'holiness churches' from the United States, which had come out of the movement to return to the New Testament emphasis on personal holiness and 'perfection' in the Christian life. These churches sent missionaries across the still expanding United States and into the Caribbean that, post-Emancipation, was seen as fertile ground for conversions. The Disciples of Christ arrived in Jamaica in 1858, the Brethren in the 1860s, Seventh Day Adventists in the 1870s, the Salvation Army in 1887, and the African Methodist Episcopal (AME) in the 1890s (Dayfoot 1999).

"The evangelical and pentecostal religion has been a movement among the underclass" (Roper 1991). The first (American) evangelicals were regarded as antislavery, though this was not the *raison d'être* of the faith, and they were not always militant in the cause. But they welcomed slaves and ex-slaves into their congregations, with seating alongside whoever else wanted to come—at the time a bold, even revolutionary, position. This 'underclass' was the first target audience in the Caribbean as well.

Ashley Smith and Garnet Roper, both clergymen, identify three factors that help to explain the widespread popularity of evangelical and pentecostal churches: leadership, worship, and language. "Unlike the normal situation among lower income members of established or mainline European type churches, Pentecostal groups are usually led by male persons from the same socio-economic sector who have had little or no exposure to life situations outside of the physical and cultural environment with which members of the group live" (Smith 1978: 4). The worship service "is characterized by simplicity of physical setting, order of worship and speech. . . . A great deal of emotional unburdening takes place within each worship service, and this is facilitated by the unrestrictive nature of the service in respect of tone and the demand for propriety in speech and physical gesture" (Smith 1978: 4). "The important thing . . . is that the liturgy and language [of the service] are understandable. This religion is very oral and understands that the Jamaican culture is an oral culture" (Roper 1991: 37). This understanding is what drives the extensive use of the electronic media by the modern evangelical churches, which has helped to further extend their influence in the society: the form and content of their services are suited to the microphone and television camera.

These factors help to explain the enduring adherence to and growth of these churches. Some of the salient features of the worship service—laying on of hands, possession by the Holy Spirit, speaking in tongues, singing, and in some cases dancing—attract many who would have grown up accustomed to or participating in Revival, but are perhaps also seeking something more organized and recognized.[14] The informality of worship—contrasting with the 'Sunday best' clothing which is *de rigueur*—invites those who are intimidated by the set-piece services of the established churches. In sum, "those alienated from sources of influence in the society and who are victimized by forces, both real and imagined, are given access to power by their religion" (Roper 1991: 38).

In the early years middle-class members of established churches, according to Smith, himself an elder statesman in one such church, responded to the evangelical churches with "a feeling of contempt and disgust." This has changed since independence in 1962, he says, since when there has been "growing appreciation for and genuine acceptance of what is 'native' in the culture" by the middle classes. In addition, "it is very evident that the movement has taken on Church-type characteristics in respect of organization, preparation for and expectation of leaders" (Smith 1978: 5).

This assumption of the outward attributes of the 'mainstream' has, if anything, helped to increase membership in the evangelical churches. They have more resources, for instance, both internally and on-call from principals and affiliates abroad, with which to move quickly into the new urban communities springing up on former agricultural lands surrounding the Corporate Area, and where the traditional churches are hardly to be found.

The issue between the faith communities can be seen as one of "indigenisation: . . . a liturgy which is culturally meaningful; and a theology which begins to reflect at least some of the spiritual values which are deeply embedded in [the] culture" (Chevannes 1991: 46). There has been significant indigenization of the liturgy: drums, guitars, Revival hymns, and, on occasion, dancing are to be found in some services of some of the established churches. On the theological level, however, "European Christianity creates a split between body and spirit, while on the other hand the Afro-Caribbean people treat them as unified wholes" (Chevannes 1991: 47). The established churches are, of course, constrained in their theological flexibility by both structure and history, which adds a 'political' aspect to the issue: their links with overseas centers of authority, with the period of colonialism, and, in some cases, with slavery. Despite indigenization of their clergy, which in all but the Roman Catholic Church is now complete, they are still burdened by the past.

Within many of those churches, however, movements of renewal are at work, with greater or lesser 'blessing' from the centers of formal authority. The so-called Charismatic Movement, a resurgence of the spirit that animated earlier awakenings and Revivals, has been quietly at work in Jamaica over thirty years or so, across denominational boundaries. It has led in some cases to the creation of new churches entirely, in the pentecostal mode. Within the Roman Catholic Church, also, there are 'faith' and 'covenant' communities that explore inner healing through experience 'in the spirit,' while at the same time reaching out to the wider society, including those in prison, in several special 'ministries.' The worship services of these communities—whose members follow the age-old Jamaican pattern of also attending the regular Sunday services in their parish churches—engage both body and spirit in a lively and authentic expression of Jamaican spirituality.

NOTES

1. In the twenty-five years between Emancipation in Jamaica and that in United States, black slave sailors on American vessels were encouraged to desert and claim their freedom in Jamaica, which significant numbers of them did.

2. Ironically, that passage of Scripture has great significance for the Rastafari as well, as we shall see.

3. Hereinafter used to mean foreign Baptist, Moravian, and Wesleyan clergymen who, upon death or transfer, were replaced from outside Jamaica. By this time Native churches were operating procedures of succession.

4. Obeah is "a set or system of secret beliefs in the use of supernatural forces to attain or defend against evil ends" (Allsopp 1996: 412).

5. The figure of John the Baptist is very important in Native churches.

6. This characteristic is not unknown today, with people moving between (Christian) churches for worship, and between Christian and African observances.

7. Similar revivals had already been observed in the United States, Britain, and Ireland in the late 1850s.

8. "The labored, rhythmic dancing associated with revivalist worship" (Bisnauth 1989: 194). Other words, such as 'groaning' and 'laboring,' are used by other writers in describing the process of spirit possession at a Revival meeting.

9. Bedward is featured in at least two folk songs that most Jamaicans know: *Dip dem Bedward* and *Sly Mongoose*.

10. Also Revelation 5:2, 5; "And I saw a strong angel proclaiming with a loud voice, 'Who is worthy to open the book and loose the seals thereof?' . . . And one of the elders saith unto me, 'Weep not: behold, the Lion of the tribe of Judah, the Root of David, hath prevailed to open the Book and to loose the seven of God sent forth unto all the earth.' "

11. "I am black, but comely" (Song of Solomon 1: 5).

12. The exposure of the slaves to the KJV, with its several references to Ethiopia, melded with this longing into what some writers refer to as 'Ethiopianism' and Chevannes calls "the idealization of Africa" (Chevannes 1995: 33–34). Ethiopia becomes the 'word' for the whole of Africa.

13. The Ethiopian Orthodox Church came to Jamaica in 1970; many Rastafari "denounced its practice of baptism . . . as being too close to the Christian and Revival traditions" (Chevannes 1998: 108). The Church also maintains "a diplomatic silence" on the divinity of H.I.M. Nevertheless, many Rastafari belong to the church, which has several communities across the island and is a member of the mainstream Jamaica Council of Churches. The most famous Rastafari of all, Bob Marley, was buried according to its rites.

14. There are several umbrella organizations for the evangelical and pentecostal churches, through which they pool some resources and also make their voices heard on a wide range of national issues.

3

Education

THE SHAPE of education in Jamaica has been determined, more than anything else, by two factors: the 'idea of education' in the mind of colonial bureaucrats and island legislators, and the (limited) resources they were prepared to allocate to education. What has resulted is a structure so set in its original purposes that, in many important respects, it stands unyielding, despite more than half a century's struggle to alter it. A look at the historical development of the education system is, therefore, essential to appreciating the problems facing policy makers and educators at the beginning of the twenty-first century.

A BRIEF HISTORY

Early Initiatives

Education in Jamaica began with a number of bequests made in the seventeenth and eighteenth centuries, mainly to provide schools for the sons of poor white families. Bequests were meant for schools to educate *free* people, so that, up to 1834, only whites—and a small number of free black and colored children—could go to school. Slave children received no tutelage other than 'minding' by older slave women until they 'graduated' to work gangs on the plantation.

Christian missionaries started the earliest educational institutions that admitted black students, running schools for free children, but also teaching slave children. They tried to start schools for adult slaves—an effort stoutly resisted by the planters who were convinced that education would encourage the slaves to consider themselves too good for manual labor. This was a position many in the elite classes supported up to the twentieth century. Several scholars consider this 'upper crust' resistance partly responsible for the limited educational opportunities afforded the black population.

Many influential persons in Britain were concerned that once the 'controls' obtaining under slavery were removed, the society would collapse for lack of a labor force since the freed blacks would lead slothful and unproductive lives. To avoid such breakdown, the Emancipation Act of 1833 provided "for the religious and moral education" of the ex-slaves by making a grant to the colonies of £30,000 a year for five years. The British government accepted the recommendation of Rev. John Sterling that the grant money be given to nonconformist missionaries to administer, rather than local legislatures. Sterling had two motives: he wished the missionaries to continue educating the ex-slaves, and he wished their education to have a religious base, thereby promoting the 'civilizing' influence of British values. In this way, church schools became the basis of a mass system of education. (After 1840 the grant slowly decreased, ceasing entirely in 1845.)

The first response to schools was vigorous; all churches reported increased enrollment since the ex-slaves expected education to improve their lot. The churches also had high expectations, anticipating that educated ex-slaves would be teachers and lay preachers. These expectations were not unjustified, for some free villages did achieve high levels of literacy.

Normal Schools

In the first two years, grant funds covered most of the cost of building schools; after that they helped cover the cost of teachers' salaries. Many teachers were brought from England (Jamaican teachers had little opportunity for training) and did not come cheap. Rev. Sterling had suggested that a 'normal school' to train teachers be established. In 1836, through the bequest of Lady Mico, the Mico Institution (now Mico College) was set up to train apprentices who were teachers. In addition, between 1839 and 1843, several denominations started normal schools to train their own teachers. Normal and elementary schools had mutual interests: the brightest schoolchildren would train as teachers and return to the schools to teach.

Sustaining the Elementary School System

At first support for elementary education was limited to the imperial government's grant (to Jamaica) of £7,500 per annum; the local assembly of legislators provided nothing. When the grant ended in 1845, some churches limped along on their own resources. Overall, however, they found it difficult to maintain schools once the grant ceased.

Though many ex-slaves continued to look to education as a way to improve themselves, the government had other ideas. As grant support waned, the assembly voted sums annually for education, recognizing ways for it to serve their purposes. In 1844, they passed an "Act to encourage Agricultural Education" and proposed a £30 incentive to schools offering "agricultural pursuits" that fulfilled certain conditions. Not many schools responded; missionary churches rightly interpreted that the move was intended to retain the ex-slaves for manual labor.

Crown Colony Government and Payment by Results

After the Morant Bay Rebellion (1865), the Jamaican legislature dissolved itself. In 1866 Jamaica became a Crown Colony with the governor exercising the greatest legislative and political power. Governor Sir John Peter Grant swiftly commenced educational reforms with a powerful socializing intent via a reformed Code of Regulations (1867). It introduced the Payment by Results system, tying government grants to achievement of specified educational objectives. 'Industrial' education was once more encouraged by special incentives, and the number of industrial schools doubled between 1867 and 1872. The schools proved ineffective, perhaps because parents continued to resist education of this kind for their children—a reasonable position, given the fact that most of the ex-slave population did not own sufficient arable land to make a living from—and eventually the grants were reduced.

In 1882 the Department of Education formalized the pupil-teacher system that had emerged out of the practice of older pupils helping to instruct younger ones and themselves benefiting by additional instruction from the teacher in charge. Upon completing school, these pupil-teachers stayed to assist the teacher for very small wages. A syllabus and a program of annual examinations were devised for them. The pupil-teacher system was to survive, side by side with intramural teacher training programs, well into the twentieth century.

Ten years later, government took over the elementary school system—a move many lament even now. Until that time, the churches had owned and managed the schools, assisted by the state; in 1892, government undertook to direct policy and provide funding, though the churches continued as owners. Government also began to set up its own schools and abolished fees. Funded by an education tax, free primary education finally became available.

SECONDARY EDUCATION: 1879 TO 1912

The initiative to establish secondary schools came from the churches: in 1850, the Jesuits established the first secondary school, St. George's College, primarily to cater to Roman Catholic exiles from Haiti. As the middle of the century approached, nonconformist missionaries began to worry about schooling for their own children. Catholic schools were not an option, and they were not prepared for their children to go to their own elementary schools. The missionaries also wished to swell their ranks with recruits with higher education. Thus, out of these partly selfish motives, the other-than-Catholic denominations started several secondary schools between 1875 and 1900.

Secondary education emerged as a direct result of the existence of primary education. Wealthy Jamaicans had always sent their children to school abroad; however, even in the heyday of sugar, not all whites could afford this. Thus, local private schools emerged at the end of the eighteenth and during the nineteenth century. As the fortunes of sugar declined in the late nineteenth century, fewer whites could afford an education abroad for their children. In 1879, government set up the Jamaica Schools Commission to administer secondary education, which was meant for the middle classes— less-well-off whites, browns, and a few blacks. The poor, it was assumed, could not benefit from education at this level; even if they could, it would threaten the status quo by raising them above "their proper stations."

EDUCATION AT THE BEGINNING OF THE TWENTIETH CENTURY

There seems to have been no 'mind' to expand secondary places so that, in time, children could move from primary levels in the elementary system into upper grades in the secondary system.[1] Instead, there appears to have been a widespread opinion that very few poor children were fit to improve their lot. Certainly the number of secondary school places remained few: in 1911, His Majesty's Inspector of Schools, H. H. Piggott, found 842 students in the 12 schools he visited—534 boys and 308 girls. This number represented a mere 1 percent of the age cohort. Another 700 were in private secondary schools.

Primary Education, 1892 to 1943

Little occurred to expand or improve the educational system between the beginning of the century and the advent of World War II. Except for a small number of scholarships available to elementary students, the dichotomy between primary and secondary sectors remained firmly in place. The Department of Education was responsible for the elementary/teachers' college level, while the Jamaica Schools Commission managed the secondary schools. There were more girls in the system than boys: most teachers' college students were female, and girls were the majority in elementary schools where they outperformed as well as outnumbered boys.

There were some gains: elementary education remained free or heavily subsidized, and enrollment increased: between 1890 and 1943, primary school enrollment went from 48.5 percent to 72.0 percent of the age cohort. Also, though white officialdom controlled the sector, blacks began to make aggressive use of the (albeit limited) advantages education afforded. During the early twentieth century, there was a stream—"never large, but . . . constant" (Knight 1990: 295)—of talented children of "the lower orders" making their way by means of scholarships into secondary schools, and from there into the professions.

Elementary education focused narrowly on literacy, numeracy, and vocational skills, with the classics, arts, and sciences introduced only surreptitiously and on private initiative. Nevertheless, because they were highly motivated, the lower classes, led by black schoolmasters and schoolmistresses, capitalized on what was available and by their considerable effort created the black and brown professional class. Eventually the will of the people prevailed: by the late 1940s, agriculture, manual training, and domestic economy began to be phased out of the primary school curriculum for pupils under 12 years of age.

Secondary Education, 1912 to 1943

Not a great deal transpired in secondary education between 1912 and 1943. Girls had equal access to secondary places, and the system expanded in 1920 by giving secondary schools grants-in-aid. Schools had to apply for grants-in-aid to the Commission, which prescribed the scheme under which they operated. An inspection process ensured that schools fulfilled the conditions of the grant. There was no prescription that any proportion of elementary students should be admitted as a condition of the grants-in-aid, nor were grants-in-aid provided to secondary schools run for profit. The consequence was that black children, many of whom had to attend private for-profit secondary schools, suffered on both counts.

Economic conditions deteriorated over the period, one consequence being that there were few jobs for secondary school leavers. The Director of Education in 1936 was alarmed that graduates seemed to want desk-type positions and to scorn agriculture; he suggested that opportunities for secondary school graduates lay in the fields of agriculture or elementary school teaching.

CONTEMPORARY EDUCATION IN JAMAICA

If any difference was to be effected in Jamaican education, history made it plain that it would have to be at the hands of Jamaicans: the story of contemporary education is essentially the account of what Jamaicans have managed to do with education since it became their responsibility.

Jamaica's first cabinet was appointed in 1953. This event can be seen as part of a process that really began with colonial administrators handing over a degree of legislative control to the Jamaican leaders elected with adult suffrage in 1944. Indeed, the self-government process can be seen as extending even further back, to the 1930s riots that prodded a lethargic bureaucracy to investigations, which produced reports, which proposed educational reforms. Though the Report of Lord Moyne's Commission was *the* response to the 1930s disturbances and was intended to include comments on the system of elementary education, it is the Report of Columbia University's Professor I. L. Kandel that first tackled the integration of primary and secondary systems.

Articulating Primary and Secondary Systems

The Kandel Report addressed the issue of integrating primary and secondary systems. One of Kandel's suggestions for reorganizing the system was that primary education should be general education, with no vocational content, while postprimary education should be offered in several kinds of schools with different curricula. However welcome these ideas may have been, they prompted no action: when the first Minister of Education took office in 1953, things were much the same as they had been before 1938.

The years 1953 to 1988 represent a roller coaster ride of gains and reversals in Jamaican education. The period of 1953 to 1978 has been characterized as "years of expansion and development," and the period 1978 to 1988 as a decade of "retrenchment and reversals" (Miller 1989: 205).[2] There were three sets of reforms in this twenty-five-year period: the 1957 Reforms, the New Deal for Education in 1966, and the "free education" reforms of 1973. In each case the year is indicative and not definite: the reforms described occur in the years following, and in the case of the 1966 reforms, co-opt some policies formulated prior to that time. Each set of reforms represented an attempt to accommodate the aspirations of a population eager to achieve a better life for themselves and their children. Each achieved some gains in one or the other sector of the system, sometimes to see them later reversed. None represented the radical restructuring required to offer all Jamaicans, regardless of social background, an opportunity for quality education limited only by the individual's ability to progress.

The Reforms

Several changes proposed in 1957 were concerned with connecting the primary and secondary subsectors: government created 2,000 additional high school "free places" (full tuition subsidies) and, as the Kandel Report had recommended, introduced the Common Entrance Examination as the basis of entry into high schools. This enlarged the bridge between primary and secondary sectors but was not a restructuring.

The New Deal for Education was the first official plan for education in independent Jamaica. Policies devised as far back as 1962 were retroactively incorporated into the New Deal. Thus, the New Deal is said to have introduced the controversial 70:30 Regulation (implemented in 1962) that tried to redress educational inequalities by reserving 70 percent of free places in high school for primary school children (Miller 1989: 211). In the 1961 Common Entrance Examination, middle-class children from private schools (5 percent of the total age cohort) had won 54 percent of the awards. The 70/30 Regulation was eventually removed in 1974 because, in that year, primary schools won 74 percent of places on merit.

It has been argued that the New Deal had a lasting impact on Jamaican education for three reasons: it represented the largest single capital expansion of the system since the abolition of slavery; it utilized international and bilateral agencies to fund the expansion of the system at all levels, and it promoted public support for early childhood education through basic schools (Miller 1989: 212).

The 1973 reforms are memorable for the institution of free high school and university education, implemented in 1975. (Both programs have since ceased.) Other developments included the Curriculum Development Thrust, intended to reform the curriculum in public elementary schools at all levels except junior secondary; the transforming of junior secondary into five-year secondary schools; the inclusion of special schools for the handicapped as part of the public system of education; the establishment of community colleges; the establishment of the Jamaica Association for the Advancement of Literacy (JAMAL) Foundation to eliminate illiteracy at all levels; and the introduction of the shift system whereby primary and secondary school plants were utilized by two sets of students and teachers each day.

The socialist experiment of the 1970s had certain deleterious socioeconomic effects, among them the flight of capital and the migration of middle-class professionals, including teachers. By 1978, the country was in trauma: gripped by unprecedented political division and a collapsing financial base, the government of the day was forced to look to the International Monetary Fund (IMF) for financial assistance. Jamaica had had some kind of agreement with the IMF since 1977. The IMF may not have prescribed educational measures, but many cutbacks in educational provision were attributed to the need to observe IMF conditions. Thus, there is little doubt that "the impact on education of the policies occasioned by IMF conditionalities [was] negative" (Miller 1989: 214).

Retrenchment

Over the next decade, retrenchment impacted teacher education most severely: between 1984 and 1986, in-service programs at training college and university levels ceased, and two intramural teacher training programs closed down. Thus, by 1988 there was once more a pervasive shortage of teachers. There were other reversals: the Ministry of Education turned a blind eye to high schools' unofficially reintroducing fees. At university level, fees were also reintroduced by way of a 'cess' levied by government. Education's share of government's recurrent expenditure fell from a high of 20 percent in the late 1970s to a low of 12 percent in 1988, as a result of which school plants fell into serious disrepair.

There were some gains: the Human Employment and Resource Training (HEART) Foundation was established to work with employers in training persons for existing employment opportunities. With donor agencies and private sector support, the government also set up the Primary Textbook Project in 1984. It ensured that, for the first time, each primary school child had a textbook in English, mathematics, science, and social studies. In addition, programs for training primary and secondary school teachers were reformed.

THE END OF THE TWENTIETH CENTURY: 1988–1998

Three developments in the period 1988 to 1998 deserve mention: the Reform in Secondary Education (ROSE) project, the retirement of the Common Entrance Examination, and the introduction of the National Assessment Program. The three are functionally related.

The ROSE Project, commenced in 1993, is "the most comprehensive of the twentieth-century reforms of education in Jamaica, and potentially the most far-reaching in dealing with the weaknesses inherited from the colonial period" (King 1998: 56). ROSE presents a common curriculum for all children in grades seven through nine (the 12 to 15 age group) in secondary schools. The proposed (2002) provision of a secondary school place for every child does not, however, eliminate variation in the quality of schools.

The Common Entrance Examination was replaced in 1999 by the Grade Six Achievement Test, part of an ambitious National Assessment Program. The availability of a secondary school place for every child makes it possible to retire the Common Entrance Examination. The National Assessment Program tests each child on the curriculum studied, rather than on a few selected subjects. Students are tested at grades one, three, and four, and an achievement test is given at grade six, replacing the Common Entrance Examination.

However, as a newspaper columnist observed, "One of the conditions for the success of the new [program] is the availability of quality Secondary School places" since, in the absence of a system of high quality secondary schools, testing will inevitably perform "allocative functions" (Wint 1998).

TERTIARY EDUCATION

There is a large postsecondary educational sector including six community colleges, eight teacher training colleges, the College of Agriculture, the Edna Manley School for the Visual and Performing Arts, the G. C. Foster College of Physical Education and Sports, Northern Caribbean University (a Seventh-Day Adventist institution), the University of Technology, Jamaica, and the University of the West Indies. Table 3.1 lists the student enrollment in Jamaican tertiary institutions in 1988–1989 and 1996–1997. Several U.S. universities offer off-shore degree programs, undergraduate and graduate, which are structured to accommodate working adults.

Community colleges were intended to prepare students for university entry, train persons for middle-level jobs, and be a training/retraining community resource to help persons keep pace, *inter alia*, with changes in technology. Some community colleges also offer the first year of a number of programs available at the University of Technology, Jamaica.

The teachers' colleges provide three years of training for teachers in the areas of early childhood, primary, secondary, and special education, though

Table 3.1

Student Enrollment in Tertiary Institutions in Jamaica, 1988–1989 and 1996–1997

Type of tertiary institution	No. of schools 1988–1989	Enrollment	No. of schools 1996–1997	Enrollment
Community colleges	4	5,851	6	4,213
Teachers' colleges	8	2,780	6	3,588
Edna Manley College/ Cultural Training Centre	1	278	1	268
College of Agriculture	1	236	1	536
G. C. Foster College of PE & Sports	1	73	1	200
West Indies College (Teachers)/Northern Caribbean U.	1	25	1	NA
College of Arts Sc. & Tech./U. of Tech.	1	4,527	1	7,102
U. of the West Indies, Mona Campus	1	5,209	1	8,274
TOTAL	18	18,979	18	24,181

Source: Taken from *Education Statistics 1988–89* and *Pocketbook of Statistics Jamaica 1998*.

not all colleges provide training in all four areas. G. C. Foster College of Physical Education and Sports trains teachers of physical education.

Students obtain a teaching diploma upon completion of the teachers' college program; certification is issued jointly by the Ministry of Education, the Joint Board of Teacher Education of the University of the West Indies and the college that the student attended.

The Edna Manley School for the Performing and Visual Arts began in 1976 as the Cultural Training Center, created out of previously existing Schools of Art and Music. Administered by the Institute of Jamaica, it is now a multidisciplinary home of schools for the visual arts, drama, dance, and music. (See also Chapters 9 and 10, on the performing arts and the visual arts.) Students accepted into the schools often have some previous training acquired at privately run dance schools and music studios. Youngsters usually acquire experience in the visual arts in school or in summer programs run in camps and at the libraries.

There is some private entrepreneurship at this level as well. Independent schools exist that provide courses in several areas including secretarial and business skills, practical nursing, computer training, management and production, automotive skills, catering, hairdressing, and cosmetology. There is an automotive school and Dental Auxiliary Training School, both government-run.

EDUCATION AT THE BEGINNING OF THE TWENTY-FIRST CENTURY

Many Jamaican children begin school before age 6, toddling off to play schools and nursery schools, or more formally structured infant, kindergarten, or basic schools, by the age of four. There are twenty-nine infant schools run by the government and attached to primary schools. The government also pays the salaries of the heads of eighteen demonstration basic schools, all of whom are trained teachers, and subsidizes teachers' salaries in the remaining basic schools. Otherwise, the entire early childhood sector is privately owned and run. Kindergartens are usually attached to preparatory schools, many of which are in turn attached to high schools. The best arrangement is for a child to be enrolled in a kindergarten attached to one of the 'top' high schools, since selection upwards is more or less automatic, once the child performs adequately. Kindergartens serve the middle to upper classes and are comparatively expensive. Kindergarten teachers are trained—often overseas—and most schools are fairly well equipped. Some parents register children as soon as they are conceived, since competition for places in the 'best' of these schools is fierce.

The Jamaican educational success story nonpareil is the revolutionizing of the basic school sector, largely through the efforts of the late Dudley R. B. Grant, with the support of the (Netherlands) Bernard Van Leer Foundation. Basic schools are preprimary schools—poor people's kindergartens. Operated by churches, voluntary organizations, and private individuals, they vary widely in resources. A few (usually those run by churches and voluntary organizations) can compare with the best kindergartens; others make do in less-than-ideal quarters, dependent on the assistance of communities that are very poor. Grant networked basic schools into local communities through sponsoring organizations and built these into an islandwide organization. Over most of a period spanning thirty years, the Van Leer Foundation helped to upgrade plants and funded teacher training (ongoing and intramural), since most teachers had only a primary school education, and, in some cases, very little of that. Parents were encouraged to help in basic schools by contributing labor, materials, equipment, and even time in the classroom, and by fund-raising and helping to maintain school plants. Basic school teachers became experts in converting any space into a classroom and using 'found materials' to make teaching aids.

Early childhood and primary education (private and public) is taken very seriously: parents are eager for children to learn to read and count, and proudly invite their children to show off their literacy and numeracy skills. There are various enrichment activities: school plays, concerts, parades, prize-giving ceremonies, and even graduations. Programs at better schools compare with the best anywhere in the world. Readiness activities in kindergarten introduce the three Rs as well as basic science, social studies, religious education, physical education (often including dance), arts and crafts, and music.

These subjects also constitute the curriculum for grades one through six. In a few schools, computers offer access to the cyberworld, and Spanish is taught. Extramural sports are emphasized, and 'sports day' is one of the highlights of the school year. Some preparatory schools have football teams that participate in organized interschool competitions. Children compete as members of 'houses'—a British tradition and a feature continuing on up through the system, till they are superseded by Halls of Residence at the tertiary level.

An annual spelling bee competition run by the Gleaner Company, the island's oldest newspaper publisher, attracts islandwide participation. Top spellers compete in the U.S. national finals, and in 1998 Jodi Ann Maxwell, the Jamaican champion, won the U.S. competition. Primary-level schools, public and private, support the Jamaica Festival Competitions that take place at Independence celebrations. They prepare dances, songs, plays, and items of poetry and prose (some original) for performance at that time.

For persons in school between 1957 and 1997, the halcyon early days began to lose their luster in grade five, when preparation for the dreaded Common Entrance Examination began. Tens of thousands of children (50,000 plus, in the case of the last examination in 1998) sat the exam, which tested mathematics, language skills, and mental ability. They competed for some 2,000 high school places in 1957, and some 17,000 places in 1998. Most children were therefore doomed to fail, a blight on their lives from which only two subsequent, narrow windows of opportunity offered escape. Because it was invidious, the pressure to remove the Common Entrance Examination was great; as we have said, it was finally removed in 1999.

High school in Jamaica lasts five years (grades seven to eleven, or forms one to five), unless students qualify to spend a further two years studying for

Advanced Level examinations, and elect to do so. There are several kinds of high schools: traditional high, technical high, agricultural high, comprehensive high, and new secondary schools. The traditional high or 'grammar' schools (which have always, like their British models, offered a classical academic education) are the most prestigious and are mostly single sex schools. Newer secondary high schools, technical schools, and comprehensive schools are coeducational.

At the end of five years, students sit an outside examination—one set by an examining body external to the school. Until 1980, most students sat the University of Cambridge Ordinary ('O') level examinations; since 1979, students in the Anglophone region have taken examinations set by the Caribbean Examinations Council (CXC). However, overseas examinations as well as others, including the London City and Guilds Examinations, continue to be available, and some candidates (including private students) do take them.

The high school curriculum is diverse and challenging. The core curriculum in the lower grades includes English language and literature, mathematics, general science, history, geography, civics, religious education, French, Spanish, art, music, and physical education. Church schools may offer religion. In higher grades (fourth and fifth forms), students can specialize in a wider variety of subjects. The Caribbean Examination Council assesses some thirty subjects.

Students and parents are usually very enthusiastic at the beginning of high school. Parents scramble to find funds for uniforms, books, and equipment. Almost all Jamaican schools require students to wear uniforms, and, for many students of both sexes, a long and wearying day ends with hours of homework and then preparation of uniforms for the next day.

Enthusiasm seems to dwindle after the first year, one sign being that figures for sales of school textbooks drop off for the second and third years of high school. (They pick up somewhat in the fourth year when students begin the syllabuses for the external examinations.) Most high schools are fully government supported or receive a grant-in-aid, though there have always been private schools, some of which are poorly resourced enterprises while others, set up and maintained by influential special interest groups, are well resourced.

Sports is the extracurricular activity that receives the most consistent support, and many students win scholarships (high school and university) to North American institutions for performance in this area. Football and track and field are especially popular and enthusiastically supported by the students themselves.

High school diplomas are awarded at the end of the first five years, once the student has satisfactorily completed the course of studies. Satisfactory completion is not necessarily tied to performance on the examinations, which is generally poor and has always been so. Data for 1945 to 1987 for percentage of students passing English in end-of-high-school exams show that passes of over 50 percent were only achieved ten times during these thirty-seven years. (Miller 1989: 221–222).[3] English is a compulsory subject, as is mathematics.

LITERACY

Literacy data for Jamaica vary greatly. A 1998 editorial in the online version of the newspaper *The Gleaner* says: "While the official literacy rate used for the assessment of the country's Human Development Index is 84.4 per cent, estimates of functional illiteracy range from 30 per cent to as high as 50 per cent" ("Banishing Illiteracy"). Still, an improvement in educational standards was observed over the period 1962–1988, using literacy as one measure (Miller 1989: 221). Illiteracy declined from 50 percent in the 1960s to 18 percent of the population over age 15 in 1987. However, results of a 1994 National Literacy Survey are not encouraging. It showed only 57 percent of the population as functionally literate, 18 percent as literate, 3 percent as having basic literacy skills, and 21 percent classified as absolutely illiterate (Boxill 1997).

Education, seen by the freed population after Emancipation as the means by which it would advance itself, continues, at least in political rhetoric and policy documents, to be considered a unifying, democratizing force in Jamaican society. Some of the facts do not entirely support that view. Studies in the last quarter of the twentieth century find that race, class, and gender impact educational achievement. Put succinctly, better-off, lighter-skinned students do better than poorer darker-skinned students. Complex patterns of achievement characterize the performance of females, but, overall, they outperform males. Scholars have yet to account for the fact that forces that originally operated to allot education (among other resources) as a scarce benefit seem still to exercise influence, never mind that the nation has been politically independent for almost four decades, with the vote being exercised by a predominantly black, mainly peasant/working-class population.

Improvements have indubitably been made since Jamaicans began governing themselves: the question is, how far-reaching have these improvements been? There has been a significant measure of integration among levels of the system, for "An educational ladder now exists. Public primary education is integrated with public secondary education. The latter is articulated with university education available locally" (Miller 1989: 224). In 1989, primary and secondary education were partially integrated. Abolition of the Common Entrance and the promise of a secondary school place for every child suggest a system that is completely integrated. However, as long as marked differences in the quality of schools remain, education will continue its historic discrimination against poor children. The several types of public secondary institutions (traditional high, technical high, agricultural high, comprehensive high, and new secondary schools) may continue to mean that "neither the lines of educational demarcation nor the social functions served by these different types of schools are clear" (Miller 1989: 224).

At the beginning of the twenty-first century, then, almost all children of primary age (6–11 years) are enrolled in school, while some 88 percent of the children of lower secondary age (12–14 years) and roughly half of the children of upper secondary age (15–16 years) are enrolled in secondary schools at their respective levels. University enrollment for 1994–1995 stood at over 14,000, and more than 10,000 students were enrolled at other post-secondary institutions.

These figures would seem to report a remarkable achievement. However, many educators' opinions on the product of two centuries of Jamaican education are unenthusiastic. One educator chafes at both the inequalities in Jamaican education—"perhaps most extreme and intractable at the secondary level"—and "widespread dissatisfaction with low levels of achievement in national and regional examinations [and] . . . dissatisfaction with the unpreparedness of . . . graduates for the world of work" (King 1998: 45).

One historian emphasizes process rather than product in measuring much the same achievement. He sees the expanded educational system that produced a new professional class in the Caribbean as one of four sources in which the democratization of regional societies was rooted. The democratic movement grew, although a small elite kept political control up to the 1940s. It was education, along with economic diversification, the expansion of organized religion, and the rise of labor unions, that Knight sees as contributing "to the formation of that strong tradition of democratic government which has characterized the English Caribbean during the twentieth century." In fact, he calls education "the great social elevator of the English Caribbean masses" (Knight 1990: 295).

Both the historian and educator would probably join a broad consensus that the problems in contemporary Jamaican education are inherited: systems constructed to serve plantation society in a British colony in the nineteenth century could not work in the twentieth century, let alone the twenty-first. Many persons expected that things would change with independence in

1962. There were indeed changes, but these tinkered with old structures rather than creating new ones. Nevertheless, if every Jamaican child has the chance of a secondary school place at the beginning of the twenty-first century, then perhaps the confidence that Jamaicans have always placed in education will finally, in some measure, have been justified.

NOTES

1. There were also social differences among secondary schools: smaller ones in rural areas drew more students from the lower social echelons than did larger schools and boarding schools. It was recommended that the smaller schools follow a more vocational curriculum and that the larger schools should follow a more liberal program (Miller 1990: 87).

2. The account of this period that follows draws heavily on Miller's work.

3. There was no examination in 1951. The highest percentage (63.1 percent) was achieved in 1974.

4

Language

NAOMI Unoo see mi dyin trial!
       Dem people yah nuh easy.
       A kill dem a go kill de man.
       How yuh mean "Which man?"
       Nuh de man Jesus. Yuh know—
       De one dat preach? And
       Tell story? Yuh never hear
       Him yet? Bwoy, me nuh
       Understand oonu young
       People. If oonu did stay at
       Oonu yard, me would seh
       Come. But oonu walk street
       And ignorant same way.

—from Pamela Mordecai, *de Man*

JAMAICA can claim international attention for at least two things: reggae music and its creole language, one of several found all over the world. *The Oxford Companion to the English Language* (McArthur 1992: 539) says that Jamaican Creole is "relatively well researched . . . because of the presence since 1948 of a campus of the University of the West Indies." Beginning in the late 1950s, scholars in the Caribbean and elsewhere became increasingly interested in the creole languages of the region—an especially promising field of study because these were new languages that had formed quickly. Thus, studying creoles might help scholars understand the processes by which children (and adult learners of new languages) acquire language, which might, in turn, throw light on how humans originally acquired speech. It was not long before the Caribbean became an exciting laboratory for the study of creole linguistics: "every sub-branch of linguistics . . . has sought and continues to seek new and powerful insights from Caribbean language data."[1]

The Jamaican language situation is complex. Jamaicans make use of not one, but two distinct languages, to varying degrees: Standard Jamaican English, a kissin' cousin of Standard British English with which it shares vocabulary and grammar; and Jamaican Creole, a comparatively new language with mostly English words but very different grammar, pronunciation, and rhythms. Jamaican Creole is thought to have developed at some point between the mid-seventeenth and mid-eighteenth centuries. Although any English speaker can understand Standard Jamaican English, the structures and pronunciation of Jamaican Creole are so different that most non-Jamaican speakers cannot understand it when they are first exposed to it. However, what is fascinating is that Jamaican speakers rarely use true Standard Jamaican English or true Jamaican Creole, operating instead at some level of a range of language in between the two. This range of language is referred to as the *creole continuum*.

The energy and creativity of Jamaican speakers make it impossible to give a satisfactory account of language in *Jah-mek-ya* (a pun on 'Jah make here' derived from Rastafarian 'Dread Talk'). Also, it is a challenge to describe any creole—or pidgin[2]—because, though these languages are fairly easy to recognize, linguists disagree on how to define them. Still, an attempt must be made, for though some may quarrel with 'creole' as a classification, this new Jamaican language is widely referred to as a creole.

Jamaicans pour body and spirit into their language, utilizing facial expression, gesture, tone and pitch, and nonverbal 'noises' that convey both mood and meaning. The fact that speakers know each other well is also important, since it allows them to refer in a kind of language shorthand to familiar persons, places, and events. To make matters more complicated, Jamaican Creole lacks a well-known, widely used *orthography* (system of writing). Orthographies exist, but their usefulness is limited because most people are not familiar with them. In this chapter, traditional English words and spellings are used to represent both Jamaican Creole and Standard English words; where the Jamaican Creole word is unique, it is approximated using phonetic spelling. Jamaican Creole appears in examples in italics, and Standard English in boldface.

THE JAMAICAN CREOLE CONTINUUM

It has been said that "the language of Jamaicans is best understood as a becoming" (Alleyne 1980: 120). This is a good way to describe Jamaican culture and language since both are constantly absorbing and refashioning things. 'Becoming' has a more specific meaning as used here, however: it signifies the continually shifting ranges of Jamaican language. No Jamaican speaker's language remains at any one level of the continuum: all Jamaicans use several levels. Ranges may be closer to Jamaican English or Jamaican Creole, but most settle in the middle, moving towards English or towards Jamaican Creole, as appropriate.

The continuum levels are not a mish-mash of randomly assembled forms; each level has its own structures and pronunciation. The following sentences represent levels of the continuum:

the men don't know what they are saying	Standard Jamaican English
the man them don' know what them sayin'	middle range, closer to English
de man dem doan know wa dem a seh	middle range, closer to Jamaican Creole
de man dem no know weh dem (d)a seh	(close to true) Jamaican Creole

Speakers often change from level to level (in a single statement or series of statements) with considerable effect, for it is not only grammar and pronunciation that alter, but most of the other 'bearers of meaning' that have been mentioned—body language, tone and pitch, and nonverbal noises.

Many Jamaicans are unable to use language levels that are near to Standard English, and fewer still use them exclusively. Language levels are, by and large, related to social behaviors and community/family origins. ('Social class' as defined by income is not a useful concept for describing Jamaican society at the beginning of the twenty-first century.) If they grow up in situations where books and learning are important, speakers are likely to be able to use a wide range of the continuum, including Standard English levels. Whatever their competence, most Jamaican speakers satisfy the needs of the occasion by shifting back and forth across 'their portion' of the continuum. Job interviews give rise to nearer-English forms, as do formal and public occasions.

Jamaican Creole is a 'heart' language—a vivid, vigorous medium used by most of the population as their language-for-living. It is increasingly widening its public domains, for reasons explored later on.

ATTITUDES TOWARD JAMAICAN CREOLE

One of the unfortunate legacies of colonization has been the negative attitude of many Jamaicans to Jamaican Creole. There is an often-quoted comment by Lady Maria Nugent (1966: 98), wife of the governor of Jamaica in 1806, in her diary, to the effect that "Many of the [white] ladies . . . speak a sort of broken English, with an indolent drawling out of their words, that is very tiresome if not disgusting." Hers was one of many such laments. Over a hundred years later, the famous Jamaican poet and folklorist, Louise Bennett, in an interview, confirmed the negative attitudes she encountered in performing and publishing her 'dialect verse' (Bennett 1968: 98).

For most of its history, Jamaican Creole has been pejoratively referred to as 'patois' or 'the dialect,' and defined as 'broken' or 'bad English.' Suggestions that it was a language in its own right were often laughed to scorn. Parents discouraged their children from speaking it, since they knew it would hamper their chances, socially and professionally. From the start, some form of English was the language of the white power holders, and Jamaican Creole—or some precursor to it—the language of the black oppressed. (Neither group were exclusive users, but, overall, English was regarded as white people's language and Creole 'belonged' to black people.) The *lingua franca* was English. Book learning was in English, since it was the language of books. The law, church, government, and commerce were conducted in English. Thus, anything resembling English that was not English had to be 'bad' or 'broken'—even if it was the language of most Jamaicans.

Not everyone felt this way. As early as 1868, Thomas Russell had produced *The Etymology of Jamaica Grammar*, a document which is "unique . . . [since] no other writer of the period attempted to give an account of the creole and none admitted to the existence of observable, systematic rules in it" (Lalla and DaCosta 1990: 185). Although Russell's grammar was intended to entertain, it does acknowledge Jamaican Creole as a *language*. Earlier in the century, James Phillippo, a Baptist missionary working primarily with black people, published a work entitled *Jamaica: Its Past and Present State*, including in it letters in creole and word-for-word accounts of conversations. Phillippo did not set out to record the language, but his renditions of it show a respect for Jamaican Creole missing in other early accounts.

Whatever the 'authorities' had to say, Jamaican language was hard to kill.

By 1966, when Beryl Bailey published *Jamaican Creole Syntax: A Transformational Approach*, many Jamaicans had concluded that 'patois' was indeed a language. Currently, in an age when mass media provide examples of British and American English, Jamaican Creole shows no signs of extinction. Indeed, it has recently generated an offshoot, "Dread Talk," the language of Rastafarians, discussed at the end of this chapter.

With political independence and an increasing sense of national and cultural identity, even greater numbers of Jamaicans have become proud of their language. Undoubtedly, the international success of Jamaican music, and in its wake, dub poetry, has done much to enhance the status of Jamaican Creole at home. Educational institutions accept and acknowledge Jamaican Creole as the first language of most Jamaicans, and as the vehicle of literary works. Since the Jamaican Creole-speaking community is comparatively small, and the language has no extensive tradition of being written down, to be able to use only Jamaican Creole would constitute a handicap socially and educationally. For practical reasons, therefore, English remains the language of all but the earliest school, where teaching is most often bidialectal. (Many would say the language of schools 'claims to be,' rather than 'is,' English, since most teachers use some middle range of the continuum and not English.) English is taught from grade one, routinely examined, and required for certification at high school and college levels.

JAMAICAN CREOLE'S EXTENDING DOMAINS

Jamaican Creole has been used as the vehicle for literature for longer than any other Caribbean English Creole. Short fiction, novels, poetry, and drama thrive on the creole—also known as 'the vernacular' and 'the demotic.' From the performances of Henry G. Murray and his sons, in the late nineteenth century (see Chapter 7), through the verse of Claude MacKay and Una Marson early in the twentieth, to, later in the century, the dialect verse of Louise Bennett, the poems of dub artists, the prose of almost all contemporary writers of fiction, and the language of pantomime as well as popular theater, Jamaican Creole has proved an extraordinarily flexible medium.

If attitudes to Jamaican Creole have changed recently, linguists must be given some of the credit. However, writers and performers saw its virtues well before the mid-twentieth century when creole linguistics came into its own. The fact that local preachers (many of whom did not speak English) used Jamaican Creole inevitably enhanced its status. Its use in broadcasting and newspaper columns also helped, though in both cases this was mostly for entertainment. In addition, the popular Christmas pantomime, begun in the 1940s, soon saw the advantage of using the full range of the language continuum. Local radio and TV soaps and a burgeoning theater tradition have capitalized on its appeal, and in the last decade of the twentieth century, the Bible Society of the West Indies began translating the Bible into a dialect of Jamaican Creole meant to appeal to urban youth.

A LIKL TAS'E OF JAMAICAN TALK

A proper account of Jamaican Creole should cover its pronunciation, vocabulary, and grammar, and would be impossible here. It is, however, possible to convey some of the flavor of the language by pointing out some features of all three. Another look at the quotation at the start of the chapter, as well as other examples, is helpful, for excerpts of 'real' speech are the best introduction. However, since dialogue on the page cannot illustrate rhythm or pronunciation, and since these help to invest Jamaican language with its special character, some remarks about them are in order, to begin with.

Pronunciation

Jamaica Talk notices the "swoop and tumble" of peasant speech, pointing out its frequent alteration of levels—often from syllable to syllable (Cassidy 1961: 26). Though this rise-and-fall is most noticeable in Jamaican Creole, it affects Jamaican English as well, and perhaps explains Lady Nugent's comment previously referred to. It has been suggested that this lilt comes from African languages, and that similar intonation features occur on the West African coast (Cassidy 1961: 31).

Jamaican Creole borrows English words but in many cases radically alters their pronunciation. It uses all except four of the sixteen English simple and combined vowel sounds, but it assembles them 'to its own suit.' Flattened open vowel sounds (*haan* = **horn;** *aal* = **all**) characterize Jamaican Creole pronunciation. Some Jamaican speakers, aware of this tendency to flatten, and anxious to use correct English forms, 'round up' the 'wrong' sounds. This phenomenon is often a source of great humor. For example, this rounding up, combined with the misapplied 'h' (discussed later), produces *hopple* for **apple,** and *hogrovate* for **aggravate.**

Consonants are the same as in English except that **th** as in **thin** is sounded as *t* (so *tin* = **thin**), and **th** as in **them** as **d** (*dem*). Examples of the latter feature occur in the excerpt at the beginning of the chapter. Curiously, **k** and **g,** when they precede standard **a,** become *ky* and *gy,* so that **cat** is sounded *kyat* and **garden,** *gyarden.* So Jamaicans use *kyarts* to go to the *kyash*-and-

kyarry where they buy *kyabbages*, *kyandy*, and *kyashews*. They also put out *gyarbage*, *gyas* the *kyar*, and visit art *gyalleries*.

Informal English usage in many parts of the world leaves out vowels that begin words if they are not stressed, and this also affects Jamaican Creole words like *bout* (**about**), *nuff* (**enough**), and *pon* (**upon**). As has been said, these can equally occur in less-than-careful English speech; however *ducta* for **conductor** and *shorance* from **assurance** are pure Jamaica Talk!

Consonant clusters at the ends of originally English words are simplified in Jamaican Creole and sometimes disappear: **crisp** becomes *kris*, **soft** becomes *sof*, **cold** becomes *col*, **sand** becomes *san*. Examples of 'disappearance' include the -z sound at the end of **because** (*becaa*), the -t in **what** (*wha*), and the -l in (auxiliary) **will** (*wi*). Nasal sounds at the end of some words (like **from, can't**, and **him**) can either disappear or add a nasal quality to the preceding vowel, to become *frong, cyaan, 'ing*; similarly, **town** becomes *tung* and **down** becomes *dung*.

The following sentence in JC illustrates several of the features mentioned so far: *me 'fraid fi go dung tung becaa ef he see me he wi kill me stone coal dead* (**I'm afraid to go down town because if he sees me, he will kill me stone-cold dead**).

The participial ending **-ing** is collapsed to *-in*—one of many old features in Jamaican pronunciation; Shakespeare collapsed these endings in exactly the same way. (Archaisms also exist in vocabulary and usage.) Indeed, many of the pronunciations already mentioned may also be archaic. The Jamaican Creole pronunciation for **woman** (*uman*) is also old: it was a feature of British English in the fifteenth century, and the 'upper crust' used it until its status fell in the nineteenth century (Cassidy 1961: 40).

This short account of pronunciation ends with two features that are often manipulated in writing to produce double meanings, or used on stage to enormous humorous effect. Transposition of sounds creates Creole words that are often identical with entirely unrelated English ones: **ask** is sounded *aks* (just like English **axe**) and **desk**, *deks* (as in English **decks**). The playful *h*, already mentioned, is perhaps the most hilarious: it attaches itself to vowels and diphthongs that are stressed (*heggs, hice, hignorant* for **eggs, ice, ignorant**) and vanishes from words where it belongs (*'ouse, 'amper, 'and*). The following exchange, with which generations of Jamaican school children have entertained one another, says a lot about about attitudes to language:

CHILD: *Teacher, 'Arry 'it me in mi 'ead, wid a 'eavy, 'eavy 'ammer. It 'urt 'ard.* (**Teacher, Harry hit me in my head with a heavy, heavy hammer. It hurt hard.**)

TEACHER: Hemphasize you' haches, you hignorant hass.
(**Emphasize your h's, you ignorant ass.**)

Overall, it is the lilt, energy, and drama of Jamaica Talk that strike listeners when they first hear it. The slaves' earliest education was at the hands of missionaries, and, for most, their first book was the Bible. Biblical rhythms ripple through Jamaican speech. Preaching also helped to nurture a dramatic sense all Jamaican speakers have: they use parallelism, climax and bathos, rhetorical questions, puns, double meanings, repetition, biblical references, proverbs, sayings, and the devices of switching and sliding between levels of the continuum.

Grammar

In the excerpt from *de Man* at the beginning of this chapter, Naomi uses the second person pronoun, *unoo* (pronounced *unu*), which probably comes from Ibo, a Nigerian language. The *Dictionary of Caribbean English Usage* (Allsopp 1996: 577) says *unu* is most often used in the plural, though it can be singular when it sometimes conveys a special derogatory meaning. As the excerpt from *de Man* also shows, *unu* is freely used with the other second person pronoun, *yuh* (you). It also gives examples of the Jamaican Creole first person singular pronoun, *me*. Like all creole pronoun forms, it serves for nominative and accusative. The third person pronouns are *him* (often *'im*), which refers to males and females; and *it*, *wi* (we), *unu* or *yuh*, and *dem* (them) are the plural forms.

Nouns form their plurals by adding *dem*; thus, the plural of **man** is *man-dem*, and of **pot**, *pot-dem*. This may be a legacy from Ewe and Twi languages. Possession is indicated by the prefix *fe* (**for**): thus, *fe-me* = **mine;** *fe-you* = **yours,** *fe-Kyarol* = **Carol's** and so on. Similarly, **my house, my car** = *fe me 'ouse, fe me kyar*. Nouns lend themselves to wonderful compounding: *eye-water* = **tears,** *dead-house* = **morgue,** *neck-string* = **tendon in the neck,** *age-paper,* = **birth certificate,** *foot-bottom* = **sole of the foot,** *meat-kind* = **meat,** as distinct from *food-kind* = **starches** (like yam, potatoes, eddoes, and so on) are a few examples. Others are considered later.

Sentence order in Jamaican Creole is subject, verb, object. Jamaican is in many ways an economical language, and its words are often multifunctional, serving in many grammatical categories. Word order is therefore important for meaning: *de bwoy, 'im sick* and *'im sick de bwoy* mean **as for the boy— he is sick** and **he has made the boy sick,** respectively. Verbs do not change to show agreement: thus, *de man run* and also *de man-dem run*. **To be** is not used to indicate a state of being, and nothing replaces it: so, *de pikni sick, de bwoy ignorant*. *a, de*, or *da* are alternative forms that indicate action-in-process: *'im a/de/da sing* = **he is singing**.

Verbs do not change form to indicate tense, the latter being shown adverbially: thus, **he came here yesterday** = *him come ya yesside*; **he gave her a hundred dollars last Christmas** = *him gi 'er 'undred dollar Christmas gone*. Future may be indicated by auxiliary *wi*; for example, **he will arrive by nightfall** = *him wi reach by night*. However, the language is rich in the expression of the future: **he will arrive by nightfall** = *him a go reach by night; him gwine reach by night*. The form *ben*, once used for the past tense (*him ben come ya befo* = **he has been here before**) has all but disappeared.

Double negatives are a noticeable feature: *mi nuh know nutn; mi neva get nuh supper* = **I don't know anything, I didn't get any supper**. Also, "one very striking feature of [Jamaican] folk speech is that verbs are used in sequences without connectives" (Cassidy 1961: 62). Called 'serial verbs,' this device is vivid: *him phone clear to foreign send go tell him mumma say him pregnant* = **she telephoned all the way overseas to let her mother know that she was pregnant**.

Rising pitch rather than inversion indicates questions: *de bwoy 'ave de bag*, delivered with a rise of pitch, changes from statement to question. There is a question marker *nuh* that occurs at the end of sentences and has the sense of Jamaican (middle range) *don't it?* which is the equivalent of English **isn't that so?** Thus, *him come here dis morning, nuh?* means **he came here this morning—isn't that so?**

Creole employs *and* as the conjunction of preference, for few subordinating conjunctions are used. Thus: *him come, and him look, and him look, and him go way, and come back, and look-look some more* = **when he came, he searched for a while, after which he went away, only to return to do more searching**. Other conjunctions are *after* (as **since** or **because**), *before* (**instead of**), *so* (**even as** and **and thus**). Examples in each case are: *you no haffi raise you vice, after me no 'ard-eaz* = **you don't have to shout—I'm not deaf**; *befo you-self heed di Lord word, you gaan fe chastise nodda man* = **instead of hearing the Lord's word yourself, you've gone off to chastise someone else**; *so me plan', so me reap* = **I plant and thus I reap**.

Vocabulary

It has been noted that "one device [of Jamaican Creole word formation] is strikingly characteristic and different [from Standard British English]; the use of . . . reduplication of form" (Cassidy 1961: 69). Simple repetition is by far the most popular kind of reduplication in Jamaican language; it is often onomatopoeic and is used to form adjectives, nouns, prepositions, verbs, and adverbs. Examples of adjectives are: *chaka-chaka* = **disorderly**, *fool-fool* = **stupid**, and *chatty-chatty* = **talkative**; of nouns: *mus-mus* = **mouse**, *su-su* = **gossip**; and *fee-fee* = **a whistle**; of prepositions: *rong-and-rong* = **around**, and *bout-bout* = **round about**; of verbs: *batta-batta* = **to beat repeatedly**, and *chop-chop* = **chop all over**; and adverbs: *lickle-lickle* = **by degrees**, and *degge-degge* = **sole, only, merely**.

Reduplication in verbs can serve more than one purpose: it may imply that the action happens over a period (*him look-look whole day, and never fin' not 'in'* = **he looked all day long but found nothing**). It may also suggest habitual action: thus, *de dawg beg-beg becaa dem doan feed 'im* = **the dog is constantly begging because they don't feed him**.

Like all languages, Jamaica Talk changes constantly in response to the needs of those who speak it. It compounds old words to make new ones, as has just been illustrated; it creates new meanings for old words (*fall* = **to become pregnant; to seduce**); preserves archaic meanings (*facety* = **insolent**); and makes new words (*rass* = **backside**). Indeed, in Dread Talk (discussed in the final section of this chapter), it creates a whole new sublanguage with a vocabulary embodying the philosophy of its speakers.

THE STORY OF THE DEVELOPMENT OF JAMAICAN CREOLE

Language anywhere in the world varies according to who speaks (e.g., king, farmer, lawyer, priest, man, woman), who is spoken to (e.g., serf, field slave, house slave, freedman, man, woman), and the context in which the conversation takes place. It was very important, in the formation of Jamaican Creole, that one set of speakers were rulers and the other set, not just ruled, but slaves. In Jamaica's case, if Africans had enslaved Europeans, the language that would have come about would have been different.

The ratio of Europeans to Africans at any particular point in the history of the development of a creole must have affected the process of development in important ways. Differing circumstances also prompted more extended or limited exchange between subcommunities of speakers (e.g., white plantation owners and their families, white tradesmen, free blacks, slaves), which also affected language acquisition on both sides. Linguists must reconstruct how, at each stage, the developing creole language, in this case, Jamaican Creole, was affected by these relations.

Though there is no proof, some people have suggested that Jamaican Creole formed within one generation—somewhere in the period 1660–1700.

(Others say the period may have been longer.) However long it actually took, we know that by the end of the eighteenth century, a new language, both like and unlike English, existed. After that, Jamaican Creole and English have lived together, each serving a particular linguistic purpose, each influencing the other to some extent, at the same time that both remained relatively intact. In time, this living together gave rise to that range of languages (some more English, others more creole) now referred to as the creole continuum.

Of special interest, because less is known about it, is what had happened to the slaves *before* their arrival in the Caribbean. It seems that they brought not only African languages but a version of English as well. An African language (Mandingo) and an English dialect (Guinea Coast Creole English) influenced this version of English. Over 20,000 slaves came to Jamaica from West African trading posts in the period 1674 to 1688, which is exactly the time when some scholars think Jamaican Creole formed. During this time the ratio of blacks to whites also changed radically: in 1673, there were 7,768 whites and 9,504 blacks (freedmen and Maroons excluded); by 1693–1694, there were 7,000 whites and 40,000 blacks.

During the next century and a half, whites became fewer and blacks increased greatly in number, mostly by importation, for the spread of plantation agriculture demanded more and more labor. Contact between slaves was therefore much more frequent than it had been when the ratio of blacks to whites was more equal. Examples of the English language that the slaves heard came from all kinds of people—speakers of 'good' English, speakers of English dialects, speakers of Guinea Coast Creole.

Many holdings were isolated small farms, so slaves on these holdings had little contact with slaves anywhere else. They would take their example of the English language from whatever 'brand' of English their owners or overseers spoke. In Jamaica's case, most English people were speakers of regional dialects related to the places in the British Isles that they came from. The first African arrivants no doubt tried to speak these dialects, and their *imitation* of what they heard became the example for the next group of Africans arriving, and so on. Thus, by a process of constantly remaking their own imitations of English, the slaves reinforced their patterns of speech—and Jamaican Creole was born.

Space does not permit our telling this story in greater detail, though it is not quite ended. For one thing, there is a belief that slaves from different ethnic backgrounds were deliberately kept away from each other and therefore could not communicate in their own languages. However, there is evidence that planters preferred slaves from the Gold Coast (Kromanti), and they were kept together and could therefore talk to each other in their own languages (Alleyne 1988: 120). This is further confirmation that African languages were spoken in Jamaica and must have affected Jamaican Creole as it developed.

Social class and regional dialects of the English language were important in 'keeping up' the status of the English language in Jamaica, though there were smaller and smaller numbers of English people. In the late eighteenth and nineteenth centuries, British-educated Jamaicans, British members of an expanding colonial bureaucracy, teachers and other professionals, and missionaries helped to keep the status of English high. In addition, the printing press had arrived in Jamaica in 1718; after that, the English of books and newspapers influenced small but increasing numbers of people who could read.

Maroon communities in Jamaica (see Chapter 1) brought together people from different African backgrounds as well as creoles, since both Jamaican-born (creoles) and imported slaves ran away to Maroon havens. There is no complete study of language among Jamaican Maroons, but the language situation seems to have been complicated and very interesting. Kromantis were the largest group in Maroon communities, and the Kromanti language is still used in Jamaican Maroon rituals. However, escapees from many other ethnicities used their own languages.

Immigration to Jamaica after emancipation in the form of indentured African laborers over the period 1840 to 1864 provided a reconnection to Africa at a time when the island had become more creole and less African, since the slave trade ceased in 1807. Though the number of indentured laborers (from Sierra Leone and Central Africa) was small, their influence was great in the areas where they settled. In the communities they joined, these post-Emancipation emigrants would have helped to emphasize the African elements in Jamaican Creole.

Finally, German settlers in the nineteenth century, and Indian, Chinese, and Lebanese Arabic immigrants of the same period, have also made small contributions to Jamaican language.

A LAST WORD: DREAD TALK

'Dread' or 'Rasta Talk' is the language of Rastafarians. Although the Rastafarian religion is a relatively recent development, it has generated great interest and a small but growing local and international following (see Chapter 2). Rastafarian philosophy embodies black Jamaicans' concern with spirituality, pride in their race, and interest in their African roots—though

Rastafarians wish to return to Ethiopia and not the West African homelands of the Akan-Ashante, Yoruba, Ibo, or Ibibio peoples.

An offshoot of Jamaican Creole, Dread Talk serves the cultural and philosophical beliefs of Rastafarians in a way that is most unusual for languages. Usually the form and function of language are quite unconnected. Even onomatopoeic words are not perfect examples of what they represent; thus, though bees everywhere buzz alike, languages represent this buzz in different words. In the case of Dread Talk, form and function are seen differently. "Rastafarian speech behavior is based on a philosophical view of language and the world in which words have an inherent power to evoke and to *be* the thing meant" (Alleyne 1983: 15).

Rasta attitudes to the name *Jesus* are a case in point. For Rastas, *Je-sus* is a false God. Rastafarians consider "the current English pronunciation . . . unacceptable because it is a distortion of the original Amharic, designed to deceive blacks. What the white man calls 'Je-sus' is actually a pseudo-divinity which he tries to foist on the black race" (Owens 1976: 106). The correct pronunciation for the name is 'Jes-us,' similar in sound to 'just us' (*jes us*), in Jamaican Creole. Thus sounded, the name conveys the fact that Christ is alive, incarnate within man.

Rasta language has modified Jamaican Creole mainly by altering some words, altering greetings, and changing address and pronominal systems. Four categories of Rasta vocabulary have been described: old words to which new meanings have been assigned; words in which phonology and intent are as one; I-words and Y-words; and new words (Pollard 1994). The word 'dread' is an example of a new significance for an 'old' word. In Dread Talk, it means 'Rastafarian' (*im is a dread* = **he is a Rastafarian**) and also describes Rasta beliefs and culture, as in 'dread culture.' 'Dreadlocks' refers to the thick locks of hair worn by Rastafarians.

Words in which phonology and intent are as one, and I-words and Y-words, demonstrate the Rastafarian sense of the spiritual in vocabulary particularly well. Where a certain sound and a special meaning have become cemented by association, Dread Talk assumes that the meaning obtains wherever the sound occurs, and derives rules that alter words to reflect this sound-signing. Thus **understand** becomes *overstand*, since to construe the meaning of something is to control or be 'over' the idea. Similarly, **oppress** is *downpress*, and **informer** is *outformer*.

Rasta philosophy attaches overarching importance to perception; this is accomplished in the physical world through the organ of the *eye*, the sound of which is identical with the word *I*. The eye permits 'sighting' (insight) by means of which the self comes to a realization of the *I* of person, the Rasta *I*. For Rasta, the homphony of **eye** and **I** is no accident. Thus, unlike Jamaican Creole, Dread Talk never uses the pronouns *me, we, unoo*. Instead, *I* or *I-man* is the first person singular form for all cases. *I-and-I* is the plural form for all cases, and is often used for the singular as well. The strategy for addressing a second person is to use the third person, a device that adds formality to Rasta speech. Thus, *I-man* would greet you, a woman: "*I-and-I hail the daughter.*" Rastafarians consider the *I* sound a 'positive vibration,' which occurs in crucial words such as *Haile* Selassie (Emperor of Ethiopia and, for Rastafarians, the Son of God), *Zion, height*. Dread Talk uses the sound to derive an entire category of words: *ailalu* = **callaloo** (a spinach-like green); *ainana* = **banana**; *iration* = **vibration**; *ital* = **vital** (in matters of food and cooking), **unsalted**.

New Rastafarian words include *irie*—a word difficult to translate outside of an understanding of Rastafarian theology, ideology, and culture. Insofar as it signifies the I, aware of the spiritual in the self and the word, and profoundly connected to both, *irie* could be said to describe, not just Dread Talk, but the whole spectrum of language alive in the mouths of Jamaicans for over three centuries.

NOTES

1. Mervyn Alleyne (1983: 1) in a lecture at the University of the West Indies, Mona. This chapter depends heavily on the work of scholars of Caribbean language and social history, including Alleyne himself, as well as the late Beryl Bailey, Derek Bickerton, Edward Brathwaite, Lawrence Carrington, the late Frederic Cassidy, Pauline Christie, Michael Craton, Jean DaCosta, Barbara Kopytoff, Barbara Lalla, Salikoko Mufwene, Velma Pollard, and Monica Schuler.

2. A simplified or reduced language containing vocabulary from two or more languages, used for communication between people who do not speak a common language.

New Kingston.

Port Royal; seventeenth/eighteenth-century Jamaica.

Statue of Paul Bogle by Edna Manley in front of the Morant Bay Courthouse.

Rural church.

Rural Baptist church.

Revival group on its way to a yard or baptism, rural Jamaica.

Teacher and students at a basic school.

Hosay (Muslim festival).

Game of cricket.

A scene from the play *Jane and Louisa Will Soon Come Home*, by Erna Brodber, which was adapted by the author from her novel of the same title.

Jamaica Orchestra of Youth.

Bob Marley sculpture by Alvin Marriott.

Jamaican folk singers in concert.

Mento dancers.

Maypole dance.

Modern Jonkunnu recreation at a heritage celebration.

Anansi: Jamaica carnival.

Chapel, University of the West Indies campus; this eighteenth-century Great House was transported stone by stone and reassembled as a multidenominational chapel.

Faculty Office, Mona Campus, University of the West Indies; a modern re-creation of Jamaican Vermacular.

Devon House.

Great House, St. Ann; still in use.

Interior of Great House, St. Ann.

Old **House** of Assembly, Spanish Town; built in the late eighteenth-century in Jamaican Georgian style and still in use by the St. Catherine Parish Council Chambers offices.

Nineteenth-century townhouse, Spanish Town; still in use.

Urban "peasant" bungalow, Kingston.

5

Social Customs

INFLUENCES

JAMAICANS are to be found working, studying, and living in practically every country and region of the world. Many of those who remain at home yearn to leave, most commonly for Canada and the United States; those who manage to do so are considered fortunate by family and friends, whatever the circumstances of their new lives.

But most of them return, if not to live, though thousands do every year, then to visit 'The Rock'—one of the many affectionate names for the island, others being 'Jamdown,' 'JA,' or simply 'Yard.' Family occasions such as weddings, funerals, anniversaries, special birthdays, and christenings exert a natural pull back; and such occasions are used to renew acquaintance with people and places across the island.

Two factors deserve to be noted. First, after a century of outward migration it is no longer unusual for almost entire families, to the third generation, to be domiciled abroad, sometimes in the same city or region. In such circumstances, major family celebrations may now take place in Toronto, or Birmingham (England), or Chicago, and the few members still living in Jamaica would travel to those centers. Second, most of the essential elements of such celebrations can be replicated wherever they take place. In the last fifteen or so years there has sprung up a network of growers, packers, and shippers at one end and wholesalers, distributors, and retailers at the other who service the Caribbean diasporic communities across North America and Europe with foodstuffs, grocery items, toiletries, music, and clothing from 'Yard.'

There are, of course, delights that only the homeland can offer: a lazy family day at the beach; a roadside meal of roasted yam and saltfish; a jelly coconut on a hot day; authentic jerk pork at a seaside village called Boston in the parish of Portland; peppered river 'shrimps' (actually crayfish) at Middle Quarters in St. Elizabeth. And there is the place itself. Jamaicans have an intense relationship with the landscape of their homeland, source of pain, fount of beauty. They are in complete agreement with Christopher Columbus's reported comment: "the fairest isle that eyes have beheld." All other landscapes are silently measured against it for beauty and found wanting.

The expatriate who remains in touch with his or her roots is a conduit of the foreign culture. One vehicle has been the 'barrel,' a cylindrical container of industrial-strength cardboard with metal top and bottom, which relatives in 'foreign' send to relatives 'a-yard.' The barrel has been a cornucopia of foreign material things—clothes, shoes, foodstuffs, and other goodies—for generations of Jamaicans, introducing new foods and fashions, and supplying much-needed items, particularly for school, to the less well-off.

Travel and the media, especially television, have also been conduits of new fashions and foods. The diet and eating habits of most Jamaicans have changed greatly over the period of the island's independence; this is especially true of the young in the larger population centers, who are as at home in the hamburger and fried chicken palaces of Burger King and KFC as their North American counterparts. But the more traditional foods and dishes have held their own.

CUISINE

The kitchen is the arena in which the island's history, from the Taino to the present day, and all the ethnocultural traditions that comprise the country come together most visibly and harmoniously. Food is an integral part of almost all occasions, private and public, even the most solemn.

Traditional Jamaican cooking has two dominant characteristics: a lot of oil is used in its preparation, and it is highly seasoned. Preferred seasonings, along with salt and black pepper, are thyme, scallion (or escallian), onions, and peppers. The favored 'scotch bonnet' pepper, so called for its distinctive crumpled shape, and a variety of 'country pepper' cousins are, for many Jamaicans, essential ingredients at every meal. Pimento, garlic, and ginger are also popular seasonings. There are regional favorites, and regional and personal variations in preparation. But there are a core set of dishes and foodstuffs that all Jamaicans would recognize as distinctively their own and that illustrate the many facets of the island's cultural history, going as far back in some cases as the Tainos.

At the top of such a list would be ackee and saltfish, generally regarded as the national dish. The ackee is a West African fruit, introduced to Jamaica in the 1770s, which grows in all parts of the island. Hardly eaten in its native habitat, its yellow flesh provides tasty counterpoint to the salted fish, cod. Ackee must be harvested and cooked only after the fruit has opened naturally; before that it is highly toxic. It is first steamed and then fried in oil with onions, thyme, pepper, and tomatoes. In the past several years, shortages of cod at the traditional source, the waters off the east coast of Canada, have sent the price of codfish out of the easy reach of many Jamaicans; the ackee is mixed as often now with other things, such as salted pork, bacon, sausage, and vegetables.

As breakfast, ackee and saltfish would generally be accompanied by one or more of the following: hardo bread, bammie, johnny cakes, or roasted breadfruit. Hardo bread is a heavy white bread in which a liberal amount of lard is used instead of butter or margarine. It remains soft and edible far longer than other breads and is favored for outings. Bammie, a round flat cake made from dried cassava, was a staple food of the Taino. It will last for several days until it is soaked in cow's or coconut milk or water and then deep fried until brown. Johnny cakes are made of wheat flour and water, with pinches of salt and baking powder, kneaded into round balls and fried. More properly known as journey cakes, they were part of the food taken by slaves and others to provision their travels. Another favorite is the breadfruit, a large fleshy fruit of a tree introduced at the end of the eighteenth century from the Pacific islands by the infamous Captain William Bligh (of *Mutiny on the Bounty* fame). It grows all over the island and is eaten boiled, roasted, or fried. But it tastes sweetest, most Jamaicans would agree, roasted in its skin in the embers of an open fire.

A standard component of the main meal of the day—whether midday or evening—is 'food.' This apparent redundancy is explained by the centrality of various 'ground provisions' to the Jamaican diet, going back to the foods grown in the provision grounds of slavery. 'Food' would be one or other of several types of yam originally brought from West Africa; other tubers and root crops such as sweet potato and yampi grown by the Taino; bananas and plantains (from the Canary Islands, originally), and the breadfruit. They provide bulk to what can be, in hard times, very modest sharings of meat or fish. Dumplings of wheaten flour or cornmeal, boiled or fried, serve the same purpose.

Without refrigeration—not widespread in the country until the 1970s— food had to be cooked fresh and eaten immediately. Otherwise it was 'enabled,' through prior curing or special cooking, to last a long time. This explains the prevalence of highly seasoned, salt- or smoke-cured meats and fish and deep-fried foods in the Jamaican diet. Corned pork and corned beef—cured in brine and seasoning, in which they traveled to Jamaica in olden days—continue to be popular, often served with broad beans and boiled green bananas. A tinned version, shredded and called 'bully beef,' packaged in Brazil and Argentina but marketed under local labels, is an enduringly popular quick meal, generally laced with onions and pepper and eaten with hardo bread or rice.

Smoked herring, fried with onions and tomatoes, is also a popular breakfast, usually served with boiled bananas and roasted breadfruit. Smoked herring is also ground fine with pepper, other seasonings, oil, and vinegar to make Solomon Gundy, a distinctive savory paste popular as an hors d'oeuvre or snack, on crackers or toast. Still popular with some is salted mackerel in 'rundown,' a sweet peppery gravy of highly seasoned coconut milk; rundown is served with boiled bananas as breakfast or main meal.

Fresh fish from the waters surrounding the island, and nowadays also from freshwater inland fish farms, provide many Jamaicans with a staple food. A variety of fish are prepared steamed, stewed, and grilled, as elsewhere. But two fish dishes are particularly popular with Jamaicans. Fleshy varieties are sometimes 'escaveitched': deep fried, then soaked in a marinade of vinegar, onions, pimentos, scotch bonnet peppers, thinly sliced raw carrots, and sugar; in that marinade it lasts for several days, even without refrigeration. Small fish, called sprats, are deep fried to a crisp in highly seasoned oil; these can be eaten whole, bones and all, as a snack.

Among people from outside of Jamaica, even some who may not have visited the island, two culinary products are particularly well known: patties and jerk chicken. The patty was fast food to generations of Jamaicans long before Macdonald's and Burger King came to the island. Essentially a spiced meat pie in light flaky pastry, it is made by everyone from individual bakers to large factory-like franchises and is to be found across the island and, these days, much further afield. Wherever in the world Jamaicans live in sizable numbers patties are made and sold, and not only in Jamaican shops or restaurants.

'Jerk,' as a style of preparation, goes back to Jamaica's slave history, to the Maroons, or even further, some say, to the Akan of West Africa, who were present in large numbers in the parish of Portland, whence jerk originated.

Once more, to answer the exigencies of the age, a means had to be found of preparing food so that it would last the several days a journey would take between villages, or for an expedition into the hills. Wild pigs were first prepared in this way, as the most readily available meat in the mountains of Portland. Though these animals are now extinct, and the necessity for long expeditionary treks has also passed, the method of preparing pork endures.

In authentic 'jerk' cooking, the meat is sliced into portions and soaked in a marinade of pepper, vinegar, pimento and other spices, and scallion. The meat is then smoked over charcoal on a barbecue grill while covered with strips of wood from the pimento tree. The meat cooks in its own juice, moist, fragrant, and peppery in the 'pit,' the hollow in the earth in which the barbecue is built. The secret is in the marinade and the wood, and there are purists who insist that *real* jerk pork can only come from Boston, the seaside village on the northeast coast in Portland. Jerk is now international: bottles of packaged jerk seasoning are sold all over the world; not all of them are even prepared in Jamaica. Jerk has found its way into *haute cuisine* while simultaneously remaining in the pit and on the roadside, increasing its popularity as it goes.

The traditional recipes and ways of cooking are still widely practiced, but they make space in the kitchen for other kinds of cooking. East Indian and Chinese laborers were brought into the Caribbean by the English authorities as a response to the cry of planters for cheap labor to replace the emancipated slaves. Neither group was very numerous in Jamaica to begin with, certainly as compared to Trinidad and Guyana, where Indians now comprise more than 50 percent of the populations. But both brought their style of cooking and in some cases foodstuffs and seasonings with them. The peoples and their cuisine have melded into the general Jamaican *mélange*, to the extent that no one today thinks of one of the most popular of local dishes, curry goat—and its derivative soup, mannish water, made from boiling the head and entrails of the slaughtered animal, and popularly held to be an aphrodisiac—as anything but a quintessentially Jamaican dish.

Interestingly, Indian cuisine has made a greater impact in the average Jamaican home than the small number of Indian restaurants around the island would suggest. With respect to Chinese cooking, however, the opposite is true. While stir frying is becoming popular in the home, few families would go to the trouble needed to prepare many of the Cantonese and Szechuan delicacies. Instead, Jamaicans go out to the scores of Chinese restaurants to be found on every corner of the island. They range from expensive food palaces to humble lunch counters and roadside cook vans. In most

Chinese restaurants, curried meats and seasonal Jamaican dishes are also served, testifying to the cross-fertilization of culinary tastes that typifies the island's culture.

A more recently introduced style of cooking is 'ital,' the gift of the Rastafari. The word denotes something natural and, with respect to food, is applied to earth-grown products—ground provisions, vegetables, sometimes fish, but never meats—cooked without salt. Stir fry and stewing are popular preparation methods, seasoned with lime juice, coconut milk, and the omnipresent country pepper. The increasing attention paid these days to the benefits of a healthy diet has made ital cooking popular even beyond the widening circle of people who adhere to Rastafari beliefs and practices. Ital food can be found in some restaurants alongside traditional staples from around the world.

Perhaps in time ital will make its way into the newest types of restaurants in Jamaica, the hamburger, chicken, and pizza fast food chains that are now ubiquitous in almost every part of the world. Nearly all the well-known American chains are to be found in the larger cities and no longer only in the tourist centers where North American visitors may have looked for them in earlier days. They are particularly popular among the young, who here, as elsewhere, are now being raised on a hefty diet of American television, commercials and all.

The invasion of fast food restaurants has provided a stimulus for older eating places. Jamaican recipes, well prepared and presented, are much more popular today than they were twenty years ago. The places where local cuisine, however defined, is served are also more attractive and numerous, from luxury hotels and the national airline, Air Jamaica, to roadside stalls.

No discourse on Jamaican cuisine would be complete without mention of drinks. Teetotalers and the health conscious have a wide range of fruit and other juices from which to choose, from pineapple to passion fruit and coconut water, and some intriguing mixes. There is also, in season, one of Jamaica's gifts to the world: the ortanique, a trademarked cross between the orange and tangerine. Although most production now goes abroad, it is a source of pride and pleasure at home. Another distinctive product is Blue Mountain coffee, grown high (over 3,000 feet) in the mountains of that name. One of the most highly prized arabica beans, it commands a premium price in the markets of the world.

On the stronger side of the bar can be found Jamaica's world-famous rums, and Red Stripe beer, all sold around the world. Rum is the base for an extensive range of liqueurs made from local fruits. At one time, many homes would offer guests a homemade pimento 'dram,' but tradition is giving way to the convenience of liqueurs purchased ready-made. These too are sold internationally. Tia Maria, originally created by Jamaican food technologists, is one of the best-known coffee liqueurs in the world.

FESTIVALS: SACRED AND SECULAR

Jamaica's calendar is a mixture of worldwide holiday celebrations, such as Christmas and Easter, and festivities particular to the island, like Heritage Week and the Jamaica Festival. While not all of them have particular foods associated with them, eating and drinking are integrally part of almost all such occasions, private and public.

Christmas

In terms of food, Christmas is the biggest celebration of the year. Families gather for a large feast on the day itself, and to exchange presents, usually at the home of the titular head of the family, or the person with the largest house. But during the course of the Christmas season, which lasts until the first week in January, other households in the family will return the hospitality with luncheons or dinners.

The main Christmas Day meal may be eaten, depending on family tradition and convenience, at any time between early afternoon and early evening. The timing of this feast determines the nature of the first Christmas meal, the breakfast. If lunch is to be early, then breakfast would be fairly light. But more often it is a substantial meal, sometimes with guests, which is not usual at other times of the year. The menu would be a mixture of Jamaican staples—ackee and saltfish, bammie, rundown, boiled bananas, and roasted breadfruit—and other favorites like scrambled eggs, bacon, sausages, and juices. On many tables, as well as coffee and tea, there would be country chocolate, made from handmade balls of cocoa, boiled in water or milk, with cinnamon and brown sugar added.

Some of these dishes would be a part of the menu for lunch as well. But smoked leg of ham would be the main meat of that meal, with chicken as a secondary dish. Accompanying the ham are rice and peas. This is one of the staples of Jamaican households, especially for Sunday luncheon or special occasions. Usually the rice is cooked with red peas, coconut milk, and seasoning. But at Christmas, and other times when the vine is bearing, gungo (Congo) peas are used; and when the ham is finished, hambone and gungo peas soup is made, a symbolic end to the Christmas season.

After the main meal, there's dessert: Christmas pudding and cake (and other sweets). Both are rich in dried fruit, which has been soaked in wine, sometimes for as long as ten months. The cake is baked in the oven; the pudding is boiled. Each family would have its recipes for the precise preparation of these specialties. The pudding, made up to a month before Christmas, to 'settle,' is doused in white overproof rum or brandy and set alight just before being eaten with a sauce of butter and sugar flavored with brandy or sherry.

Not all of these dishes would be on every table. There would be individual variations according to preference (vegetarian dishes are increasingly popular, throughout the year), economic circumstance, religious belief, and family tradition. But many of them would be on the menu of every family, except the very poorest.

Christmas is also a time for visiting friends and relatives; unofficial open house is held everywhere during the week between Boxing Day (the day after Christmas) and New Year's Day. At every home the visitor would be offered a glass of sorrel, a deep red drink made from soaking the leaves of this relative of the hibiscus in hot water, and then flavoring with sugar, ginger or lime, and rum (if desired). The sorrel plant blooms only at Christmas-time. There would usually be rum punch at this time also, made to the traditional formula: "one [measure] of sour [lime juice], two of sweet [strawberry syrup], three of strong [rum] four of weak [water]." The guest would also be offered a slice of Christmas pudding or cake.

New Year

The new year is welcomed by most Jamaicans in much the same way as in the rest of world, with parties in private homes, clubs, and hotels on the one hand, and in churches with services and midnight vigils—called Watch Night—on the other. But a large and increasing number of Jamaicans welcome the new year quietly, at home with family and a few close friends, in a simple celebration that doesn't go much beyond midnight. No special foods are associated with modern New Year; it is the end of a season of much, often too much, feasting, and most people are a little tired of food and concerned about weight by then.

Easter

The faithfulness with which the traditional Lenten dietary strictures are adhered to is decreasing steadily in Jamaica. In many households a generation ago, there would be no cooking between Holy Thursday afternoon and Easter

Sunday morning, when Christ's resurrection would have been celebrated by an early church service followed by a large breakfast with many dishes including meat. During the preceding two and a half days even the nonchurch-goers in the house would have to live on fish (escaveitched or fried beforehand), hardo bread, and bun-and-cheese.

In the minds of all Jamaicans, however, the food most associated with the season of Easter is bun-and-cheese, eaten together in this instance though both are eaten separately throughout the year. The bun is a loaf-shaped spiced bread, with dried chopped fruit (the same as is used in the Christmas cake and pudding, but not soaked in wine), and with molasses and/or stout added. The cheese of traditional preference is a processed cheddar, golden-colored and highly salted. Packaged in tins, it is shipped wherever in the world Jamaicans are found in numbers. Bakeries in Jamaica also send their Easter buns to shops in these communities, or Jamaican-owned bakeries abroad make their own versions. Smaller spiced round buns with wedges of processed cheese provide a filling snack or light lunch throughout the year.

Jamaica Festival

The Jamaica Festival, which has been staged yearly from 1963, is an island-wide mixture of competitions and exhibitions in the major areas of the arts—music, dance, literature, speech, fine arts, photography—as well as the culinary arts, a very popular competitive platform for chefs in hotels and restaurants. Thousands of people, young and old, from schools and community groups, as well as individuals, are involved in preparing for 'Festival,' as it is colloquially known. An exhaustive series of eliminations begin at the zone and parish level several months before the national finals, which take place during the final two weeks in July, in time to showcase winners at special concerts and exhibitions during the period of independence in early August.

Despite suffering from the funding cutbacks that have plagued other government-sponsored activities over several years, the Jamaica Festival has endured and become an integral part of the cultural calendar of the island. Countless numbers of Jamaica's stellar performers in the artistic fields covered in the competitions started as unknowns in Festival. It remains the only regular opportunity many have to display their art and skills.

Emancipation and Independence

The anniversaries of Emancipation and Independence both fall within the first week of August. Historically, August 1 had been celebrated as Emancipation Day from the first such day in 1838; in the 1890s, when legislation created the first public holidays, Emancipation Day was one of them. Over the years it became arguably the most emotionally resonant anniversary in the entire calendar. In 1962, however, when the country gained its independence from Britain, the public celebration of Emancipation was set aside by the-powers-that-be in favor of independence, which also arrived in August. The date for this new holiday was set as the first Monday in August, a floating date. Subsequently, even in those years when the holiday happened to be August 1, Independence was emphasized over Emancipation.

Observance of the Emancipation anniversary never ceased, however, especially among the Baptist, Moravian, and Methodist churches, whose missionaries had been very involved in the agitation for 'Full Free.' In 1997, for the first time in thirty-five years, Emancipation Day was celebrated with the organizing support of the government; the following year it was established once again as an official public holiday. At the same time Independence Day was set as August 6, the date on which independence was first proclaimed in 1962. Thus there are two holidays within one week—at least until the next change of policy. Eventually there may well be three in the month of August, as there has been persistent lobbying for August 17, the birthday of Marcus Garvey, to be made a public holiday as well.

The first weekend in August is also the time for the All-Island Agricultural Show at a huge fairground in the center of the island called Denbiegh. Farmers great and small congregate from across the island with their vegetables, fruit, flowers, and livestock, to show off and compete. Every company and state agency having the slightest connection to agriculture is represented there, and thousands of visitors pour through the gates every day. They come to see and to buy, and to enjoy the stage shows and other entertainment and food on offer.

Heritage Week

Following a quiet September, when children go back to school, National Heritage Week is celebrated in mid-October. Originally begun as the centenary celebration of the 1865 Morant Bay Rebellion, the holiday became, as the company of National Heroes grew in the 1970s, National Heroes Day and eventually National Heritage Week. The observances are arranged by an official committee to illustrate different themes from year to year.

Official sponsorship, while limiting spontaneity and structuring peoples' observance, serves a useful purpose. The celebrations, whether Festival, Emancipation, or National Heritage Week, expose regional customs to other

Jamaicans, especially in Kingston, thus widening the sense of cultural community. Also, by providing encouragement (and funding) for those who have retained some of the folkways which would otherwise wither, the prospect for continuity is strengthened.

These are the major secular, state, and Christian holidays. But other ethnic and religious groups have their own celebrations, some of which have come to be enjoyed by the wider community. Diwali (Hindu) and Hosay (Muslim), especially Hosay, have become community festivals in those areas in which Indians are numerically strong. Some aspects of their observance in Jamaica would differ, for instance, from celebrations in Trinidad and Guyana because of the local infusion. The Chinese New Year, also set by the lunar calendar, is celebrated predominantly by the Chinese-Jamaican community, but not exclusively so. Jewish special days are observed more intimately within that community, centered as they are on the ritual practices of the faith.

RECREATION

Most Jamaicans take their recreation very seriously. The "Jamaica—No Problem" image on T-shirts and advertisements, which draws so many visitors to the island and which has served only to reinforce the traditional notion of the happy-go-lucky native, is not one to which Jamaicans themselves subscribe. They are aggressive, competitive, and, in sports as in many other areas of endeavor, successful out of all proportion to size and population. Enthusiasm for sports, especially among the young, is fueled by heroes, and Jamaica has had its share of those.

Football (Soccer)

There is evidence that the Taino played a game that involved manipulating a round object with their feet, but there is no indication of continuity to the modern game of football. That was brought to the island by the British troops stationed there from the 1870s onwards to keep the peace of the Crown Colony. Matches between regimental teams were grand social events, watched from the sidelines by Queen Victoria's loyal subjects. It did not take long for the game to penetrate into every corner of the island.

By the early years of the twentieth century, club teams were playing in competitions organized across the country, fed by the nurseries of the high schools, who also competed amongst themselves. By the 1920s Jamaican national teams were venturing abroad to do battle against neighbors like Haiti, Cuba, and the Dominican Republic, and playing host to their teams as well.

There are now islandwide competitions at all levels of the educational system, from primary schools to universities and other tertiary institutions. Adult club competitions are organized across and between parishes, and also within special interest groups, like private sector companies. The players for the national side are drawn from the clubs.

After World War II, the various soccer organizations of the Caribbean and Central American region, including Jamaica's, began organizing subregional and regional competitions. These eventually came to be recognized and promoted by FIFA, the world federation of soccer organizations, and the competitive purview eventually widened to include the United States and Canada. Steadily improving performances from the Jamaican national team in these international competitions planted the ultimate dream of soccer-playing nations: a place in the World Cup finals.

The fulfillment of that dream required a paradigm shift in the approach to 'the beautiful game.' A haphazard constellation of individually skilled stars capable of occasional acts of brilliance had to become a team of interdependent players on their toes for the full ninety minutes of a game. Players had to be prepared to endure arduous training sessions over several months, while observing dietary and curfew restrictions. Not all who began the course finished it. Also, it was not achieved without outside help from several players of Jamaican birth and/or parenthood who played normally for soccer clubs in the United Kingdom. The whole effort, including several Jamaican coaches, trainers, physiotherapists, and managers, was presided over by a technical director from Brazil, the 'holy land' of football for many in the developing world.

It culminated in success. Against all odds, Jamaica's Reggae Boyz (the name was eventually trademarked) was one of three teams from the regional group to reach the finals in France in June–July 1998, the other two being Mexico, perennial finalists, and the United States. Although they were soundly beaten in the round-robin first round by their first two opponents, Croatia and Argentina, they rallied in their final match to defeat Japan. They went no further in the competition but finished points ahead of several more highly fancied teams, including the United States.

The effect on the country of the long campaign of ups and downs, with nail-biting finishes to almost every match and near disasters a-plenty, was salutary. Soccer replaced politics as the leading spectator sport. More than any single phenomenon in memory, it united the disparate citizenry across class, shade, and income level in a single aspiration—the 'Road to France 98,' as thousands of bumper stickers proclaimed it. There was, on this issue at least, the kind of camaraderie and sense of purpose that only duress of the worst kind usually engenders.

Schoolboys now have a team of heroes to emulate in their favorite sport, and in its aftermath France '98 has added the tincture of money to the equation, as several Jamaican-based team members have received contracts to play for professional clubs in Europe and the Far East. Of such things are dreams made.

Cricket

Long before soccer was of the standard to support such ambition, the game of cricket provided the platform for dreaming on that scale. Someone familiar with baseball may have an easier time understanding cricket than someone completely new to both games—*maybe*. Both games take place on grass fields; in both, players with gloves use bats to hit hard balls, and an umpire presides over both; nowadays both are often played under lights. But there the similarity ends. The bats are differently shaped, the balls differently sized and composed, only three players on the cricket field are allowed to wear gloves, and you argue with the decision of the cricket umpire at peril of being banned from the game. The rules of cricket are as subtle and complex as a catechism, and the simile is not inappropriate: to the initiated (fan or player), the devotion to cricket is worthy, lifelong, and paramount.

Most games can serve as metaphors for life, but only in the case of cricket is the metaphor extended over five seven-hour days of play for a single contest (a Test Match). And to the fan, every moment of those hours, even when nothing seems to be happening on the field of play, is fraught with tension, drama, possibility, and, underlying it all, history.

Cricket is also a metaphor for much of the social history of the West Indian islands, going back into the last century. Like soccer, it was brought to the islands by the English, but on a completely different basis. Conventional colonial wisdom decreed soccer as a game for the masses. English 'gentlemen' didn't play soccer, either at home or abroad. Thus it was acceptable, even desirable, for English regiments, made up mostly of working-class professional soldiers and conscripts, to teach that game to the masses in the Empire. Cricket, however, was bound up from the first in notions of the proper relationships between ruler and ruled. In the mother country, participants in the game were divided (they even used different changing rooms) into Gentlemen and Players. The latter were paid for playing and were in fact the backbone of any team but would not, until well after World War II, be made captains of teams that included Gentlemen.

That ethos was transported, in the baggage of colonial bureaucrats, to the Empire. There, the key organizing principle of the game was differentiation based not on skill but on class and color. (It is more than coincidence that cricket was most popular, and best played, in those countries where social class and/or color defined private relationships and public affairs: England, South Africa, India, Pakistan, Australia, and the West Indies.) Differentiation went hand in hand with the glorification of certain personal qualities: sportsmanship ("it's not whether you win or lose, it's how you play the game"), loyalty to team, and, above all, restraint ("the stiff upper lip"), on and off the field. Such qualities, in fact, exemplified the behavior expected of its subject members by the Empire ("England expects every man to do his duty"). The duty of the dark-skinned ruled, the Players, was to submit to their fair-skinned rulers, the Gentlemen. Cricket reinforced the status quo; it was an ineluctable part of Empire.

Inequalities of status notwithstanding, West Indian islanders took to the game with verve, determination, and flair, and quickly set about overturning the hierarchies. Organized on a regionwide basis, as teams in many other sports once were for international competitions, cricket is the only game in which a "West Indian" side still participates, more than seventy years after its first international series. The great West Indian writer C.L.R. James says that

> the clash of race, caste and class did not retard but stimulated West Indian cricket. . . . [I]n those years [the 1920s and 1930s] social and political passions, denied normal outlets, expressed themselves so fiercely in cricket (and other games) precisely because they were games. . . . Class and racial rivalries . . . could be fought out without violence or much lost except pride and honor. Thus the cricket field was a stage on which selected individuals played representative roles which were charged with social significance. (1994: 72)

But pride and honor comprised *the* most treasured currency in the colonial interchange between the races. To this day there is a special flavor to a West Indies victory over England, among the seven other teams that comprise the aristocracy of the sport.

Although there were dark-skinned members of the very first test team fielded in 1928 against England, it was not until 1948 that a black man— George Headley of Jamaica, for some aficionados the greatest batsman in the history of the game—was allowed to captain a Test side, and then for one match only, as a token of esteem for his remarkable twenty-year career that was then drawing to a close. The West Indies won their first Test series (five five-day matches over a period of two to three months) on home grounds as early as 1935, a mere seven years after entering the international arena. But it was a series victory in England in 1950 that heralded the arrival on the international scene of a group of players who would redefine the game. While observing its courtly, even archaic protocols, West Indian bowlers, batsmen, and fielders electrified crowds wherever they went, which from the 1950s onwards included Australia, New Zealand, India, and Pakistan; more recently Sri Lanka and South Africa have joined the cricketing fellowship.

West Indian crowds themselves played no small part in this. They knew, as James says, "the code as it applied to the game" (1994: 48) and expected their players to maintain it. But unlike their English counterparts, they themselves "shouted and stamped and yelled and expressed themselves fully in anger and joy . . . whether they [were] in Bridgetown or Birmingham" (James 1994: 48). Nowadays they also blow trumpets, conch shells, and cow horns; ring bells; shake rattles and tambourines; and beat drums in pyrotechnic displays of joy and displeasure carried around the world by ubiquitous television cameras. They have influenced the behavior of all other crowds, even the once restrained English.

Nowadays, too, teams have colored uniforms plastered with sponsors' logos, and although the cognoscenti still cherish the five-day Test battle, the one-day match, a relatively recent innovation, is more popular with the crowds. One-day matches are sometimes played at night, under lights—unheard of in the glory days of cricket as the quintessential summer game. The West Indies team, after reigning supreme in the world game from the mid-1960s—when it sent its first team abroad with a black captain, Frank Worrell of Barbados—to the end of the 1980s, is in a period of retrenchment and rebuilding mirroring the economies and societies from which their players come.

Track and Field

Cricket and soccer are not the only sporting activities in which Jamaicans have excelled on the world stage. From the period immediately following World War II, Jamaican track and field athletes have been world champions at the international level, including the Olympics: Herb McKenley, Donald Quarrie, and Merlene Ottey are numbered among the great sprinters of the modern era; Arthur Wint, among the greatest middle distance runners. In the 1996 Olympics, Jamaica ranked in the top five in the world in the number of medals won per capita of population.

Over the years Jamaicans have also claimed a number of front-line athletes who compete under other flags, on the basis of their Jamaican birth or parenthood: most recently and proudly, Donovan Bailey of Canada and Linford Christie of Britain, but also, less proudly, Ben Johnson of Canada. An extensive network of interschool athletic competitions supports the development of this remarkable stream of talented individuals. Many schools now have the benefit of the experienced athletes who have represented the island in earlier days and have returned as coaches. Past and present stars, it must be noted, are often the beneficiaries of scholarships to colleges in the United States that have a particular interest in track and field and have long-standing links with the Jamaican athletic fraternity. There, the Otteys-in-the-making are able to take advantage not only of training facilities superior to those available in Jamaica but of a more intense competitive schedule with which to hone their skills.

Track and field, cricket, and, more recently, soccer are the three sports at which Jamaicans are in the top ranks in the world. At the regional level the island's fortunes wax and wane in several other sports: tennis, table tennis, netball, swimming, golf, badminton, and squash, among others. All of these are pastimes for thousands of devotees who never make it to the national teams.

As elsewhere, games and sporting activities in general often carry social/class overtones. Thus tennis, golf, squash, and badminton are still perceived as enjoyed by middle-class and upper-middle-class persons, although this is not necessarily any longer true for all of them. Tennis in particular, once the preserve of expatriates and affluent white Jamaicans, has changed its complexion in every respect. Because of the costs involved, golf is still for the fairly affluent, but it is also true that former caddies have represented the island in international competitions.

Dominoes

Two pastimes cut across all class and income boundaries: horse racing and dominoes. The sharp crack of domino cards on wooden tables is heard in rum-bars and on verandahs across the island, as rich and poor alike pursue their avocation with passion and skill. The complexities of the game are 'read' and manipulated by men who may not recognize their own names on a page. All the guile and bravado that are integral to the Jamaican personality, especially the male of the species—women play at their peril, receiving no quarter—are brought to the domino table for affirmation and challenge. Triumphs are remembered for years, and lovingly detailed, especially in the presence of the vanquished. Rivalries between pairs of partners go on for decades and are an important feature of many friendships.

Horse Racing

Horse racing is both a sport and a multibillion-dollar business. A huge industry radiates across the island from the center at the Caymanas Park race track, located on the site of a former sugar estate across the harbor from Kingston. From stable hands and grooms to bookmakers' staff in the betting shops (not all of them licensed), in every corner of the country tens of thousands are dependent on the horses and those who gamble on them. The government provides a network of agencies to ensure, not always successfully, a measure of honesty and fairness in the conduct of business in the various sections of the undertaking, and to regulate the division of spoils.

The ingredient essential to most Jamaican entertainment, whether social or activity-related, is communality. Pastimes such as chess are not widely popular. Whether playing, spectating, or just 'hanging,' Jamaicans like to be in a group, beginning with family or friends—but beyond that, the larger the group, within reason, the better.

6

Media and Cinema

NEWSPAPERS

THE FIRST Jamaican printery was established in 1718. By May of that year, the island's first newspaper, *The Weekly Jamaica Courant with News Foreign and Domestick*, rolled off the licensed press; before the end of that year the first book had been published. It proved impossible, and impolitic, to restrict the technology to a single practitioner, and within the next several years a myriad of competitors sprang up. The function of a government printer, however, solely responsible for the publication of official documents, persists to this day, as it does, in one form or another, in many former British colonies.

At any given time in those early days, and indeed until the end of the nineteenth century, there would have been up to a dozen newspapers and journals appearing in the various towns of the island, serving the communities around their point of publication. Most of them emanated from Kingston, the commercial center of Jamaica and, after 1874, the political capital and the largest city. They were for the most part weeklies, but a few were dailies; most lasted no more than a few years.

As a colony tied to the metropole by trade and affairs of state, the doings of planters, merchants, and state officials, in the island and abroad, formed the main substance of the newspapers of the day. In coastal and inland towns alike, information on the arrival and departure of ships was the most eagerly awaited news. Coverage of the goings-on at Jamaica Assembly, the elected body that with the English governor administered the state affairs of the colony, was always careful. The concept of freedom of the press was not seriously entertained, even by the press, in eighteenth- and nineteenth-century Jamaica, and the constitutional power of officialdom was great. While printers, acting often as their own publishers, did not require a license to produce a newspaper, they did depend on the goodwill of their readership and their advertisers, including the government, to survive in both their chosen fields. So a delicate balance had to be maintained between the interests of the various groups in the society: officialdom, the plantocracy, the professionals, and the merchants, who were the main source of publishing revenue.

The issues of the period on which all parties of consequence were agreed, however, and to which there were few references in the newspapers—save for notices of arrivals, sales, and runaways—were those relating to slavery. The reality under the noses of the whites of the colony was not discussed in print, except for preemptive excoriating reviews of those publications in England and the United States that supported the abolition of the trade and/ or institution. The French Revolution and the upheaval of the Haitian Revolution were closely followed by the Jamaican press, some of which carried articles and advertisements in French for the benefit of the white refugees who took shelter in Jamaica. The literate blacks among the slaves and freedmen, some of whom would have read these publications (the slaves surreptitiously), were left in no doubt as to prevailing opinion about their condition and the prospects for its amelioration.

Over time, other currents of opinion in the society came to be represented in the press, as ownership widened to include groups other than the white printers and entrepreneurs. The first notable example of this was *The Watchman and Jamaica Free Press*, a weekly started in the 1820s in Kingston by two colored men, Robert Osborn and Edward Jordon. At that time the colored progeny of white fathers, and black, usually slave, mothers were a distinct class in the colony: they were often educated (some of them in England), and had professions, property, and in some cases wealth. What they did *not* have, until 1831, was the right to vote or to sit in the Assembly.

The Watchman was closely allied, through its founders, with the missionary effort for abolition in general and the Methodist Church in particular. As such it was in contradistinction to prevailing opinion expressed by its competitors. When, following the Great Christmas Rebellion of 1831–1832, *The Watchman* printed an article calling on "friends of humanity to give a long pull, and a strong pull, and a pull altogether, until we bring the system [of slavery] down" (Black 1983: 107), Jordon was arrested and charged with "constructive treason." He was acquitted of that charge, but convicted of other, trumped up charges that were eventually dismissed, but not before he had served six months in the penitentiary. Interestingly, Jordon went on to a distinguished career as a 'radical' member of the Assembly, much of the time a thorn in the side of those representing conventional opinion. He resigned in the early 1860s to become island secretary, eventually serving under Governor Edward Eyre, of 1865 fame.

The Watchman was the first in an important line of newspapers owned by Jamaicans who stood outside the current of 'official' opinion, and who, by virtue of their economic independence and forceful eloquence, could not be silenced or ignored. For five years on either side of the twentieth century century, there was The Advocate, published in Kingston by Robert Love, born in the Bahamas and trained as a clergyman and medical doctor in the United States. In the pages of his newspaper and from the platforms of organizations such as The People's Convention, of which he was a founder, Dr. Love and like-minded black Jamaicans pushed for change in the structures of the crown colony and in the economic conditions of the rural poor in particular.

Three years after the demise of The Advocate, and eighty years after Osborn and Jordon, Marcus Garvey, Jr., by profession a printer, started a paper, also called The Watchman. The venture did not last very long, perhaps because by the following year Garvey went to Panama, where he published La Prensa. He returned to Jamaica and then went to the United States, to more successful and significant ventures in the medium, such as The Negro World, which was published between 1918 and 1933. Upon his return to his native land in the late 1920s, he put out The Black Man and The New Jamaican. While these were popular publications, they did not long outlast the tenure of their publisher and driving force; when Garvey left Jamaica for England in 1935, his legacy remained in the hearts and minds of thousands of his readers and followers, and endures to this day; but the publications of the Universal Negro Improvement Association (UNIA), at least in Jamaica, soon ceased.

One of the places at which Marcus Garvey learned his profession of printer was the Jamaican Government Printing Office; another was The Daily Gleaner. It began life as The Gleaner and Weekly Compendium of News in 1834, the same year that slavery was abolished, and still exists, one of the longest continuously published newspapers in the Western Hemisphere. Originating in the efforts of two Jewish brothers, and with effective control remaining with prominent members of the Jewish community until the third quarter of the twentieth century, The Gleaner, by dint of longevity and business acumen, has cemented its place in the Jamaican psyche to the extent that the name is synonymous with 'newspaper' for countless generations of Jamaicans, at home and abroad (*The Gleaner* had an overseas edition as early as 1866 and has several today).

For years at a time over its long history, *The Gleaner* has been the only regular morning daily and at times has had itself as its only competitor, through its sister paper *The Star*, which first appeared in 1951 and is still the only afternoon daily. Both *The Gleaner* and *The Star* provide information on everything from world wars and cataclysms to personal triumphs and tragedies, from school concerts and tea parties to political analysis and currency movements. The company also produces a weekly newspaper for Jamaican schools during the school year, one for visitors to the island during the tourist season, and a weekly racing guide for the thousands of turfites.

The Gleaner has used—some would argue abused—its dominant position to further the particular interests of its owners and/or editors, to influence policy at the national and parochial levels, and to promote campaigns that satisfy its particular view of the national interest. Along the way it has made strange alliances: Marcus Garvey, for instance, the champion of the black poor, found an advocate in his court battles in the scion of the wealthy Jewish family that owned the newspaper in the 1920s, even while the paper itself railed against his policies. It has also been a training ground for most of Jamaica's journalistic fraternity, as well as a showplace for the work of its literary figures.

It is fair to say that from the mid-1940s, when party politics was born, to the present, *The Gleaner* and its competitors have been in contradistinction to each other—'the Old Lady of Harbour Street,' as it was called, monopolizing the middle-to-right of the spectrum and the others scrambling to establish themselves in what ideological space was left in a fundamentally conservative society. There have been a few organs that would have been radical in any society, but they have not lasted more than a few years.

The 1990s was a fertile period in the media field, including newspapers. Computer technology in general and desktop publishing in particular, as well as streamlining the operations of large dailies like *The Gleaner*, have facilitated the creation of three new national dailies. One, the *Jamaica Record*, failed after three years; another, the *Sunday Herald*, has become a weekly; and the third, the *Jamaica Observer*, with the substantial resources of the Sandals Hotel group behind it, continues at time of writing to compete with *The Gleaner*.

The affordability of desktop publishing equipment has made possible the proliferation of small weeklies serving regional or even smaller communities, or particular interest groups. These papers, some substantial and well produced, provide readers in the communities and interest groups served with pertinent information and viewpoints that may be ignored by the larger papers; in a sense, they are descendants of the small, localized newspapers of the eighteenth and nineteenth centuries. One of the first community newspapers of the modern era was *The Boulevard News*, begun in the mid-1980s as a newspaper for the communities along the Washington Boulevard, the major artery out of the capital city to the west and home to a mix of people in the trades and professions, small businesses, light and heavy industry, and, inevitably, the unemployed. Its founding editor, Clarence Brodie, would regard his newspaper as in the tradition of Marcus Garvey's *Watchman* and *The Advocate* of Robert Love. Indeed the newspaper, now known simply as *The News*, carries selections from the writings of Garvey in every edition. The names of other newspapers tell the areas and interests they serve: the *Western Mirror* (a weekly), the *Mid-Island News* (biweekly), and the *Twin City Sun* (biweekly), which serves two satellite cities on the edge of the capital.

In recent years there has also been something of a revival in magazine publishing, focusing on entertainment—mainly popular music—and sports. Economic uncertainty renders publishing a risky venture, and many magazines appear irregularly and fade from the scene. The Institute of Jamaica continues to produce the *Jamaica Journal*, a remarkable compendium of timely research on an array of subjects in the arts and sciences, written by specialists for the layman. *The Jamaica Naturalist*, published by an environmental nongovernmental organization, made its appearance in 1991 and has secured a niche for itself as the voice of the growing movement for environmental preservation.

The local efforts struggle against the deluge of glossy magazines published in the United States and Britain, appearing regularly and at competitive prices throughout the island in supermarkets, pharmacies, and hotels. These cater to the innate curiosity of many Jamaicans about goings-on and fashions 'in foreign,' inspiring fads and styles that can be seen in the shops and homes a few weeks later.

RADIO AND TELEVISION

Nine radio and two television stations provide service to all but the most inaccessible parts of Jamaica; in addition there are about thirty licensed subscriber television systems and several unlicensed ones. There are thousands of 'dishes' perched atop apartment blocks and condominiums and decorating the yards of private homes. Jamaica is surely one of the most wired small societies.

Broadcasting began in Jamaica in 1939, when a private transceiver was pressed into service by the British authorities in order to broadcast to an anxious public information about World War II, which had just begun. In 1950 the British Rediffusion group was given a license to establish Jamaica's first commercial radio station, on the AM frequency range. Eventually Jamaican-owned, the station continues today as Radio Jamaica Ltd. (call sign RJR). After a slow start—there was some initial resistance to the commercial interruptions—the new service became extremely popular.

From the start, however, there were those who felt that a privately owned broadcasting company, operating primarily for profit and depending entirely on commercial revenue to finance its operation, could not be depended upon to meet "special needs . . . in the fields of self-expression, culture, information and entertainment," in the words of a government policy paper on the matter in 1958 (Ministry Paper No. 5, January 13, 1958).

Out of the desire to meet those needs, a public broadcasting service was set up in 1959, known as the Jamaica Broadcasting Corporation. Without the resources to provide full funding to the new entity, the Jamaican government of the day had no choice but to have JBC operate on semicommercial lines; meaning that the government would provide some of the necessary funding, but the rest would be obtained through the sale of commercial time and program sponsorship.

For the next thirty years, JBC and Radio Jamaica enjoyed a duopoly in radio, and JBC, for a similar period after 1963, a monopoly in television. The government-owned station tried to live up to the high ideals of its founders, and its early days are regarded by many older media heads as the golden days of Jamaican broadcasting. Plays and serials were commissioned from Jamaican writers and produced in-house by staff directors, actors, and technicians. Live concerts of Jamaican music were broadcast weekly.

JBC also became the hub for other publicly owned media operations. An educational broadcasting service producing programs to curriculum requirements, one of the first in the world, was formed by the Ministry of Education. A government information service was established that produced printed material on government programs, but whose main focus quickly became outreach through radio and, eventually, television.

But success was uneven. Production efforts were costly, and JBC's revenue base became increasingly uncertain. The station's biggest problem, however, the one that eroded its credibility even faster than its revenues—though they were not unrelated—was political interference. By the end of its first decade of life, JBC was firmly established in public perception as a government mouthpiece; incipient and increasing cynicism about successive governments took its toll on listenership and advertising. In 1997 the government of the day faced the inevitable, and, in an ironic twist, sold almost all the assets of the JBC to RJR, its historic rival.

By then, the world of communications and media had been transformed by new technologies that permitted a wider array of programming to be offered in a variety of different ways, especially on television. Service providers in the United States led the way, and Jamaicans were not slow to appreciate the advantages of living in the broadcast shadow of that huge engine of production. In the 1980s, while the government bolstered the television monopoly of its station, dishes proliferated in the homes of the Jamaican middle class. Encryption of the signals by the broadcasters caused hardly a pause and created a new industry: the acquisition and installation of code-breaking chips. The story was the same wherever a country or community (including within the United States) found itself in the footprint of a broadcasting satellite.

In 1989 the first tentative steps into the new communications world were taken by the authorities. Three licenses were issued in that year for new FM radio services; two years later a license for a second television service and another FM radio service were issued. All the new licensees were private companies, and there were specific requirements as to ownership of these companies to prevent their control by individual investors, especially persons already involved in media operations. Many of these controls have been abandoned as unworkable.

Other licenses were granted, one awarded jointly to the University of the West Indies and the University of Technology for a low-power station that would cover their virtually adjoining campuses and the surrounding communities. Another license, a controversial one, was granted for religious broadcasting on radio; eventually one was also given for television.

The controversy began before the first religious license was even drafted. There was concern that the station would be a conduit for the kind of electronic evangelizing already available on programs sponsored by some churches on existing stations, furthering what was deplored as an already high level of cultural intrusion. At least partly in response to this concern, the licensing authority required that all registered churches, Christian and non-Christian, be given the chance to participate in the entity to which the license would eventually be given. In the event, not all of them took the opportunity, but the policy created a series of internal checks and balances within the station and ensured a trouble-free beginning to religious broadcasting in Jamaica. While foreign matter is not absent, fears of American overkill have largely subsided, as programmers, especially in radio, have created a wide range of local material to fill the airtime.

Subscriber television grew out of the fascination of the Jamaican middle class with things American and took off like wildfire after the introduction of the first TVRO (television receive only) receiver, or 'dish,' in 1980. There are now tens of thousands of dishes; no one knows exactly how many because registration is not required. The growth in numbers has slowed somewhat because of natural saturation of the market and because of the expansion of organized subscriber systems, legal and otherwise.

PROGRAMMING AND LOCAL PRODUCTION

High production costs, lack of easily available venture capital, small domestic audience, and few distribution linkages to overseas markets affect production output for the audio-visual media, especially television. At the same time, Jamaica's stations have eagerly adopted the concept of '24/7' programming beloved by their North American counterparts. The two challenges, taken together, leave television stations with little recourse but to foreign programming. Excepting news, sports, and current affairs, programming on Jamaican television consists of up to 90 percent imported programming, almost all of that from the United States. On cable systems there is nothing local at all, not even the advertisements.

On radio the situation is, to some extent, reversed. Music is the staple of radio stations everywhere. The United States is the largest producer of recorded music, and Jamaica's proximity to that source ensures that a great deal of American music is played on most Jamaican stations but not by any means as much as was the case a decade ago. Record production and distribution can be profitably accomplished on a much narrower economic base than is needed for films and television shows. Lower capital costs and skilled engineers and studio musicians allow for the existence of several world-class recording studios in Jamaica that not only attract a host of international pop stars but, with the abundance of local talent available for all phases of music creation, underpin a quantum of Jamaican musical production out of proportion to the size of the society.

Most of this production, past and present, finds outlet on the radio stations. One of those, IRIE FM, devotes its programming entirely to Jamaican music, broadly defined. The rapturous reception given it when it began in 1989 and its sustained popularity since then have transformed the radio landscape and boosted appreciation of Jamaican music and music-related programming.

Music, news, and current affairs are the core programming of most radio stations. Paramount in the last category are phone-in talk shows, on which hosts and guests air their views on issues of personal and/or popular concern. Political matters dominate these discussions, which are free-wheeling and boisterous, often generating more heat than light. Party and government operatives monitor the shows to gauge public opinion; they also use the shows to try to mold that opinion and to embarrass their opponents.

Media in Jamaica operate without overt statutory controls except for licensing in the case of radio and television stations. But an out-of-date law of libel, based on an English law of the nineteenth century, protects public figures, especially politicians, from the kind of scrutiny and criticism that are de rigeur in some countries.

The popularity of talk shows has extended the use of telephony as part of broadcasting. Radio doctors and radio psychiatrists—licensed practitioners—counsel callers on their personal problems over the air; family counselors advise parents and children; spiritual counselors discuss matters of faith with the troubled. Radio in Jamaica is a highly interactive medium.

It is also a *Jamaican* medium, far more so than television. Its beginning in colonial times meant, perhaps inevitably, announcers who were hired for their apparent ability to sound English or North American and playing mostly foreign recorded music and introducing taped foreign programming. Today's *mélange* of stations with distinctive programming and presentation styles makes for a media landscape that is recognizably Jamaican. A person from the United States watching television in a hotel room, on the other hand, could be forgiven for wondering if he or she had left home.

CINEMA

Jamaica is better known as a location for feature films and television programs than as a producer of its own cinema. From the 1950s, when Hollywood producers began to search for locations away from their own country, until the present day, Jamaica has provided the setting for a wide range of feature films, including the latest version of *Lord of the Flies*, which was able to claim verisimilitude for its hurricane scene, filmed during and after Hurricane Gilbert in September 1988. Along the way, Jamaicans have developed a range of professional skills on both sides of the camera, which adds to the value of the island as a location. In the absence of local or overseas capital, however, those skills have not been harnessed toward sustained indigenous production in the medium.

The notable exception remains *The Harder They Come*, the first feature-length movie made entirely by Jamaicans for international release. Its story of a Jamaican country-bumpkin-come-to-town, who became a pop music star and, eventually, hunted murderer and icon, featured the singer Jimmy Cliff in his first film role and a driving reggae soundtrack that introduced Jamaican music to millions of people outside the island. The movie, directed and co-written by Jamaican Perry Henzell, has been playing steadily in art house cinemas and on specialty television channels around the world ever since its release in 1972.

The Harder They Come, made at a time of hopeful political change and cultural renewal, has inspired two generations of audio-visual artists. One of the authors of its screenplay, Trevor Rhone, a leading Jamaican dramatist, went on to produce a film version of his stage play *Smile Orange* and was the writer for a Canadian film, *Milk and Honey*, describing the travails of a Jamaican domestic worker in that country, which won a Juno, the Canadian Oscar award.

Other Jamaican efforts—*The Children of Babylon, Countryman, The Lunatic*—have been less successful. More recently (1997) the potent mixture of music, violence, and the urban ghetto setting, which worked so well in *The Harder They Come*, was harnessed by producers in Britain for *Dancehall Queen*, which has had success in Jamaica and in the cities that host the far-flung Jamaican community abroad, and for *Third World Cop* (1999), a scorching depiction of violence, corruption, and redemption in 'paradise' directed by a nephew of Perry Henzell, Chris Browne. The movies make good use of the most readily available Jamaican ingredients: great music, picturesque settings (natural and man-made), and a reputation for violence that dogs the country and its nationals wherever they live. Attempts to show the everyday realities of everyday people, however adept artistically, have failed to ignite marketers and audiences at home and abroad.

Third World Cop may, ironically, point the way to a genuine indigenous film industry. With no in-country processing facilities, making films in the traditional way poses huge logistical problems, adding to already high costs. *Third World Cop* was shot using digital video technology, which allows instantaneous review as a basis for quick decisions on reshooting—thereby cutting costs substantially. With the appropriate digital technology already in the country—along with actors, musicians, and behind-the-scenes crew—one can expect to see a greater number of Jamaican productions, and a wider range of treatments, beginning to emerge.

7

Literature

IT IS NOT EASY to say when Jamaican literature began, nor indeed what has comprised it at any given moment. Scholars are only now addressing the task of recovering and making available written-down works, many of which are still to be collected from the newspapers and little magazines in which they first appeared. At the beginning of the twenty-first century, many writers who publish outside of Jamaica must accept that their books will take a long time to 'get home' and may reach there in very small numbers. Also, any accurate account must include both oral and literary texts. Sadly, preserving the *oral* aspects of Jamaican literature is a case of too little, too late, since much of it is probably irretrievably lost. Our discussion will thus concern itself largely with written-down texts.

In his novel *Tom Cringle's Log*, an adventure story set mainly in Jamaica and the surrounding seas, Michael Scott describes a sailor singing about "how dat Corromantee rascal, my fader" (1836: 83) sold him on the Gold Coast—an instance of the breaking apart of family, kinship, and nation. Every other dislocation is a more or less violent version of this one; the players may be different, but the effect is the same. Beginning with the idea of transplanted Jamaicans as people separated from family-kin and/or nation-kin, we can discuss Jamaican literature as the journey back to reconstituted kinship. Interpreted in this context, words like 'displacement,' 'alienation,' and 'fragmentation' point to brokenness but also to a possibility for wholeness: thus, "In Jamaican fiction, a shifting emphasis from exile, loss and displacement to nationalism is ongoing" (Lalla 1996: 89).

Beginning in the 1930s, and paralleling developments in the decades thereafter, Louise Bennett's stories and dialect poems united spoken and written traditions[1] in hilarious recitals that poked fun at pretension and celebrated the ingenuity with which poor people 'made life.' Bennett's work harked back to the storytelling tradition of the Murrays in the nineteenth century (see Chapter 9) and ushered in both the writing of the women and the tradition of dub. Way ahead of her time, she lighted the way for the literature, joining an oral tradition from Africa and a literary tradition from England, in a unique body of work that is essentially creole and insists on our Jamaican 'generation,' never mind where we came from:

Back to Africa

Back to Africa, Miss Matty?
Yuh no know what you da seh?
You haffi come from somewhe fus
Before yuh go back deh!

Me know seh dat yuh great great great
Granma was African,
But Mattie, doan['t] yuh great great great
Granpa was Englishman?

Den yuh great granmodder fader
By yuh fader side was Jew?
An yuh grampa by yuh modder side
Was Frenchie parlez-vous?

But de balance a yuh family,
Yuh whole generation,
Oonoo all bawn dung a Bun Grung—
Oonoo all is Jamaican! (Bennett 1982: 104)

Bennett enlarged the tradition of Jamaican poetry-in-creole begun earlier by Tom Redcam, Claude McKay, and Una Marson. An actress and folklorist as well as poet (see Chapter 9), she published several collections in the early years, as well as *Jamaica Labrish* (1972 and 1975), *Anansi and Miss Lou* (1979), and *Selected Poems* (1982) and *Aunty Roachy Seh* (1993) more recently. Though her poetry has seen increasing discussion, that and many other aspects of her contribution are still inadequately represented.

It is appropriate to begin with Miss Lou (as all Jamaicans know her), for, as we say elsewhere, she reconciles, in her person and her work, an endless variety of family *bruck-up*—fragmentations of color, class, mores, and language. Miss Lou not only gathers Jamaicans into a family, she also calls them to their 'best behaving.'

Accounts of the beginning of Jamaican literature often start in 1759, with Francis Williams, a black Jamaican, who wrote an ode in Latin dedicated to the newly arrived governor of Jamaica. Williams was a free-born black Jamaican, educated in England as part of an experiment to prove blacks were as teachable as whites. "Welcome, Welcome, Brother Debtor," another poem that Williams may have written, mockingly celebrates his time in prison. If nothing else, the two poems together make an indigenous beginning.

The first Jamaican prose narratives are travelogues or diaries and are mostly by non-Jamaicans with distinctly foreign perspectives, some of whom had never been to Jamaica. Two significant exceptions were Monk Lewis's *Journal of a West Indian Proprietor* (1834) and *Lady Nugent's Journal* (1839). Both provide catalogues of daily life in Jamaica by persons who despite being foreigners, were keen observers of the local scene.[2] There were accounts by black people from other countries, too—Nancy Prince's *A Black Woman's Odyssey Through Russia and Jamaica* (1799), for example. *The Wonderful Adventures of Mary Seacole in Many Lands* (1857) was an account of travels abroad by a Jamaican nurse, Mary Seacole.

There were novels as well, exclusively from foreign hands. Among them were Michael Scott's *Tom Cringle's Log* and other nineteenth-century novels, including the anonymous *Hamel, the Obeah Man* (1827), *Marly; or, the Life of a Planter in Jamaica* (1828), also anonymous, and, later in the century, Mayne Reid's *Maroon* (1862). *Hamel, the Obeah Man* is "unique . . . in that it demonstrates what a white writer . . . could achieve if he went beyond the superfices of the 'System' and tried to enter the imagination of at least a single slave" (Brathwaite 1970: 72). *Hamel* was an aberration in this regard, but, despite its feat of imagination, it did not agitate for change. Thus, concern for the lot of the slaves in nineteenth-century prose was, at worst, entirely absent and, at best, an acknowledgment of a hideous system of oppression—nothing more.

The situation was different with *oral* literature: "In this pre-twentieth century period . . . most extant verse is folk song, and so preserves the perspective of slaves in a voice that is not only dislocated and alienated, but also dissatisfied and often antagonistic" (Lalla 1996: 7). Free, educated black writers were "as isolated as the uneducated" and so shared the outcast's perspective. Still, they, like the prose writers, did not attack the status quo.

In 1889, a long poem entitled "Jamaica" (by 'T. R., a Jamaican') was published, which reflected the nationalist feeling abroad even before the end of the nineteenth century. It described the island's history and tenuous political and economic state, anticipating what the future might bring. A "significant document in the history of the nativization of Caribbean poetry in English . . . it is remarkable for its nationalistic sentiment, and for the way it speaks for the underdog and the coloured people of Jamaica" (Baugh 1994: 1242).

Whether he was 'T. R.' or not, at about the turn of the century, Tom Redcam,[3] a near-white Jamaican, had started to write patriotic verses that attracted attention. Redcam's poems were a call to recognize and celebrate Jamaican-ness as something unique. Unfortunately, his poems largely imitated Romantic and Victorian English nature poetry and they influenced many early Jamaican poets.[4] The poems did achieve vitality in their occasional use of Jamaican Creole, but these were not the ones that were imitated.

An important contribution to the development of Jamaican literature was Redcam/MacDermot's All Jamaica Library, which began serious literary publishing in Jamaica. The All Jamaica Library was an effort to publish affordable works written by Jamaicans dealing directly with Jamaica and Jamaicans. Although it set out to produce poetry, history, and essays, money proved a problem, and only four works of prose fiction (in five volumes) appeared. Whatever its failings—the standard of the four works was not high—the All Jamaica Library put cheap editions into the hands of Jamaicans. It also began the work of turning the focus of 'written-down' literature away from Europe.

There were political stirrings at this time, and the beginnings of cultural awareness. Black nationalist Marcus Garvey who was also a poet and prodigious writer had begun to hold lectures, conferences, and cultural shows as early as 1913. There were other initiatives to organize groups and societies, some devoted to literary activity. Books on Jamaican culture were also appearing: Walter Jekyll, an Englishman, published *Jamaican Song and Story* (1907); Astley Clerk published an account of Jamaican music and musical instruments in 1913; and later, American Martha Beckwith published *Black Roadways: A Study of Jamaican Folk Life* (1929).

A novelist from a comfortable middle-class background, H. G. de Lisser cannily had all ten of his novels serialized in Jamaica, either in *The Daily Gleaner*, of which he was editor, or in a magazine he owned, *Planter's Punch* (they were all subsequently published as books). *Jane's Career* (1914), de Lisser's first novel, has the dual distinction of having the first black central character (in a novel by a Jamaican writer) and being "the first West Indian novel in which the peasant is given full status as a human person" (Ramchand and Gray 1971: xiv). Critics also credit him with successfully handling creole speech. De Lisser represents the society quite accurately; however, like the nineteenth-century 'foreign' writers, he did not question the status quo. Ironically there is little doubt that his solid middle-classness is what enabled him to break ground by "represent[ing] the working-class folk as literary subjects" (Donnell and Welsh 1996: 30).

Claude McKay, the first published black Jamaican writer, was also the first to achieve international acclaim. McKay hailed from the country (Clarendon). He worked early on as a policeman and developed a great sympathy for those unfortunates who broke the law. Encouraged by folklorist Walter Jekyll, he produced two books of poetry, *Songs of Jamaica* (1912) and *Constab Ballads* (1912), both in Jamaican Creole. They were well received, and he was awarded the Institute of Jamaica's Silver Musgrave Medal that year. He emigrated to the United States in 1912, where he achieved a substantial reputation and became part of the Harlem Renaissance flowering of black letters. Though the form of his later poetry is more conventional, it has a depth of feeling that is rare in Caribbean writing. He is especially well known in the United States for his sonnet "If We Must Die."

Despite his poetry's being better known, McKay's fiction is more important. His published writing includes three novels, *Home to Harlem* (1928), *Banjo: A Story Without a Plot* (1929), and *Banana Bottom* (1933), and a collection of short stories, *Gingertown* (1932). "The [Harlem] world McKay presents is alive with stevedores, railway workers, waiters, prostitutes, pimps, homosexuals, brothels, fornication, adultery, venereal disease, drugs, brawls, laughter, sensual dancers, soul food, the rhythm of the blues, the music of the soulful ghetto" (M. Morris 1975: 36–37). This level of honesty brought him angry responses from many critics, including W.E.B. DuBois and Marcus Garvey.

McKay never came back to Jamaica. In 1924 he took up residence in France, travelling between there and Germany, Spain, and North Africa in the following years, and writing his major novels. He eventually returned to the United States where he died in reduced circumstances in 1948.

THE 1930s AND 1940s

Garvey's determined efforts in the 1910s and 1920s to help uplift black people and reconstruct their idea of themselves through education and cultural awareness had some effect, as did other efforts at cultural and political organization. By the middle of the 1930s, it was clear that, where creative writing was concerned, things were changing:

Caribbean poetry . . . took a decisive turn in the later 1930s and early 1940s. This development was related to the general socio-political thrust of this period, manifested in the labour unrest that swept through the Caribbean in the late 1930s.

• • •

Anti-colonialism, the necessity for Caribbean self-definition, protest against social ills deriving from considerations of class, colour, and economic status, assertion of the dignity and beauty of the black person, willingness to take poetic nurture from local cultural roots—these were some of the themes that brought a new immediacy to Caribbean poetry. (Baugh 1994: 1243)

The early poets whom Tom Redcam had influenced (many were women) were concerned with writing verse in conventional style (sonnets, odes) and showed no desire to experiment—their introduction of local material was largely for decoration's sake. Two important poets who began to publish in the 1930s and who broke these imported molds are Una Marson and George Campbell.

Marson experimented with form, writing poems in Jamaican Creole about passion, frustrated love, loneliness, and racism. Her focus was on being Jamaican, being black, being racially proud, and being an independent woman, well before any of these was fashionable. She went to England in 1932 (she travelled widely) where she worked for the BBC and conceived the radio program "Calling the West Indies."[5] Between 1930 and 1945, she published four poetry collections[6] and was awarded the Institute of Jamaica's Silver Musgrave Medal in 1930 at age 25. She also wrote three plays (see Chapter 9). An enigmatic character who suffered from depression and was as capable of being devastated by loneliness and unrequited love as of being independent and self-motivated, Marson died in 1965 at age 60. The Una Marson Prize for Adult Literature in Jamaica's National Literary Awards is awarded biennially in her memory.

The writing effort at this time was assisted by the many little magazines that appeared throughout the region. In Jamaica there were *Focus, Planter's Punch,* and the University College of the West Indies' (UCWI) *Caribbean Quarterly. Bim* in Barbados, *The Beacon* in Trinidad, and *Kyk-over-al* in Guyana also published Jamaican authors. The magazines featured poetry, prose, and articles and, in a region where there was no publishing industry to provide an outlet for writers, performed (and still perform) an invaluable function.

No poet more clearly embodied the radical changes in Jamaica than George Campbell. He was part of the political ferment of the 1930s, part of the Drumblair group (see Chapter 10), and an intimate of the Manleys to whom he has remained close (see Chapter 10). He influenced Nobel Laureate Derek Walcott who, in Chapter One of his autobiographical poem, *Another Life*, explicitly mentions reading "Holy" from Campbell's book *First Poems* (1945).

"Campbell's poetry meditates upon what it means to be 'West Indian.' . . . 'Holy' is is an acknowledgement and benediction of the ethnic plurality on which a Caribbean nation could be built" (Donnell and Welsh 1996: 117). "Holy" begins with a powerful oxymoron: "Holy be the white head of a Negro." Thereafter it uses the litany prayer form to invoke blessings on various heads: "the black flax of a black child"; the "down" that is golden and that streams "in the waves of the wind"; the calm, impersonal "sea[s]" of heads of Chinese hair. As he affirms the holiness of Indians' heads, he ascribes to them a "feeling of distance and space and dusk." In the last line, all these heads are swept into oneness with "the earth and the sun"—their holiness at once imbuing and blessed by all of creation.

Rather like Claude McKay, Campbell integrates issues of ethnicity and socioeconomics in the service of a utopian vision for humanity, which he allies to an idyllic vision of possibility for Jamaica. He clearly calls Jamaicans to be a family, using metaphors of house and home to encourage them to think again about the ways in which they understand themselves, one another, and the island they live in.

Two important writers to emerge at this time were Roger Mais and V. S. Reid. Mais published two collections of short stories, *And Most of All Man* (1942) and *Face and Other Stories* (1942), and Reid published *New Day* in 1949. Mais was a brown Jamaican who was continually writing—articles, short stories, poems, plays. Involved in the political upheavals in Jamaica that culminated in the riots of 1938 and 1939, he committed himself passionately to the nationalist cause. At least thirty-eight of his stories appeared in *Public Opinion*[7] between 1940 and 1950, many of them still uncollected. His novels—his major literary contribution—all appeared in the 1950s, and are therefore discussed with other works appearing at that time.

Reid's *New Day* was published in 1949. He wrote it to debunk the idea that Bogle and Gordon, two of the 1865 'rebels' who were hanged, were criminals. A watershed work, it traces Jamaica's history, from the 'Rebellion' of 1865 to the new Constitution in 1944, through the character of the narrator, Johnny Campbell. The novel is innovative both in its use of language and its treatment of a historical theme. Reid speaks of "stylizing the dialect, keeping the atmosphere, keeping the syntax as much as possible" (Reid 1988: 4) in an effort to write in dialect but make the novel accessible to a wider audience. His approach to history was to adopt the point of view of the persons involved in the tumultuous events of the time—essentially, a Jamaican look at a Jamaican struggle.

THE 1950s

Several West Indian writers (including Jamaicans Neville Dawes, John Hearne, Roger Mais, V. S. Reid, and Andrew Salkey) went to England in the course of the 1950s, all driven there—or so we are told—by the lack of a receptive audience at home.

Ironically, there was growing interest in things cultural in Jamaica at the time. By then, Kingston had at least one bookshop, and the Institute of Jamaica and its library were flourishing. The UCWI had started in 1948. In 1957, Pioneer Press published Louise Bennett's[8] *Anansi Stories and Dialect Verse*. (A Jamaican initiative begun in 1950 by the Gleaner Company, the Press had produced several titles by then.) In the Caribbean, the little magazines continued to publish, while in Jamaica outlets like *The Gleaner, Planter's Punch*, and especially *Focus* (which appeared twice in the fifties and was edited by Edna Manley) and *Public Opinion* paid attention to things Jamaican and seriously discussed literature and the arts.

Mais had written his three novels before he left Jamaica; his achievement in *The Hills Were Joyful Together* (1953), *Brother Man* (1954), and *Black Lightning* (1955) is beyond question. Like McKay, he looked close-up at the lives of ordinary people, thus causing considerable controversy among the Jamaican middle-class audience. This comment on *The Hills Were Joyful Together* represents Mais's intention in all three books: "In his portrayal of . . . a Kingston slum, Mais transforms the yard into the world of man, and the condition of the yard-dweller [to] the human condition. Herein lies the vision he is attempting to express" (Daphne Morris 1981: vii). This vision was consistent with his commitment to nationalism and to the ideals of truth and justice, all of which lend his work extraordinary passion. The poet's instincts invest his prose with a sure sense of the rhythms of Jamaican speech, and his dramatic sense ensures keenly observed *realités*. These voices are from the "Chorus of People in the Lane" who offer a running commentary throughout *Brother Man*:

—Goin' have 'nodder hurricane dis year shore, Massa God don' done wid we yet, hm! goin' blow we down flat dis time!

—Man too wicked in de world, mek Big Massa sorry de day him ever try wid him. Man! jus' like bad, bad pikney a-yard, can't do nutt'n wid him 'tall-'tall.

—Ax pardon, seems Ah tek up wind in me belly again, caan get no ease whatever sake of de wind.

—Tek *ciracee*,[9] bile it mek tea, best t'ing fo' belly-wind. (Mais 1970: 106)

The rumble of wind in the belly is the microcosmic, human echo of the cosmic disturbance of the hurricane.

John Hearne's *Voices Under the Window* was first published in 1955, the year of Roger Mais's death. It was rapidly followed by *Strangers at the Gate* (1956), *The Faces of Love* (1957) (published in the United States as *The Eye of the Storm* in 1958), *The Autumn Equinox* (1959), and *The Land of the Living* (1961). Of the four novelists, Hearne was perhaps least kindly treated by the critics, one of whom commented: "I've often wondered whether Hearne's theme, with the loaded concern . . . for a mythological, colonial squirearchy, is not [why] his work is at present less energetic than the West Indian novels at their best" (Lamming 1978: 26). Hearne's writing over the next twenty years was confined to popular fiction: three thriller-type parodies of detective novels coauthored with journalist Morris Cargill. *The Sure Salvation* (1981) would be his vindication.

Andrew Salkey was a poet, novelist, essayist, children's writer, prolific anthologist, and academic. His first novel, *A Quality of Violence* (1959), was lionized as an audacious work. In it, he did as Mais had done, venturing outside his experience to explore a world of poor country people, peasants, small farmers, planters, and poco jumpers (see Chapter 9 for a description of the pukkumina dance ritual). Twenty-five years later, the assessment was less enthusiastic: "in relation to pocomania, the narrative eye . . . is an outsider's. . . . The narrative tone is often distant and critical" (Mervyn Morris 1994: 62). At the time, however, Salkey could not have made a bolder entrance: with a Guggenheim Fellowship awarded on the strength of the novel, he launched into a highly productive career.

V. S. Reid published *The Leopard* in 1958. A *tour de force* of the imagination, for Reid never went to Africa, *The Leopard* is set in Kenya at the time of the Mau Mau uprisings. Arguably his best book, it tells the story of a mixed-blood child who is rescued by his African father after his white mother has been murdered by the Mau Mau. (The child is unaware of his relationship to his father.) Reid uses their situation, their oneness as prey for the leopard (the father has been wounded), to explore political, social, racial, and familial issues in an inspired poetic prose.

One poet worthy of note who published his first collection in the early 1950s is Basil Clare McFarlane. A slim volume, *Jacob and the Angels*, was published by Miniature Poets (Georgetown, British Guiana) in 1952. Few other poets published in the 1950s; the flowering of poetic talent awaited the 1960s and 1970s.

THE 1960S AND 1970S

These two decades are especially important for the emergence and rapid consolidation of five fine poetic talents: Edward Baugh, A. L. Hendriks, Anthony McNeill, Mervyn Morris, and Dennis Scott. Together, these poets move Jamaican poetic considerations firmly in the direction of 'home'——closely conceived as family, extending into community, and directly addressing nation-family, as in Baugh's "People Poem (The Leader Speaks)":

People Poem (The Leader Speaks)

In the name of the people
I give you the People's Constitution
in which the rights of the people
have been enshrined.
So now that the people's rights
are enshrined, meaning dead,
let us get on with the business
of building the nation
for the good of the people.
But remember: be vigilant.
Anybody who trouble me trouble you
for *you* is *me; I* am the people—
in the name of the people
and the people
and the people. (Baugh 1988: 46)

The poem code-switches from English into Jamaican Creole, uniting the separate traditions in a powerfully ironic statement. It is a strategy which, after these poets, is increasingly employed.

A. L. Hendriks, the oldest of the five, published his first book in 1965 and three other collections in the 1970s. Lyrical and sometimes metaphysically crafty, Hendriks's poetry resonates with a powerful sense of the Jamaican place, and the poetic statement often reaches out beyond local resonances to themes and preoccupations that are universal.

Dennis Scott, dancer, playwright, critic, teacher, and actor as well as poet, was a rigorous craftsman who wrote about the 'dread' aspects of Jamaican life in startling, often harsh, surreal images. He broke new ground in the reintegration of folk and 'high' poetry traditions by using the creole for *serious* purposes. "Uncle Time," his most famous poem in that regard, supplies the title for his first collection (1973), which won an International Poetry Forum Award. "Birdwalk," a poem of deadly social comment, is also entirely in creole. Craftily, it employs the "Sing a Song of Sixpence" nursery rhyme to make its point:

Birdwalk

Sing a sang a dunny[10]:
belly full a win'
scrubbin' all de mawnin,
ole, an thin.
'Now de day is ova . . . '
tryin nat to cry
black bird in de gyaden singin,
hanging out to dry.

Mister in de countin house
countin up de money,
Missis in de dinin room
eatin off de honey.
Gatta in de gyaden
prayin nat to dead
waitin fe de blackbird
walkin through she head. (Scott 1989: 46)

These five poets not only unite the nationalistic sentiments that began early in the century with the social and political concerns of McKay, Campbell, and Marson, they go beyond both, anticipating the more personal concerns of writers at the end of the twentieth century. All five write poems about home and family, the ties of affection, the trivia of everyday life. Sometimes, as in Morris's "Windscreen" a perfect match is made between the personal and the communal. The poor chap with the widening crack in his windscreen represents any institution, community, or society that is putting some crucial whole at risk (the environment, cyberspace, mental health, etc.) by not fixing the 'cracks.'

Windscreen

De garage people
seh de neat
crack in mi window
bound to grow

an though it hardly showin
now, between vibration an de heat
it noh mus grow?

I climb inside
an measure. So I know:
de crack is growin. (Morris 1992: 50)

A Morris poem is, more times than not, a nugget of few words: "Good sense and wit, sharpened by the increasingly minimal art of his later works, are among [Mervyn] Morris's prime virtues" (Baugh 1995: 73). Like Scott and Baugh, Morris can use the creole to great effect: it invests the character in "Windscreen" with a personality and wry sense of humour, at the same time that his story resonates with impending danger in ever widening domains.

Though they are all, to some degree, lyric poets, "McNeill's is the pure lyric cry, of grateful wonder and dreadful apprehension: His work bears the raw nerve scars of one who has looked into the 'Black Space' " (Baugh 1995: 70). ("Black Space" is the title of a poem in his second book, *Reel From a Life Movie* [1975].)

Some critics consider McNeill the most original poetic talent to have emerged in the West Indies. A poker player and jazz and reggae fan who 'knew' the drug culture, McNeill's poetry has profound spiritual dimensions at the same time that it is located in the most painful and disturbing personal and social realities. Influenced by American poet, W. S. Merwin, among others, he spoke of poetry as the "noise in the street," and, true to that insight, his poetry has strong oral qualities, and he uses virtually any experience as grist to his poetic mill.

A superbly able craftsman, he code switches from creole to Standard Jamaican English with ease and authority. He experimented with concrete poetry: for example, a poem (untitled and dedicated "to my family living and dead") is composed of a (slightly extended) em-dash, followed by a colon in the next line which is centered immediately below the dash, with the last line the same as the first. Poems run the gamut of length as well as subject matter: they may be composed of only one line

the light around god is too dark

or may run to several pages. Extraordinarily prolific, he left over twenty unpublished manuscripts when he died in 1995.

Jamaican anthologies tend to bracket each decade: the 1962 publication of *The Independence Anthology of Poetry* and the *Savacou* 'New Writing 1970' double issue helped to identify the directions in which poetry was going. Kamau Brathwaite and Derek Walcott had both come to prominence in the decade, and Brathwaite was working at the UWI in Jamaica, where his poetry had begun to influence many new poetic voices.

Andrew Salkey was enormously prolific at this time, editing several anthologies and producing four new novels, travel journals, and several children's stories.

Peter Abrahams, one of the original crop of African writers in English (which included Chinua Achebe), came to Jamaica in the early 1960s. His first novel, *Mine Boy* (1963), was the first ever published by a black South African. Subsequent novels such as *The View from Coyaba* (1985) have dealt with Caribbean concerns, but he is not generally treated as a Caribbean writer.

There were books from some people who had not published before. Neville Dawes, one of the writers whose work was accorded the Lamming accolade of being "shot through with the urgency of peasant life" (quoted in Donnell and Welsh 1996: 256), published *The Last Enchantment* (1960) and later *Interim* (1978). Maroon artist and sculptor (see Chapter 10) Namba Roy's novel, *Black Albino*, appeared in 1961. Orlando Patterson published his first and most memorable novel, *The Children of Sisyphus*, in 1964. A disturbing portrayal of a prostitute's struggle to free herself from the lowest kind of slum life in the city's 'dungle,' the novel tackled subjects not unlike those addressed by Mais and Salkey. Patterson's characters are far more wretched, however, and their circumstances more hopeless. *An Absence of Ruins* (1967), a less successful work, followed, and after that *Die the Long Day* (1972).

Sylvia Wynter's *The Hills of Hebron* (1962) interrupts the voicelessness of women in Jamaican fiction up to this point and is the first novel published by a Jamaican woman of color in the twentieth century. A study of Alexander

Bedward, the revival leader, it focuses on a community of revivalists strug-
gling to survive in relative isolation in the mountains. "In its recognition of
a tendency to substitute one form of self-deception for another, the novel
presents a grim picture of betrayal within betrayal—betrayal of black by white
and black by black, of the individual by the community . . . of woman by
man" (Lalla 1996: 179). In other words, it is a novel concerned with nation-
family business.

In the 1970s a growing number of women placed their work in journals
and little magazines, especially *Jamaica Journal*, which regularly featured fiction and poetry. Rachel Manley made way for the women by publishing two
collections of poetry, *Prisms* (1972) and *Poems 2* (1978). Kraus Reprints
(1970) reprinted Basil McFarlane's *Jacob and the Angels* (1952), and, after a
long silence, John Figueroa's *Ignoring Hurts* (1976) appeared. The most accomplished of the McFarlane trio,[11] Basil McFarlane is yet to have a representative collection published.

It is perhaps appropriate to mention Michael Thelwell's novel at the end
of this account of the 1960s and 1970s, though it was published in 1980.
He reversed the usual order, writing *The Harder They Come* (1980) *after* the
famous film, scripted by Trevor Rhone and Perry Henzell. Though he has
published no other creative work, Thelwell is the only Jamaican and one of
only six West Indians mentioned in Harold Bloom's *The Western Canon*
(1994).

THE 1980s AND 1990s

Several important writers have lived and worked abroad for many years—
in some cases, since they were quite young. The question therefore arose as
to whether to include writers like Louis Simpson (United States–Pulitzer
Prize winner) in this account, or younger writers like Lucinda Roy (Namba
Roy's daughter), the child of Jamaican immigrants to Britain, who has since
migrated to the United States. The rough criteria decided on were (1) time
spent in Jamaica and (2) extent of the country's influence on the work. Still,
there is no satisfactory resolution, so, to some extent, these decisions have
been arbitrary.

John Hearne spent twenty years working on *The Sure Salvation*, the story
of what happens to the very last slave ship when it is becalmed on the Atlantic.
"From the very first sentence, Hearne stamps on the reader's senses the feeling
of seething, unhealthy tension, of festering paralysis and doom in which the
ship is held. . . . The twenty years which Hearne kept his readers waiting . . .

were . . . like the long wait of the Sure Salvation . . . not in vain" (Baugh 1983: 61, 63). Hearne died in 1994.

Up to the 1980s, most of the poetry and prose that had been published in Jamaica was by men. Among the few exceptions were poets Una Marson, Louise Bennett, and Rachel Manley and novelist Sylvia Wynter. "However, the 1980s saw a remarkable burgeoning of women poets, to parallel a similar upsurge in the appearance of prose fiction by women. . . . Together [poets like Jean Binta Breeze, Christine Craig, Lorna Goodison, and Pamela Mordecai] have affected an act of women's self-definition, articulating woman's concerns and culture and claiming woman's necessary role in the social and historical process" (Baugh 1994: 1244).

Many of the Jamaican women poets were prose writers as well, part of the "upsurge of prose fiction" to which Baugh refers. Other women fiction writers of all ages and stages were claiming a space as well. Among them was Erna Brodber whose first novel, *Jane and Louisa Will Soon Come Home*, arrived without fanfare in 1980. It would in time be discussed as a landmark work in Caribbean literature. By the end of the twentieth century, "the increasingly confident voices of women writers [had] insisted that the *patriarchal* bias of the West Indian literary canon be challenged and women's stories be written back into the representation of the quilt/braid/mosaic/ hybrid" (O'Callaghan 1999: 172).

Several anthologies of women's writing in the 1980s and 1990s confirm their increased presence. Roughly bracketing the 1980s are the *Savacou* 1979 special issue *New Poets from Jamaica*, in which seven of the thirteen poets are women; *Jamaica Woman* (1980; 1985), which anthologized the poetry of fifteen women,[12] and *From Our Yard* (1987), in which eleven of twenty-eight (Jamaican) poets are women. Interestingly enough, only one collection of Jamaican prose exists for the period of the 1980s and 1990s, the *Festival Literary Anthology* (1987) presenting a selection of gold and silver award winners in the 'Festival' short story competition over some twenty years. Anthologies are important because "only a small proportion of interesting writers in the region will ever be in a position to publish their work in book form" (Breiner 1995: 79).

Six of the poets in *Jamaica Woman* had individual collections of their work published in the next ten years: Lorna Goodison's *Tamarind Season* (1980), Christine Craig's *Quadrille for Tigers* (1984), Olive Senior's *Talking of Trees* (1985), Gloria Escoffery's *Loggerhead* (1988), Pamela Mordecai's *Journey Poem* (1989), and Velma Pollard's *Crown Point and Other Poems* (1988) appeared. Goodison went on to publish two more collections, *I Am Becoming*

My Mother (1986) and *Heartease* (1988) in the 1980s, and *Selected Poems* (1992), *To Us, All Flowers Are Roses* (1995), and *Turn Thanks* (1999) in the 1990s. Of contemporary Jamaican poets, Goodison has been the most celebrated.

Escoffery, Mordecai, Pollard, and Senior each published another book in the 1990s—*Mother Jackson Murders the Moon* (1998), *de Man, a Performance Poem* (1995), *Shame Trees Don't Grow Here* (1992), and *Gardening in the Tropics* (1994), respectively—and Heather Royes published her first collection, *The Caribbean Raj* (1996).

The most notable prose writer of the poet-prose-writers is Olive Senior whose first book, *Summer Lightning and Other Stories*, was awarded the inaugural Commonwealth Writers' Prize in 1987. Senior has subsequently published two other acclaimed collections, *Arrival of the Snake Woman* (1989) and *Discerner of Hearts* (1995). Her fiction has received international attention; her poetry, equally accomplished, is perhaps not as well known. "Do Angels Wear Brassieres?," perhaps the best known story of her first collection, displays, from the beginning, her talent for humorous writing and her facility with the creole: "Becka down on her knees ending her goodnight prayers and Cherry telling her softly, 'And ask God to bless Auntie Mary.' Becka vex that anybody could interrupt her private conversation with God so, say loud loud, 'no. Not praying for anybody that tek weh mi best glassy eye marble' " (Senior 1987: 67).

Pollard, Goodison, and Craig published collections of short fiction also: *Considering Woman* (1988); *Baby Mother and the King of Swords* (1990) and *Mint Tea and Other Stories* (1993), respectively. Pollard won the Casa de Las Americas prize for *Karl* (1993) and subsequently published *Homestretch* (1994). Brodber produced a second novel, *Myal* (1988) which was a prizewinner in the Commonwealth Writers' Competition (1989), and a third, *Louisiana* (1994). Goodison won the 1988 Commonwealth Poetry Prize (for the Americas region). Rachel Manley won the Governor General's prize (Canada's highest literary award) for *Drumblair* (1997), a compelling memoir about growing up in her famous family.

The prizewinners have not all been women. With an accomplished first collection, *Progeny of Air* (1994), Kwame Dawes claimed the Forward Prize (UK) for best collection of 1994. He has published seven other collections, most recently *Shook Foil: A Collection of Reggae Poems* (1997), a chapbook, *Mapmaker* (2000), and *Midland* (2000). It is a confident body of work that is revelatory of self-in-society in ways that perhaps link him to the integrating tradition of the women's writing. Playwright, critic, and academic as well as poet, Dawes recently edited *Wheel and Come Again* (1998), a collection of "poems mixing all the resources of language with the reggae mood, the reggae intelligence and the reggae aesthetic" (Dawes 1998: cover blurb).

Dawes's definition of reggae poems is perhaps intended to separate them from 'dub.' However, reggae poems may well be a kind of dub, for dub is no longer any single thing: a host of dubbists currently perform in many styles in many countries. Thus, concerning dub poetry, about all that can safely be said is that it is poetry in performance often backed up by rhythms, especially those of reggae music. (Some dubbists also work in the scribal tradition into which many of their performed poems happily fit.) Thus, reggae rhythms[13] plus a highly energized word-in-the-air are dub's essential elements.

The original generation of dubbists includes Oku Onuora; Linton Kwesi Johnson, a distinguished practitioner in the United Kingdom; Mutabaruka, perhaps the most famous dubbist internationally; old timers Bongo Jerry and Brother Resistance; Lillian Allen who has performed in Canada for many years; Jean Binta Breeze, undoubtedly the most famous female exponent of dub; and Mikey Smith. A somewhat later generation includes Afua Cooper—another Canadian performer—Cherry Natural and her daughter Little Natural, and M'bala and Malachi Smith of Poets in Unity.

The community of dubbists suffered a tragic loss when Mikey Smith was stoned to death in 1983. An extraordinary performer, Smith's poems also work on the page. Recognition of Smith's achievement has been unstinting: "Both spoken and written, Smith's poems have a special urgency about them, a sense that the poet is chronicling events with ruthless accuracy because telling the truth—and having it heard—will make a difference" (Chamberlain 1993: 237). A few dub poets have collections in print. *It A Come*, a slim volume of Mikey Smith's poems, appeared in 1986. However, cassettes and CDs are largely the repositories of the dub *oeuvre*.

This discussion has been framed within the idea of the reconstituted family, one way of establishing kinship being the speaking of a common language. The dubbists see themselves as operating in Miss Lou's tradition, one aspect of which is using the creole. Most other writers deploy the continuum range—from Standard English to Jamaican Creole—in both prose and poetry. Valerie Bloom and Pamela Mordecai are among a few poets who have collections written exclusively in creole. Bloom has written poetry firmly in the tradition of Miss Lou. Mordecai's *de Man*, an eyewitness account of the crucifixion of Jesus Christ, breaks new ground by extensively using the creole to treat not just a serious but a sacred subject.

There were some splendid new voices in the 1980s and 1990s, not all of them young. Charles Hyatt's memoir of his childhood, *When Me Was a Boy*

(1987), is one of the most successful Jamaican-published books, having been reprinted several times. Edward Baugh, one of the poetic talents emerging in the 1960s, published his first collection, *A Tale From the Rainforest* (1988). Hazel Campbell, who published *The Rag Doll* in 1978, published *Singerman* (1992). Evan Jones published *Stonehaven* (1993), a fictionalized modern historical epic of three recent generations of his famous political family.[14] Easton Lee penned a runaway bestselling collection of poems called *From Behind the Counter* (1999)—the counter being the shop counter in his father's grocery store in rural Jamaica. *The Denting of a Wave* (1992), Ralph Thompson's first collection, presented poems from a considerable poet who had long published regionally and internationally. It was followed by *Moving On* in 1998.

An important new prose writer emerging in the 1980s was Anthony Winkler, whose novel *The Lunatic* (1987) is "a delightfully original [one] about a sweet Jamaican madman who talks to trees and has adventures with an insatiable German tourist. It is unpretentious and has been made into a feature film and perhaps for those reasons has been largely ignored in literary circles; yet the Jamaican comic novel is a sufficiently rare breed for Winkler to deserve critical encouragement" (Breiner 1995: 84). Encouraged or no, Winkler subsequently published three other novels in this genre.

Among younger emerging writers, Kwame Dawes (son of novelist, Neville) has already been mentioned. Earl McKenzie is unusual among contemporary Jamaican *male* writers for spanning genres. He has published one collection of poetry, *Against Linearity* (1993), and two collections of stories in which a fresh, sturdy, carefully observant vision distills his rural experience. Honor Ford Smith, lead author in the bestselling anthology by the Sistren Theatre Collective, *Lionheart Gal* (1986), published an impressive first collection of poetry, *My Mother's Last Dance* (1997). Barbara Lalla published *Arch of Fire* (1998)—like Jones's *Stonehaven*, an epic tale across generations of Jamaican families.

The end of the twentieth century saw prose writing move into a new genre. Marcia Douglas's first novel, *Madame Fate* (1999), contains elements of the fabulous and fantastic, of myth and magic realism. (She also published her first collection of poems, *Electricity Comes to Cocoa Bottom*, in 1999.) Nalo Hopkinson's *Brown Girl in the Ring* (1998) is placed more firmly within the speculative fiction genre. A gripping reconstitution of the folk tale of Ti Jean and his brothers, it won several awards including the Locus Award for Best First Novel in the genre. Hopkinson's second novel, *Midnight Robber*, was published in 2000.

Discussing poems by Caribbean women, one critic has noted that "Given the rich contextuality of poems by Caribbean women, simplistic divisions between the personal and the political become meaningless" (Juneja 1995: 100). Joan Riley and Michelle Cliff have been among the writers to grapple with the intersections of personal and societal distress. Cliff began to publish rather earlier than Riley and has a larger body of work.[15] She locates her stories in Jamaica and across the United States, her adopted country, addressing painful and contentious issues of race, class, gender, and not belonging. *The Unbelonging* (1985) is, coincidentally, the title of Joan Riley's first book. It is a heartrending tale of double exile, which raises issues of sexuality, alienation, and child abuse. Her other novels[16] explore similar territory. Patricia Powell's three novels also deal with issues of gender, rejection, exile, and displacement.

Erna Brodber's novel *Jane and Louisa Will Soon Come Home* (1980) was not a prizewinner—indeed, Brodber had difficulty finding a publisher. It also seemed to take the critics (some of them) a while to fully recognize its importance. Ten years later, it was being described as "the consummate text of growing up female in the Caribbean" (Cooke 1990: 29). It is above all, as the title says, a description of homecoming: the woman's journey, the women's journey, and the community's journey—all one and the same way home. Brodber walks Louise Bennett's path, stepping her own steps, bringing to her narrative the craft and sensibilities of poet *and* folk-storyteller. See Nellie watching dancers at the First of August country fair:

> Rock the lady. Rock the lady on your toes. Walk like you going somewhere and yet is only behind her and around to come right back to your space. With one hand behind your back, kick the knee and stick out the heel. O Mass Stanley, toe it. She to the right and you to the left and let that square of a shoe box into a parallelogram and back. O. Look at her cross your shoulder. She pretty eh and she so light and is only Miss Rose in her coarse boots tomorrow. (Brodber, in Mordecai and Wilson 1987: 44)

It is a pathfinding work. Two other novels, *Myal* (1988) and *Louisiana* (1994), were also enthusiastically received.

A summation of the 1960s suggested that "Most of [Jamaican] literature has so far concentrated on defining and assessing the society out of which it grows" (Baugh 1978: 141). Up to that time, it had been male writers who had done the defining and assessing. In the remaining three decades of the twentieth century, the literature broadened to include the socially conscious messages and driving rhythms of dub poets, and more important, the complex visions of women. Dub poets have a lot in common with the women writers; if they revel in the oral tradition, the women write in a way that makes the spoken word live on the page, resounding as it does in street and home and hillside. Both put family business—the ordinary lives of ordinary people—front and center, focusing on what Lorna Goodison calls, "the condition of [our] part of this yard." (1992: 100)

It is as well, then, to end the story of the long journey of Jamaican literature to reintegrate its imposed and indigenous traditions with some comments on the work of this remarkable Jamaican woman poet: "Goodison's voice is . . . the voice of a woman for whom home is a place where simple things are central, a place located here and now . . . a place that nourishes the spirit and the imagination. . . . It is in Goodison's language as much as in anything else that she combines the ordinary with the uncommon." Also, she "brings grace and understanding to the plainness of things and of people" (Chamberlin 1993: 196–197, 198).

So perhaps the terminus of the Jamaican writer's journey is in sight. At the end of *Jane and Louisa Will Soon Come Home*, Nellie Richmond's belly is imagined as in labour with a parrot fish, which "no amount of bearing down could give birth to" (Brodber 1980: 147). Nellie feels neither sadness nor frustration, however, for the possibility of its being born exists. Perhaps Nellie, in the last words of this book, speaks for all Jamaican writers, men and women, when she says, "We are getting ready."

NOTES

1. See Mervyn Morris (1967).

2. Both works have remained important sources for social historians and continue to figure in accounts of the history of literature in the region.

3. Thomas Henry MacDermot is better known as a poet by his pen name, "Tom Redcam"; he is less well known as MacDermot, the novelist and publisher.

4. Redcam was a playwright as well. See Chapter 9.

5. It started as a program on which West Indians serving in World War II sent greetings home. It later became "Caribbean Voices" and was produced by Henry Swanzy between 1945 and 1951. It exposed talents like V. S. Naipaul and John Hearne to, among others, their home audiences.

6. *Tropic Reveries* (1930), *Heights and Depths* (1932), *The Moth and the Star* (1937), and *Towards the Stars* (1945).

7. *Public Opinion* was a weekly paper, founded and published for most of its life by O. T. Fairclough, also a founding member of the People's National Party.

8. She was now officially Louise Bannett Coverley, having married Eric Coverley in New York in 1954.

9. A climbing vine of the cucumber and pumpkin family, it is the most popular of Jamaica's tea bushes and is widely used in folk medicine.

10. "Dunny" is money.

11. His father was poet laureate J. E. Clare McFarlane, and his brother was poet R.L.C. McFarlane.

12. None of these writers had a collection of their own published at the time.

13. The verse itself makes them, and the poet may also be backed up by taped or live music.

14. Since republished (1998) in a revised edition in Heinemann's Caribbean Writers Series.

15. Her recent works include *Bodies of Water* (1990), *Free Enterprise* (1994), and *The Store of a Million Items* (1998).

16. *Waiting in the Twilight* (1987), *Romance* (1988), and *A Kindness to the Children* (1998).

8

Music

THE WORLD knows Jamaica for reggae music in the way that, a century ago, it knew the island for rum. Even those who may not be familiar with this type of music know that reggae comes from Jamaica. They know Bob Marley: his handsome, dreadlocked face with uplifted arm has become an icon of contemporary black self-recognition. People who know nothing else about Jamaica, even its accurate location, recognize Bob Marley and his music.

Reggae music has a history, both social and musical, that extends beyond Jamaica's shores and deep into its soil. Musically, reggae is thoroughly modern: electronic, urban, shot through with influences from African-American rhythm and blues music. But its language, of rebellion, caustic commentary, exhortation, and longing, taps the ancient themes of Jamaica's traditional music, grounded in the rural experience.

TRADITIONAL MUSIC

"To understand Jamaica's traditional music," according to Dr. Olive Lewin, the leading Jamaican ethnomusicologist and an acclaimed composer, arranger, and performer, "one must understand the total environment of the people who create, adapt and use it" (1983: 33). Music knits together the different aspects of Jamaican life, the internal life of the person and the communal life of the group. The different African ethnic groups brought almost nothing of their material culture with them, but they brought their memories and their beliefs. Differences in language made communication difficult and sometimes dangerous for them; they learned to speak to each other through music. Work and living conditions were brutal; music made them less so. Leisure time was scarce; music was central to its enjoyment. Music was organic to the re-creation of their life and culture on this side of the ocean. It remains important to daily life and culture.

Much traditional music has no doubt been lost, since it is only in the twentieth century that the songs and tunes have been written down, and only in the last quarter of that century has there been any intensive recording of material. What survives would seem to fall into three broad categories: music for/as worship, music for/as social occasion, and work music. These categories are not mutually exclusive of each other since many social events have religious significance, are celebrated as such, and work is social. There is, Lewin says, "the belief in one all-encompassing and eternal life, which includes the various levels of society: Gods, Saints and Heroes, Ancestral Spirits, human beings, animals, plants and the elements. The prime aim of life at all levels is to maintain and, when necessary, re-establish harmony between all its manifestations, seen and unseen" (1983: 33). In such a belief system, the spirit life and the temporal life "interpenetrate" each other (Brathwaite 2000: 46). Music, vital to both, is in a continuum from the sacred to the secular, from ritual to entertainment and performance, in ways that sometimes erase classification boundaries. In the case of some rituals—those associated with Kumina,[1] for instance—music is organic to invocation: without music, especially drumming, there is no communication with the spirit world. The types of drums played, the rhythms, and words vary according to the purpose of the ritual.

Other ceremonies surrounding important observances in the life cycle— birth, puberty, death, mourning, thanksgiving, and so on—would be social events with spiritual components. The formal period of mourning, for instance, most commonly nine days and nights, has several customs associated with it. They vary from place to place but have similar purposes: comfort to the bereaved and ensuring safe journey of the departed soul to the spirit world (for slaves, Africa, where one was reunited with one's family and God) rather than have them lingering in the 'limbo' of this life as a 'duppy.'[2] The comfort is offered during all-night 'set-ups' in the home of the bereaved— whose family provides the 'bickle,' or very specific food, for the mourners— through hymns, songs, dances, and games, interspersed with remembrances of the departed and sometimes a look ahead, to the effect of the death on those left behind.

Mi Bigga Bredda (brother)

When mi fahda a go dead
Im neva mek no will
But im lef one cow
Fi de whole a we (all of us)
An mi bigga bredda
Rob i' wey from we
Glory be to God
Mi have fi mi own, (my own cow)
Mi own a mi own.

Social songs—of courtships, mishaps, some associated with certain foods and trees—were (and are) popular, and told stories whose genesis we can only guess at now. Significant events—the uprising of 1865 in St. Thomas, the collapse of a tunnel being built on the railway—were celebrated in songs that are still sung today.

Work, often back-breaking, was the central reality of life for blacks, slaves and free: ground to be cleared, ploughed, and planted and then reaped; houses to be built; roads to be cut through hillsides and paved with stone, marl, and asphalt. Both men and women did heavy labor, though not necessarily at the same tasks. Singing, in time to the heave and bite of the pickaxe, cutlass, or mallet, made the work go faster; work songs were therefore encouraged by the planters. But some of the songs were commentaries, too, in codes that the singers alone understood:

Chi-Chi Bud O

Bud O! Bud O!
Chi-chi bud O!
Some a dem a halla
Some a bahl (bawl)

Cling-cling, pitchary,
Some a dem a halla,
Some a bahl

Chi-chi bud O!
Dacta bud a cunning bud,
Hard bud fe dead
Cling-cling, groun' dove, hawk, stark

John-crow, duck,

Toady, John-to wit, hoppin dick

This apparent litany of Jamaican birds—sung in a rhythmic call and response to the heaving of picks, and with much miming—is in fact a mocking list of people, whites and blacks, whom the singers would all know.

Parody and imitation came easily to the slaves, whose interaction with the white world was fraught with ambiguity: there was hostility on both sides, but also a keen awareness of interdependence. Parody was a survival tactic, which over time became part of the musical weave. Imitation had practical roots. There would not have been enough white musicians on the spot to provide music for the balls and other entertainments that the planters loved. So they turned to their slaves, putting violins, guitars, and other 'Western' instruments into their hands and exposed them to English, Scottish, and Irish music. Adaptations were inevitable. The instruments became part of the folk orchestra. The slaves also brought their drums into the ballrooms.

Music and dance, in traditional Jamaica, are inseparable (see Chapter 9). Social music-and-dance was known as mento, "Jamaica's indigenous dance style, whether for song, instrument or dance" (Lewin 1998: 50). Mento uses a 4/4 rhythm, with an emphasis on the last beat of the bar, and can be played fast or slow, depending on the song and the occasion. There is a lot of room for improvisation: in rhythm, instrumentation, even words, as new verses might be improvised to old songs to match the moment. The movement is mainly sideways and winding; feet often 'rent a tile,' the hips and arms doing most of the work.

Basic instrumentation in a traditional mento band would be a guitar and/or banjo and a rhumba box, on which the drummer sits and plucks four metal strips of differing length, to provide a bass line. There would be various percussion instruments, such as graters and gourds—in some cases seeds or peas inside a calabash. There might also be a violin, a flute, a penny whistle, or a saxophone. In the 1950s and 1960s large orchestras played mento in concerts alongside jazz and American dance music. No such orchestras exist today, and only the older musicians would be comfortable playing mento. But traditional bands still exist, and there is a determined and fairly successful effort, focused on the annual Jamaica Festival competitions, to keep the music and dance alive in the young.

Academics argue about the details of European and African influence on Jamaican (and Caribbean) traditional music. Nevertheless the "process of intermixture and enrichment, each to each," which social historian and poet Kamau Brathwaite terms "interculturation" (Brathwaite 2000: 11), remains important because it informs a wider ongoing debate, at the end of five centuries, about Jamaican/Caribbean identity and cultural space in a spreading monoculture. It is therefore necessary to recognize the African foundations of Jamaican music, especially as it is concerned with rhythms, ritual, and ceremonies. It is equally important to identify the reels, quadrilles, polkas, maypoles, and other dances, melodies, and games originally from Europe that are now an organic part of Jamaican/Caribbean music, as well as the fiddles, guitars, penny whistles, rhumba boxes, gourds, and drums from both continents that make the music.

Like other cultural expressions of black Jamaicans, their music was disregarded and denigrated until well into the twentieth century by the elite and the aspiring elite—including other black Jamaicans. But the music, the Anansi stories,[3] and other aspects of traditional culture remained alive among the people for whom they were part of everyday life: peasant and working-class people whose rural roots remained alive even after they moved to the towns. Rural-urban migration brought the traditional culture closer to the center stage of mass entertainment. There it met not only mutations of itself but also music and styles of dance, dress, and language from across the sea. These were brought by returning migrants and also, over time, transmitted by movies, records, radio, and, eventually, television.

POPULAR MUSIC

Pre-Independence

Before World War II, traditional Jamaican music co-existed quite comfortably with foreign, largely American, popular music forms. Both were presented in vaudeville-type concerts and stage shows. There is some evidence of the two merging, most notably in a duo known as Slim and Sam, street troubadours who accompanied themselves on a guitar and were popular throughout the 1930s. They were distinguished by the wit and topicality of their songs and the fact that they sold broadsheets of their creations on the streets and at their more formal appearances, and they appear to have made something of a living from their endeavors, no mean feat in those days. Some of their songs were based on traditional tunes with which their audience would have been very familiar and to which Slim and Sam wrote new words about everyday events around them—court cases, society scandals, political events—with idiomatic expressions and double entendres that their audience would recognize.

Slim and Sam called their songs 'blues'—as in "Balm Yard Blues," about outrageous happenings in an obeah yard, and "Depression Blues," about the hard times of the early 1930s. Few if any of their songs would have fit the pattern of classic blues from the African-American tradition, but the name shows that entertainers and their audiences were familiar with black American music of that time. It would have been brought back or sent by Jamaicans who were moving between the two countries in considerable numbers, notwithstanding periodic efforts by the U.S. federal authorities.

Musicians earned a precarious living, working with several groups according to the occasion; those who had a full-time job outside of the music industry managed better. There were dances held in exclusive clubs and homes, with attendees expecting the latest dance music (by definition, from the United States and England). Many of these musicians, the wind players especially, were graduates of a remarkable institution now over a hundred years old, the Alpha Boys School. Within two years of its founding in 1890 by the Sisters of Mercy (who had earlier established preparatory and secondary schools for girls), the school had a drum and fife corps, which was transformed soon after into a brass band. It remained the largest (and at times the only) structured music teaching program in Kingston until the establishment of the Jamaica School of Music in the 1960s. In the countryside, most boarding schools had music as part of the curriculum, their proximity to the rural sources of traditional music influencing the music taught and performed.

The movie theaters, which sprung up quickly in urban centers across the country, required musicians, sometimes orchestras, to play before and during films. As well as showing movies, the theaters mounted stage shows, some of them talent competitions, which were hugely popular and became nurseries for a plethora of entertainers, especially singers. The annual popular song competitions have been the best-attended events in the contemporary Jamaica Festivals, and the judging is subject to intense, sometimes physical debate between fans.

The introduction of commercial radio in 1950 carried music into homes across the country. For the most part this was recorded music, and therefore foreign; in 1950 there *were* no Jamaican-made records because there were no recording studios and pressing facilities until 1954. The closest thing to local dance/social music was calypso from Trinidad, which was very popular through the 1950s and 1960s, at least partly because records were available from Trinidad and from the United States during the calypso craze popularized by Jamaican-born Harry Belafonte. Otherwise, it was the popular music of the United States and, to a lesser extent, Britain that dominated the airwaves. The most popular Jamaican singers of the era, who performed at the stage shows and, occasionally, on radio (live), were billed as 'the Black Bing Crosby' or 'the Jamaican Sinatra.'[4]

In the early 1950s a form of entertainment developed that swiftly became the major influence in Jamaican music: the sound system. Essentially, sound systems are mobile discotheques providing recorded music for dancing, which was, in those days, rhythm and blues, be-bop, and boogie-woogie, the dance music of America, especially black America. The phenomenon began with paying dances staged by the owner-operators of powerful sound systems, usually in open air settings colloquially called 'lawns.' These events quickly evolved into a culture encompassing music, behavior, language, and dress.

Success or failure depended on the right combination of equipment— huge boom-boxes that delivered gut-tremors of bass and ear-piercing treble, with minimum mid-range—and music. Much of the latter was stuff familiar from the local station(s), and from AM radio stations in Miami and New Orleans. Each system would also have a trademark repertoire that had to be fed with a constant stream of the latest titles, which involved 'scouts' in the United States sending back just-released material.[5] Stories abound of owner-operators erasing the labels of discs so that rivals' spies could not identify the music being played and so source it for themselves.

Each 'sound' developed faithful followers, like the groupies of rock stars of a later age, who could be counted on to turn up at every venue. Followers and hangers-on were not above sabotaging rivals' dances with acts of provocation or outright violence, laying the foundation of the reputation for unspecified 'bad behave' (to use a Jamaican expression) that hovers over the Jamaican music scene.

The Jamaican 'Sound'

The insatiable appetite of sound systems for danceable music hastened the development of a local recording industry. The two recording studios of the 1950s—one owned by a young sociologist who would become prime minister, Edward Seaga—mainly pressed records under license for the big U.S. and U.K. labels. These would include the latest rock-and-roll hits from the United States, which were popular on radio and among middle-class young people who bought records but never found a mass audience. Sound system operators began producing their own tracks for their own systems, straight covers of American hits, and local imitations of music by the likes of Fats Domino, Johnny Ace, Brooke Benton, Clyde McFatter, and The Platters. Eventually, the big operators built their own studios, created their own record labels, and became producers of original material.

The sound system operators in their role as studio producers each created distinctive sounds, based on in-house session players and a stable of singers. The early years of recorded Jamaican music began with the 'sounds' of people like Duke Reid, an ex-policeman and liquor store owner, and his Treasure Isle label; Reid also owned Trojan sound system; Sir Coxone Dodd, who also owned a liquor store and produced early hits for the Wailers, which included Bob Marley, at Studio One; and Prince Buster, one-time bouncer for Dodd's sound system, then a producer at Studio One, before creating his Power to the People label.[6]

Buster was the producer, in 1960, of the landmark record *Oh Carolina*. Under the words of a conventional love song, after a two-bar R&B piano intro, are heard Rastafari drumming and chanting and hand-clapping, led by legendary Rastafari drummer and musician Count Ossie. *Oh Carolina* was years ahead of its time in using such rhythms. It remains one of the most frequently played records precisely because the layering of U.S.-pop rhythms and a variety of singing styles over foundation Rastafari rhythms is where Jamaican popular music went in the 1970s and 1980s.

On the eve of the country's independence, the recording studio was the crucible where traditional Jamaican music met 'foreign'; where mento, revival, and Rastafari drums mixed with rhythm and blues, boogie-woogie, and jazz. At some point someone in a recording studio—the identity of player and studio differs according to who retells the legend—emphasized the afterbeat (the second and fourth beats) rather than the traditional downbeat (first and third), and the Jamaican 'sound' was born. In one form or another, the emphatic afterbeat defined Jamaican popular music for the next thirty years.

At first the music was named 'ska.' Commentators since have ascribed ska's hard-driving rhythms, brash horn-dominated sound, and exuberant dance steps to the optimism Jamaicans felt about their future after independence.

Ska reached its apogee internationally when, in 1964 a fresh-faced young girl from 'Yard,' Millie Small, elbowed her way through The Beatles and The Rolling Stones to the top of the British pop charts with *My Boy Lollipop*, a snappy ska with a crisp big-band arrangement by another legend-to-be, guitarist Ernest Ranglin.

The early years saw a tremendous outpouring of recorded music, not all of it ska. Producers took a gamble on any number of would-be vocalists. Studios had their own session bands with instrumentalist-arrangers (Ranglin was one such) who could put together a backing for a song almost off-the-cuff. These were the best musicians in Jamaica, accustomed to playing a wide variety of music day after day, and oftentimes the backing was far superior to the song. Many songs had at most two verses, leaving plenty of room for instrumentalists like Ranglin, Tommy McCook, and Roland Alphonso on saxophone and Don Drummond on trombone to lay down solos that aficionados remember note for note forty years later. Indeed the most memorable music of the early 1960s was provided by a big band of outstanding jazz-oriented soloists and session musicians, many of them alumnae of Alpha Boys School, brought together by McCook and given the emblematic name the Skatalites. They were managed for a time by another future prime minister, Percival (P. J.) Patterson.

But the Skatalites were not the most popular band of the time, nor were Carlos Malcolm and his Afro-Jamaican Rhythms, another jazz-flavored ensemble that played highly original and danceable arrangements of Jamaican folk music, ska and American pop. American pop, especially R&B as it was morphing into soul, was still the dominant musical fare—on radio, on the jukeboxes, and in the nightclubs around Kingston and in the other towns. The Jamaican bands, like the Mighty Vikings, Lyn Taitt and the Comets, and the perennial Byron Lee and the Dragonnaires,[7] who concentrated on that repertoire were the ones with the following of middle-class patrons who could afford night clubs and records. Ska and its variants—Blue Beat, Rockers—was 'downtown' music.

For many of those actually living downtown, the promise of independence, if it existed, faded as the decade progressed. Kingston drew in more and more people, mostly young, looking for work; but there was no more work there than in the towns and villages left behind. Most ended up in the slums of west Kingston: in Trench Town, Denham Town, or, the poorest of the poor, Dungle. The disillusionment and anger were reflected in the 'Rude Boy' or 'Rudie' culture. Rude boys, according to one song popular at the time, "don't fear" anyone including the police, because they were "tougher than tough" and "strong like [a] lion."

The music itself had begun to change: the heavy, driving beat of ska, carried forward by emphatic blasts on the horns, was softened. The guitar, especially the bass, took over the afterbeat, lightened it and slowed it down. For a brief period, 1967–1968, the prevailing mood was slower, calmer, more conducive to close dancing than ska. The beat became known as 'rock steady,' after a song of that name.

Most memorable for its love songs, this transitional period could perhaps be accounted for by the hope engendered by the first postindependence election in 1967. This interpretation could also explain the river of protest songs that followed the election, which returned an unpopular government to power after upwards of 200,000 young people had been rendered unable to vote despite a new law that lowered the voting age from 21 to 18.

The beat picked up again, with a touch of mento flavoring the early reggae songs. But the overall sound—better recorded, as studio technology improved—was, like the songs, 'tougher.' The massed horns of ska mostly disappeared; they would return when Reggae went international in the late 1970s. The rhythm was driven by the guitars in increasingly complex patterns, which sometimes mimicked the Rastafari drums, more and more evident in the studios.

Reggae

"The reggae song has no beginning, no middle and no end," writes Pamela O'Gorman, one-time head of the Jamaica School of Music and a prolific writer on Jamaican music.

> The peremptory up-beat of the traps [a common opening for early reggae songs] . . . is less an introduction than the articulation of a flow that never seems to have stopped. There is no climax, there is no end. The music merely fades out into the continuum of which it seems to be an unending part. Like the blues, which shares with it this same characteristic, it lies outside the post-Renaissance sense of time and in this it is essentially non-European. (O'Gorman 1972: 51)

One important aspect of the continuum was the community from which reggae grew and in which it and its successor musical styles remain rooted. That community was western Kingston, embracing a number of distinct communities whose geographical boundaries were well known to inhabitants of the area, since they sometimes crossed them at their peril. The community was black, predominantly young, with the highest unemployment rate in the country and the highest level of violence. In the lexicon of the time, they ascribed to 'yout'-man' (young people) the role of "sufferer"; the instruments of the wider society, especially the police, were, in the inverted prefix common in Rastafari-talk, 'down-pressors.'

Numerically, Rastafari were not dominant in western Kingston, but they were very visible, with their distinctive dreadlocks and African-inspired garb. Rastafaris were physically part of the community but were distinct from it in their habits relating to food, worship, and language. They were distinctive, too, in locating the seat of their authority, collective and individual, outside of Jamaica, in the person of His Imperial Majesty Haile Selassie of Ethiopia (see Chapter 2). The proclamation of Africa as the motherland and Jamaica as the place of Babylonian captivity, the insistence on repatriation, and above all the centrality of race in their world view placed Rastafari in contradistinction to the prevailing, or at least 'official,' view of Jamaica as a society "Out of Many, One People," as expressed in the national motto.

Babylon, in the main, returned the disdain in which it was held by Rastafari. Their philosophy struck at the root of Jamaican nationalism and perceived identity. Their appearance offended middle-class sensibilities. Glorification of marijuana, ganja, as the weed of wisdom challenged specific laws. But Rastafari presented "a distinct culture with its own traditions, heroes, God and an explanation for the lower-class status of most of his race and color" (Brodber 1985: 61). All these factors made Rastafari attractive to the victims, real and self-ascribed, of 'down-pressors.'

Reggae is urban music, and the people involved in its creation were to be found in Kingston. The first recording studios were on the fringes of the depressed area; almost all the 'stars' of reggae began their climb to fame in western Kingston, many of them having come there from the countryside. One such was Robert Nesta Marley, born in St. Ann parish of a black mother and white father, who came to Kingston with his mother as a teenager. There he became friends with Neville O'Reilly Livingston (Bunny Livingston, later Bunny Wailer), whose father lived with Bob's mother for a time, and Winston Hubert McIntosh (Peter Tosh). They formed the group that became— after several name changes in the first years—the Wailers. Until they dissolved in 1974, the Wailers had more hit records in Jamaica, through all the genres of ska, rock steady, and reggae, than any other aggregation.

Their stories, individual and collective, contain all the salient elements of the story of reggae itself. They recorded scores of songs for several producers—some covers of popular American hits of the times, others originals— for pocket change. Despite sometimes having several hit records on the charts simultaneously, beginning with their first, "Simmer Down" (in which they were backed by the Skatalites), there was not enough money to hold body and spirit together.

Performers, including song writers, were paid for studio sessions, like the backing musicians. It was almost impossible to collect royalties, owing to an archaic copyright law and the virtual absence of collective agreements for artists. Arrangements, especially about money, were informal and one-sided. The producer put up the money and provided the studio, and expected to keep all the profits. The profits, less than bountiful in the early days because of the small size of the Jamaican record-buying public, increased exponentially after the mid-1960s, when ska and its successor beats established themselves in the Jamaican communities in Britain and the United States.[8] Artists' rights, on the other hand, continue to lag behind, despite the passage of modern copyright legislation in 1993.

In the years of hardship the Wailers turned their hands to other pursuits. Marley had some training in welding (as did Desmond Dekker who, with Jimmy Cliff, got Marley his first gig in a recording studio in 1960) and spent nine months in the United States, in Delaware, where his mother had gone to live with her second husband, in an assortment of jobs. He returned to Jamaica after receiving a draft notice and regrouped with Tosh and Livingston. They formed their own record label, Wailing Souls, and opened a record store. Their recordings again became fixtures on the charts but still brought little profit to the three young men. Their collective music-making was further interrupted when Livingston was sent to jail for possession of ganja, a fate he shared with another icon of reggae, Toots Hibbert of the Maytals, whose prison experience, retold in "54–46," his prison number, provided one of the enduring anthems of the genre.

Fortune smiled on them briefly in the form of Johnny Nash, a black American soul singer, who in 1968 revived his own career with the album *I Can See Clearly Now*, for which the Wailers provided instrumental and vocal backing tracks, and which included a cover version of "Stir It Up," an earlier Wailers hit, and "Guava Jelly," by Marley.[9] This was reggae tailored to the American market, as much soul as reggae, but it introduced the music to segments of the United States market, and brought the names of Marley and the Wailers to attention. "Guava Jelly" was covered by Barbara Streisand, and Eric Clapton had a number-one hit with "I Shot the Sheriff" (1973).

There followed a fertile period for the Wailers, in company with producer Lee Perry, formerly with Coxone Dodd's Studio One label. Perry's Upsetter label put out some of the songs—"Duppy Conqueror," "400 Years," and "Small Axe" among them—that cemented the Wailers' standing as a top group at home and, recorded and performed live around the world, established the credentials of Marley, and of Tosh and Livingston (hereafter Bunny Wailer) in their solo careers, on the international stage. Purists regard the Jamaican recordings up to the early 1970s as the core of the Marley/Wailers legacy, not to be matched in rerecordings and remixes, 'enhancements' that, in this view, softened the edge of the message.

The message was rebellious, even revolutionary, and Rastafari. The three men, none born Rastafari, had drawn closer to the faith and the lifestyle during their hard apprenticeship in the 1960s, as had many other artists. Though not yet sporting the long dreadlocks of later years, the group's profile[10] and the language of some of the songs fused the Rude Boy posture of earlier years with the philosophical world view of Rastafari.

Though the 'political' songs are what Marley and the Wailers are best remembered for, love songs constituted much of their output, as was the case with other songwriters and performers. In the tradition of Slim and Sam and the calypsonians of Trinidad, trenchant and often humorous comments on everyday events were made. "Mr. Brown," for example, based on contemporary street lore, traces the antics of a possibly apocryphal clownish Mr. Brown and pokes fun at police efforts to catch him.

Not all music was made to the reggae beat. American soul music was very popular in Jamaica in the late 1960s and 1970s; groups like the Impressions, the Drifters, the Four Tops had many fans and exerted influence on Jamaican groups, including the Wailers. Soul, fast and slow, provided alternative music for dancing and was well covered on the radio and by the numerous dance bands.

In 1970, the Wailers again formed their own label, Tuff Gong, which later, after the breakup of the group, added a recording studio. Today, under astute management by Marley's widow, Rita, and their children, Tuff Gong is an important player in the multinational music business.

Two years later the Wailers signed with Island Records in London. The Jamaican-born son of an English father and a Jewish-Jamaican mother, Chris Blackwell started Island Records in 1959 and had operated mostly out of the United Kingdom, where he was better known than in Jamaica. Blackwell's label was better equipped than the Jamaican ones, including Tuff Gong, to make the Wailers international stars, which is what they wanted and what Blackwell did, with two albums in 1973, *Catch A Fire* and *Burnin'*, and another in 1975, *Natty Dread*. Blackwell also provided the kind of business-like context that resulted in realistic royalties.

Catch A Fire and *Burnin'* were released as being by the Wailers. *Natty Dread* was the work of Bob Marley and the Wailers. Not only had Marley assumed front-and-center-stage in name and voice, but the Wailers were different people.[11] Peter Tosh and Bunny Wailer had departed the group, amicably by most accounts, including Tosh's, for their own successful careers. Tosh—whose *nom de guerre* as a solo artist was Stepping Razor, after his song of the same name—maintained a faithful cadre of fans with his hard-edged baritone voice and defiant stance. Wailer's stature has been enhanced by time, as the only member of the trio surviving at the end of the twentieth century. Tosh was shot dead during a break-in at his house in 1987.

Marley died from cancer in 1981, a legend, as they say, in his own lifetime;

his funeral was a state occasion. In the major music markets he was, at the time of his death, least popular in the United States, though his status and influence there have increased steadily since his death. In Europe he was *the* reggae artist. In remote parts of the world people who did not speak a word of English knew the words to Marley songs. In Africa, the words of "Get Up, Stand Up" were a battle cry to the bush fighters of then-Rhodesia and South Africa. Marley was the featured guest at the independence celebrations for the new nation of Zimbabwe a year before he died.

As well as taking reggae to the world, Marley helped to take it into the living rooms and consciousness of middle-class Jamaica. In 1968, a maturing political awareness, fed by the black power movement of North America, had come together in protests by university students over a ban by the government on a history lecturer, Walter Rodney, who was prominent in the ghetto for teaching classes on West Indian and African history to the functionally illiterate. The opposition party of the time, the PNP, identified with the discontent. Music was an integral part of their election campaign in 1972: Delroy Wilson's hit "Better Must Come," written a year before, became the campaign song.

In the campaign and in the conduct of government afterwards, there was a deliberate use of Rastafari symbols, dress, and language, self-conscious appeals to the 'yout' man-dem' by middle-class, middle-aged politicos whose own children were absorbing and reflecting, more and more, an awareness of the 'other' society.[12] This "cross-class cultural form" (Brodber 1985) was categorized as "the culture of Dread" by a leading economist and Marxist theoretician of the time, George Beckford. The culture of Dread, said Beckford (in 1977) "is the most positive and dynamic factor within the Jamaican body politic and body social at this time . . . because it provides a hope for revolutionary change." That hoped-for political change did not take place, but for that moment in time music could appear as a credible instrument of its possibility.

If Marley's music and life bridged social and economic, even political, gaps, the sense of loss at his death created a one-ness in the society that was not to be replicated until Jamaica gained a hard-fought place in the finals of the 1998 World Cup of soccer, a sport Marley loved.

Marley's fame overshadowed a wealth of other talent. Jimmy Cliff developed a huge following in Africa and South America while Marley was becoming famous elsewhere. His role in the movie *The Harder They Come* and the music he wrote for it have assured him a prominent place in reggae history. A Muslim, Cliff's was not the loud rebel voice of his friend Marley, but the intensity of his distinctive tenor carried sometimes complex messages directly to the heart.

His "Many Rivers to Cross" (1972) is used to celebrate deaths, hard times, promises of love, even birth. Bob Dylan is reported to have described Cliff's anti-war "Vietnam" as the finest protest song he had heard.

Frederick "Toots" Hibbert, of Toots and the Maytals, delivers a wide range of messages with a distinctive musical voice that comes out of the Baptist/Revival tradition of his rural background. His musical sensibility is wide ranging and his persona sufficiently distinctive for him to cover John Denver's "Country Roads" over a reggae-mento beat and make it sound like an original composition. Less of a *griot* or seer, perhaps, than either Marley or Cliff, Hibbert nevertheless speaks from a self that has never strayed far from its roots.

There are also 'mainstream' reggae stars, singers who are not as well known outside the reggae community as those whose work we have mentioned, but whose output, some over more than thirty years, provides other insights. These are the balladeers of reggae, who deliver even their 'message' songs with a keen awareness of their own lyrical skills, which in some cases match the best voices of North American pop music. The songs of Dennis Brown, the Crown Prince of Reggae to his fans (Marley being always the King), Gregory Isaacs (the Cool Ruler), Freddie McGregor, and Beres Hammond enrich the catalogue of the reggae genre. The death of Brown in 1999 at age 42 silenced perhaps the best vocal instrument reggae has known, while it was still improving.

'Reggae' After Reggae

By the time of Bob Marley's death, reggae was spreading out in several directions from its distinctive roots. Marley's success inspired a number of artists to ride the Rastafari 'boat' into overseas markets, where the money was, with uneven success. Rastafari, while part of the fabric of modern Jamaica even for those who know or care little for its beliefs and practices, can be nothing more than a passing fad for outsiders, especially in North America. So with its song messengers.

Back 'a-yard,' rhythm was still the important factor. The genius of reggae artists like Marley, Hibbert, Tosh, Cliff, and a few others was that their message was conveyed in music that kept people dancing. Sound system was still the baseboard of popular music, and, with or without 'conscious lyrics,' the patrons wanted dance music.

From its earliest days, sound system had been more than just the playing of recorded music. Distinctiveness inhered in the particular choice of music made by the 'selector,' the person operating the turntables, and also in the commentary of the 'toaster,' more popularly named for his radio counterpart, the disc jockey or DJ. The DJ in the early days fulfilled the function of the barker in a country or state fair in the United States and Europe: attracting patrons who might be passing by, chanting of the delights within.

With the advent of locally recorded 45 rpm records, the convention of 'version' became popular. A version was the rhythm track of a song, without the words. Sophisticated sound system amplifiers would peel off the vocals and leave the rhythm for dancing. Soon, record producers started putting the rhythm tracks on the flip side of the discs, and the toaster/DJs would improvise words—rhymes, social commentary, jokes—to entertain and encourage the dancers. Early masters of this art-form in the 1960s had the *noms de guerre* U Roy and Big Youth. Eventually DJ-ing went into the studio, and records of 'improvised' lyrics were produced, sometimes over original rhythm tracks, sometimes over tracks that may have served earlier song hits, and would therefore be instantly recognizable to the patrons. U Roy, Big Youth, and other early DJs were progenitors of what became 'rap' music in the United States twenty years later.

Dancehall, the reigning 'sound' at the end of the twentieth century, descends directly from version, sometimes called dub, and differs from the earlier genres mainly in employing digital technology for the creation of rhythms and in the multiplicity of rhythms used. Entire albums can comprise a singer and a sound engineer deploying his computer skills. The production of rhythm tracks *qua* rhythm gave rise to new-style producers, those who understood not only music but also computers. Of these, the most notable to date are Sly Dunbar and Robbie Shakespeare (Sly and Robbie) and Wycliffe Johnson and Cleveland Browne, known as Steelie and Clevie. Both pairs of men come from a background of providing conventional rhythm backing (bass and drums) as session musicians for most of the great names of early reggae in various studios. Both harness a variety of rhythms, from rock to techno to hip hop to latin, and filter them through their Jamaican rhythmic sensibility, from mento to gospel to revival, and through a blend of real instrumentation (by themselves and others) and digital effects, to produce music that is uniquely theirs. Mastery of computers means that these producers can operate from almost any adequately equipped studio, wherever located. A number of North American and European rock stars of the 1980s and 1990s have employed their talents.

The technical wizardry of Jamaican producers is widely acknowledged, as is their sophisticated use of rhythm. The context, the Jamaican context at least, in which these skills have been deployed, however, raises questions for many people. The violence that has been a hovering presence from the beginning of sound system—Duke Reid, a one-time policeman, was famous for the weaponry with which he surrounded himself—moved center-stage in dancehall, with offending lyrics and crowd behavior. The gun salute that is given by some members of an audience to a particularly pleasing performance is of the same order as given to a local drug 'don' upon his arrival, say, at a community function. The DJs defend their lyrics as one of 'giving the people what they want' and reflecting the society's now-ingrained culture of sexuality and violence.

The other controversial face of dancehall is 'slackness': sexually explicit lyrics, performances, and dance routines that outrage the middle class and the older generation but appear to enchant the 'massive,' a dancehall riff on 'masses.' DJs of both sexes—women having moved into what, until the late 1980s, was a men-only club—try to outdo each other in the outrageousness of their language.

All is not violence and slackness. There are self-described 'cultural DJs,' who 'big-up' (promote) respect for elders, women, and children. There are commentators who provide witty takes on the news of the day and on the foibles of their fellow Jamaicans. And there are a few who tread in the footsteps of older heads like Cliff, Burning Spear, Gregory Isaacs, and Bunny Wailer, who are themselves still making records and touring: prophets and teachers who now seem old-fashioned in the digital age. The crowds, as in the earliest days of sound system, follow whom they like, to the virtual exclusion of everyone else.

Dancehall/sound system is a culture—not only music but language, dress, 'style,' world view; it is also big business. Dancehall infuses the commercial and cultural images of the society in advertising, fashion, the media, the language.[13] But it is not a culture shared by all levels or tastes in the society. It is primarily a young working-class urban culture and is seen as violent, outrageous, and not 'nice' by 'uptown' circles—this despite the economic changes in the society over the past thirty years that have erased the class geography of earlier days. The successful DJ will share an exclusive residential street with the banker, the businessman, and the government minister.

OTHER MUSIC

Other musical genres—jazz, 'classical,' liturgical—while observing the universal protocols of the forms, have, like reggae, drawn inspiration from the country's traditional music. Not surprisingly, reggae itself has also been an influence, especially in jazz and gospel, the latter of which has seen tremendous growth in Jamaica over the past twenty years, to the point where gospel music figures large in the island's exports of recorded music, a multimillion dollar enterprise.

The pervasiveness of reggae and related forms tends to overshadow jazz and classical music. The two have devoted audiences, which overlap. But together they are not large enough to sustain the plethora of groups, venues, recordings and related activities which attend the more popular musical forms; the exception is the Jamaica Jazz Festival, held every summer for the past several years on the north coast.

The small home audience and limited training facilities—private tutors, the diploma-granting School of Music—while adequate for the journeyman, oblige the very talented and/or ambitious musician, whether performer or composer, to seek his or her fortune in North America or Europe. Jazz musicians can more easily build a career through travel between home and the metropolitan centers on both sides of the Atlantic, and many do. Guitarist Ernie Ranglin, known around the world, is one such. Monty Alexander, a U.S.-based jazz pianist who heads his own trio, performs quite frequently in his homeland, whose musical language infuses his compositions and improvisations.

For the classical musician, the prospects are less promising if, through choice or circumstance, one lives in Jamaica. For the performer devoted to classical music alone, one must be prepared for a heavy teaching schedule to survive between seasonal (Christmas, Easter) performances, when remuneration is token, if at all. For the composer, one's main income would likely be advertising jingles: there is simply not enough of a performance and audience base to nourish a classical composing career.

As a result many of Jamaica's finest classical musicians live abroad and return home only for occasional special performances. Willard White is one such: an operatic bass living in Europe and well known in the United States for his performance in the title role of Gershwin's *Porgy and Bess*, and other roles, he also appeared on both sides of the Atlantic as Othello in an acclaimed production of Shakespeare's play. White often includes arrangements of Jamaican and Caribbean folk songs in his recitals. Oswald Russell, a pianist and composer who teaches in Switzerland, Eleanor Alberga, a composer with a growing reputation in the United Kingdom, and Nerine Barrett, a pianist living in Germany, are other outstanding Jamaican musicians who have chosen to pursue their profession abroad.

But a surprising number of gifted performers and composers *do* return, many of them, like Olive Lewin and Steven Woodham, a violinist, deriving their greatest satisfaction from teaching and working with young people. Lewin, for instance, as well as forming the Jamaican Folk Singers for which she arranges, also formed the Jamaica Orchestra of Youth, a string ensemble of young children, which plays traditional Jamaican music as well as the classics.

The importance of religion in Jamaican life, and of music in religious observance, provides the background for a more encouraging picture with regard to liturgical music. There are at least five full Masses by contemporary Jamaican composers written since World War II. All of these are what would be called, generically, Folk Masses, though two carry the name "Mento Mass." All of them use the structure of the traditional Latin mass, but bend the language and rhythms to fit the culture of the congregation.

A number of the Psalms, Jamaicans' favorite biblical literature, have been given choral settings by Jamaican composers, among them Barry Chevannes, a former Jesuit seminarian, and Noel Dexter, who teaches music at the University of the West Indies Mona campus and directs the University Singers, a leading choral group that provides a showcase for traditional and popular music from across the Caribbean. A Roman Catholic priest, Richard Ho Lung, and Chevannes, have enriched the daily worship of many churches with numerous original hymns in the language and music of the people; guitars and drums are now common accompaniment to worship.

This genre-crossing by composers and performers, common across the region, arises naturally from "a musical world whose sheer diversity is paralleled in few other parts of the globe," according to an American musicologist (Bilby 1985: 202).

> This has led to the development in many areas of a phenomenon that may be referred to as polymusicality. In a musical environment in which it is possible for one to encounter virtually back to back the buoyant strains of string bands and the drumming of possession cults, the call-and-response of field hands and the layered harmony of a Bach chorale, it is not surprising that individuals acquire competence in more than one tradition. (Bilby 1985: 203)

The abundance of 'polymusicians' allows one to widen the category of 'serious' or 'art' music beyond the European tradition, which then reveals a fairly large amount of music composed in Jamaica outside of the pop genres, or the liturgical mode. Every year the annual Pantomime is produced to a full musical score that runs the gamut from reggae to light opera. Jamaican dance companies, preeminently the National Dance Theater Company, have commissioned several works from Jamaican composers. Jazz groups and orchestras, many of whose members are musically highly literate and trained, create original scores for performance and recording, often incorporating other Jamaican musical forms.

NOTES

1. Kumina, perhaps the most 'African' of Jamaican cult groups, had its origins in the central part of Africa, where Angola and Congo now exist. It is found most strongly today in the eastern and far western parts of the island, where indentured laborers from that part of Africa were forcibly settled by colonial authorities, though that influx may have replenished something already there.

2. A 'duppy' is the "Jamaican ghost or spirit of the dead . . . based on the African belief that man has two spirits, or souls. On death, one soul goes to Heaven to be judged, the other lingers on earth for a while—or for ever" (Senior 1983: 52).

3. Anansi (also Anancy and Ananse—West African) is the God-spider of West African religion and the principal character in the extensive folk tale mythology of Jamaica (and other parts of the Caribbean settled by Asante [Ashanti] peoples). A trickster spider, Br'er Anansi personifies the triumph of guile and 'brains' over the raw power of the plantation; he has survived as a hero of the 'little man' in the modern world. But the myth-making power of television and other media is threatening Anansi, whose pranks were a staple of Jamaican childhood just two generations ago.

4. The station made some effort to bring Jamaican musicians into the broadcast studio, if they were, according to the station's (British) owners, of a sufficiently high standard. And there were plenty of aspirants: a radio talent competition would routinely draw over 200 contestants to its weekly auditions. In 1959, when a second station began with a more Jamaican orientation, there was for a time a director of music, Sonny Bradshaw, now the elder statesman of Jamaican popular music, then as now a trumpet-playing band leader, composer, and arranger, who brought whole orchestras into the broadcast studio.

5. In an ironic turn, the 'flow' of music associated with early sound systems is now mainly in the other direction. Systems in the large Jamaican communities abroad are fed by their scouts in Jamaica, who send the latest releases by overnight courier service.

6. Buster, a performer himself, added such classics as 'Hard Man fe Ded,' 'Al Capone, and 'Judge Dred' to the catalogue.

7. Lee, a Chinese Jamaican guitarist, is also a long-time producer with his own studio, Dynamic Sounds.

8. Britain has a 'Jamaican' music industry possibly larger than the one 'a-Yard,' with alternative but related 'sounds.'

9. In retrospective albums, the writing credit for most songs by The Wailers is given to Marley. But the writing was a collective effort, and the royalties, when they began to trickle in, were shared.

10. The two LPs of this era were called *Soul Rebel* and *Soul Revolution*, the latter's cover art showing the Wailers armed with (wooden) guns.

11. In 1970 the trio, who had relied on the session musicians of whatever studios they were recording on, took from one such band the talents of brothers Aston (drums) and Carlton (bass) Barrett, who became permanent members of the Wailers until the death of Marley. After the departure of Tosh and Livingston, "the Wailers" referred to the instrumentalists backing Marley. Back-up singing was provided by The I-Threes: Rita Marley (Bob's wife), Marcia Griffith, and Judy Mowatt, individually the three top female vocalists in Jamaica in the 1970s, with successful recording careers of their own.

12. In fact the Third World band, a group formed in the mid-1970s and who have had signal success among middle-class Jamaicans and with reggae enthusiasts abroad, includes Stephen Coore the son of the then-deputy prime minister and a leading classical music teacher, who plays guitar and cello.

13. There is now a cottage industry of publications about Jamaican music, including academic papers and a few books. The University of the West Indies, Mona, recently set up an Institute of Reggae Studies.

9

Performing Arts

ALTHOUGH THE TAINO danced just as a pastime, on ceremonial occasions they combined music, dance, and song to produce Jamaica's earliest indigenous theater. Drums, timbrels, flutes, and trumpets accompanied these festivals that celebrated the heroic deeds of caciques (headmen), and were related in a sort of poem-song. They set an example that Jamaican theater would begin to emulate 450 years later.

A leading authority on Caribbean theater observed long ago: "I see as inseparable in folk theater, music, dance, song, speech, mime, choral response; but we . . . compartmentalize these . . . modes following alien practise" (Hill 1972: 38–39). Imprisoned by 'alien practise,' we are forced to discuss drama and dance separately.

DANCE

Jamaicans love to dance. Indeed, the development of Jamaican music is intimately tied to dance forms (see Chapter 8). This chapter is concerned, however, not with social dance, but with performed dance—choreographed, costumed and 'staged' before an audience. Since the 18th century when Haitian 'set-girls' provided entertainments for the great plantation homes, audiences had paid to see dance presentations. However, performed dance really came into its own in the 1920s and 1930s, with the coming of the motion picture. Motion pictures presented current North American and European social dance styles, choreographed sequences in musical extravaganzas, theatrical forms like tap dancing, and foreign folk and ethnic dances. Movies thus helped to push the development of performed dance: by mid-century it had consolidated, and by the end of the century, it was firmly established.

Jamaican dance has its main roots in Africa and Europe, and there is some East Indian influence. As with other aspects of Jamaican culture and custom, it is difficult to establish discrete categories with which to discuss dance. Nevertheless, performed dance may be broadly classified as traditional and modern.[1] Traditional dance is heavily African in influence, with one or two exceptions like the quadrille and maypole dances. Modern dance is eclectic— a recognizably Jamaican style heavily influenced by traditional forms but embracing contemporary American techniques (Martha Graham, Arthur Mitchell, Alvin Ailey) as well as European classical ballet.

Traditional Dance

Traditional dance exhibits both *syncretized* (culturally joined) and relatively uncontaminated original features. There is a melding of spiritually based dance elements from Europe and Africa; there are retentions that represent transplantations of ritual forms, held almost entirely intact; and there are creole forms, arising from the circumstances of the new (Jamaican) place, which are neither European, African, nor Asian.

Dance in the Caribbean has been described as having two main foci: strengthening the forces of Earth and the fertility of Earth and Man; and reaffirming the ties of the ancestral spirits and the community, and the Earth, through possession in the dance (Wynter 1970: 37). These foci apply to rituals originating in both Africa and Europe (Morris dances), which share, for example, a tradition of masking.

The mask is central in African dance. Once the masquerader begins dancing, he enters the life force of rhythm, and the god/ancestral spirit possesses him. Thus, dance is essentially religious, joining natural and supernatural worlds in life-affirming rituals, often connected with feasting. In many ways, African masquerades were like the Morris dances brought to Jamaica by English, Scottish, and Irish indentured servants. Morris dances were also part of life-affirming spring rites. The (Morris) horn dance was a fertility dance. Like Jonkonnu masqueraders, Morris dancers were all male, and each group had a leader and several characters, some of whom were animals. These similarities sometimes enabled a fusion that made it impossible to disentangle sources.

It is impossible to discuss all traditional dance forms, many of which have lost earlier social or religious purposes and are revived mostly in performance. Some thirty-nine dances have been identified and classified according to seven core types, each of which is characterized by the name of a certain dance type (Rhyman 1980: 3–14). Maroon, Myal, Kumina, Revival and Rastafari, and the dances associated with them, are classified as religious types, while Jonkonnu and Hosay and the dances associated with them are classified as secular. Jonkonnu and Pukkumina (not to be confused with Kumina—see Chapters 2 and 8) are described here because, as dance-theater combinations with significant sociohistorical content, they illuminate the process of interculturation. Christmas entertainments including Jonkonnu-Masquerade-Set Girl parades were important elements in the slaves' self-expression, which continued after Emancipation and up to today. Pukkumina,[2] a legacy of Revivalism that persists, is now interpreted on stage: for example, "Pocomania" is a dance in the repertoire of the National Dance Theatre Company (NDTC).

Jonkonnu,[3] the oldest recorded traditional dance form, is a combination of European and African forms—melded in some aspects, identifiably different in others—with further addition of creole elements. Its essential features are costume and masking, special fife and drum music, dance, and mime (Baxter 1970: 220). There is also a strong element of satire: *inter alia*, pink mesh masks worn by black people clearly signify some form of ridicule. Jonkonnu is also known as 'Horse Head,' one type of the central figure in the troupe. Hobbyhorse, a Morris animal figure, probably evolved into the character Horse Head.

Modern Jonkonnu starts by joining two old traditions: "distinctly African" Jonkonnu groups, and "Masquerade actor groups" derived from English folk theater (Bettelheim 1980: 83). The actor groups recited dramatic excerpts, many from English plays. Jonkonnu players enacted many types of mime, but "there was one playlet that occurred over and over again . . . the revival of the sick and dead patient"—a possible remnant of old fertility rites (Baxter 1970: 227).

Though it has no Christian religious significance, Jonkonnu takes place at Christmas. It almost certainly commemorates John Konny, a celebrated African trader on the Guinea (Ghanaian) Coast in the mid-eighteenth century whose fame as a fighter was so great that just mentioning his name struck fear in people—perhaps one reason for the terrifying aspect associated with Jonkonnu. This may also be because African masquerades were connected to secret societies, agencies of magic and sorcery.

Writers have described Jonkonnu (not very accurately) as a sort of horn pipe or jig. Dancers sometimes perform in lines, sometimes separate from the group for individual shows. Masqueraders dance according to their roles: Pitchy Patchy (similar to "Jack-in-the-Green") dances with small rapid jumps, flexing his shoulders, making large circular patterns and turning cart-wheels; Devil alternates quick springy steps with long ones, jabbing his pitch fork and making quick turns; Cow Head makes bucking motions with body bent low; Belly Woman amuses by moving her belly in time to the music.[4] Fertility aspects are manifest in the sensuality of many dance moves, in par-ticular, rotary pelvic motions and the *cotch*—a sudden stop, hips forward.

The Set Girls, members of blue-clad and red-clad sets (costume groups), constitute a third (creole) element in the Christmas parades. Sources offer varying accounts of their origin, but they were mixed-blood women—house-keepers and, often, mistresses, of planters, attorneys, and overseers, and per-haps also proprietors of bawdy houses and their 'girls.' There is a 1790 account of splendid dresses at grand balls for the Sets, and alliances among the slaves to the blue and red sets, demonstrated in their dress. The influx of Haitian refugees encouraged the Sets, which later extended to other colors and loyalties. Set Girls began in Kingston and spread rapidly through the whole island.

The Jonkonnu character of Babu, also evidence of cultural joining, tended to appear in communities of East Indian indentured laborers. 'Red Indians,' too, may represent original Tainos but are more likely the contribution of wild west plays and stories.

Jonkonnu was such a popular part of Christmas in the nineteenth century that in 1840, and again in 1841, when Kingston authorities tried to ban the parades, there were riots in which police confronted the crowds, killing two people in 1841. In the first half of the twentieth century bands were seen less and less frequently in the streets of the capital but remained alive in the countryside. Resuscitation was partly due to an islandwide competition in 1951–1952 sponsored by *The Daily Gleaner* newspaper, which brought both masquerade and Jonkonnu traditions together. (Set Girls are now rarely seen.) It is now most often revived at organized heritage celebrations.

Pukkumina (coloquially, 'puko' or 'poco'), a ritual form still in use, has often been recreated on stage and in Jamaican art. Influenced by Myalism, poco is one of two main Revival groups, Revivalism being "the cult form which has persisted as the main heir of the Great Revival [in 1860–1861] in so far as Afro-Christian religious sects are concerned" (Seaga 1969: 4). Dis-tinct from Zion, another Revival cult, "Puk-kumina [*sic*] is noted for its dealing with ground spirits—ancestors and fallen angels, possession, and the rich variety of dance styles exhibited by a number of 'functionaries' " (Rhy-man 1980: 13).

These functionaries include leaders called Shepherds and Shepherdesses or Mothers, attached to the bands, and various "officers[5] [who] perform ritual acts and characteristic movements in connection with the calling of the spirits and the care of the devotees into whom the spirits come after possession" (Baxter 1970: 141). Possession can last for a short time or several days. Immersion baptism is central to pukkumina, as are rituals known as 'tables,' conducted about a carefully prepared table covered with a white cloth and adorned with candles, flowers, fruit, and ceremonial objects. 'Tables' can be held for positive (for example, healing) or negative (to thwart an enemy) ends.

Dance plays a crucial role in pukkumina by helping to induce possession. It is married to improvizations of melody and harmony. "It is chiefly clapping, stamping and other percussion sounds made by the worshipers that supply the rhythmic background" (Lewin 1970: 69). Other sources contradict this, contending that poco uses drums throughout the three-day ritual. Another erroneous belief is that the drum (an East Indian drum) is used only to summon the Indian spirit (Nettleford 1969: 22). Members wear pure white garments and red or white turbans, the leader's being the largest. However, at least one source reports many solid colors—reds, blues, purples, yellows. Clearly, the ritual differs from place to place.

The ceremony involves the 'blessing' and 'breaking' of the table on the first day, the sacrifice of a goat on the second day—the high point—when the worshippers begin to 'labor' for their journey to the spirit world, and a quieter third day.

> Tramping, laboring, or drilling takes place when [worshippers] move around in a circle, counter-clockwise. . . . [As they step, bent forward] they exhale more forcibly than the corresponding intake, as the body rises. [In time] the lungs become hyperventilated, the consciousness becomes less. After performing the reacting counter motion of wheeling or rapid spinning some persons may fall. . . . the shepherd stands in the middle of the circle and cymbals [that is] he complements the beat of the tramp by recital of tongues or syllables in the form of a chant. . . . The possession stage . . . is . . . accompanied by only the gutteral breath sound of the trampers and the cymballing. (Baxter 1970: 143)

It is the wheeling and the form of the ritual—dancers surrounding the central figure of the 'cymballing' leader—that suggest a connection to the whirling dervishes of Turkey. The turbans are also a possible further East Indian influence. Although it is known that there were Muslim slaves in Jamaica who knew and recited the Koran, any more certain connection to the dervishes remains to be established.

Modern Dance in Performance

The story of the development of creative dance catalogues a small miracle. In 1950 there was no such thing; by 1985, there was a touring National Dance Theatre Company, at least three smaller companies, vibrant dance activity in the schools, a vigorously contested dance category in the Annual Jamaica Festival Competition (known as 'Festival'), and a School of Dance.

Forms of dance remained tied to color, class, and status well into the twentieth century, with traditional dance continuing as the province for the black majority. When, in the 1930s and 1940s, a number of teachers of classical ballet held classes, they were for fair-skinned children. Still, as Jamaicans would say, 'good come from bad': Herma Dias, a pupil of Mrs. Margaret Squire (one of the early dance teachers), in her turn, taught Hazel Johnston, and she began the work of training dancers, thus laying the foundation for a serious dance tradition. Johnston was a brown Jamaican from a family of substance. She studied dance briefly in Jamaica then continued her training in London, where she also studied music. Returning to Jamaica in 1937 as a rare bird—a qualified teacher of dance and music—she started classes in a friend's drawing room, since she could find no one to rent her a hall. She became the first dance teacher to build her own studio, and one of the first to envision a dance theater based on indigenous culture.

Johnston became a renowned classical ballet teacher and a pioneer of dance theater, but an early death prevented her from seeing her pupil Ivy Baxter make the connection between indigenous dance and classical ballet by creating dances in "the spirit of Jamaican realities, drawing on stories and folksongs as well as street gestures and the life of the marketplace" (Nettleford 1985: 28).

Baxter started the Ivy Baxter Creative Dance Group in 1950. When the group gave its first show, after returning from a successful visit to Puerto Rico, a critic commented, "here lies the vital force that can combine the graceful talent of the orthodox classical schools [with pure folk dance] and produce a Jamaican combination" (Milner 1952: 20) A young tutor at the University of the West Indies' (UWI's) Extra Mural Department, Rex Nettleford, joined the group at about that time, and when the 1950 pantomine ended, Eddy Thomas, a member of the pantomime chorus, also joined. Twelve years later, they would write a new chapter in Jamaican dance history.

To nurture skills, the Baxter Group initiated summer courses in dance held at UWI in conjunction with the Extra Mural Department. At the same time, on another front, the Jamaica Social Welfare Commission succeeded in encouraging rural people to revive traditional dances.

In 1962, the year of Jamaica's Independence, the government sponsored various festivities including a dance production called "Roots and Rhythms" in which five dance studios took part. The group performed works by Nettleford, Thomas, and Ivy Baxter. Then:

> out of the dance-show "Roots and Rhythms" emerged a group of trained and serious dancers . . . [who felt] there was need for a company which would provide a vehicle for well trained dancers who wish to perform and create works of excellence. Some wanted to further experiment with dance forms and techniques of all kinds but were pledged to the task of developing a style and form which would faithfully reflect the movement patterns of Jamaica and the Caribbean. (Nettleford 1968: 31)

Thus was formed the National Dance Theatre Company, with artistic directors Rex Nettleford and Eddy Thomas. The NDTC has presented a season of dance in July/August of every year since then. An eclectic company, it uses Martha Graham and modern jazz techniques to creolize and syncretize, creating its own idiom as it embraces diverse classical, ritual, traditional, and folk forms from Europe, Africa, and North America. In 1985, Nettleford offered this thematic classification of the company's repertoire:

1) Commentary on the social scene
2) The African presence
3) Caribbean religion and ritual
4) Jamaican history and legend
5) Plantation society and culture. (Long 1997: 71)

Long pointed to other themes such as matriarchy and explorations of romantic love, and dances that explored 'pure movement.' The classification is useful because it typifies not just NDTC's repertoire but, by and large, those of the other Jamaican companies.

Dances like Nettleford's "Plantation Revelry" and Eddy Thomas's "Country Wedding" were early staples of the NDTC repertoire. Nettleford's "African Scenario" (from the "Roots and Rhythms" show) would lead to his brilliant dance exposition "The Crossing," which charts the Middle-Passage-to-New-World experience.[6] Dances often cover two themes: Eddy Thomas's "Games of Arms" uses rivalry between children in a schoolyard to shape biting commentary on the Cold War; Nettleford's "Two Drums for Babylon" examines Rasta religion and Jamaican class attitudes. The NDTC has consistently brought the popular 'street' dances—ska, rock steady, reggae, dancehall onto the concert stage, often using them to make trenchant points about the society. Nettleford's "Dialogue for Three"—one of the most popular repertory items—is a comment on the love triangle and the *tallawa* (toughminded, forceful) Jamaican woman. "The ballet seeks to underscore the dominance of the woman in Jamaican society" (Nettleford 1968: 33).

As a matter of policy, the NDTC is a company in which none of the performers is paid; nevertheless, the company aspires to the highest professional standards. They have developed a vast repertoire: the Souvenir Programme from the thirty-fifth season (1997) lists 173 dance works from 23 choreographers. The troupe has made some 70 overseas tours to North America, Central and South America, Europe, and Australia. The NDTC Singers accompany them, along with a small orchestra.

Several smaller dance companies have come into being: L'Acadco, Movements, and The Company, among them. UWI has a dance group, as do many other schools and colleges. Several amateur groups exist—important feeders for the companies. The annual pantomime or 'panto' continues to be a showcase for talented dancers, and concerts in schools and communities feature increasingly polished dance items.

NDTC has always had a close relationship with the Little Theatre Movement (LTM). The LTM, which started the Jamaica School of Drama in 1968, "nurtured" the NDTC, which in turn started the Jamaica School of Dance in 1970 (Nettleford 1992: 6). The process culminated in both schools joining the School of Art, to eventually become the Edna Manley School for the Visual and Performing Arts. All NDTC annual seasons have been presented in LTM's Little Theatre in Kingston. The LTM has been instrumental in assuring that NDTC and other companies have the support of stage managers and lighting, sound, and wardrobe crews. Dance companies also have administrative backup in the form of management committees and voluntary contributors.

As in other fields, Jamaican dancers have also distinguished themselves abroad, two in particular: Clive Thompson, who as a youngster danced with the Ivy Baxter group, went north for further training and danced lead roles as a member first of the Martha Graham dance group, and then of the Alvin Ailey Dance Theater; Garth Fagan, who runs his own company, the Bucket Dance Company, and teaches at the University of Rochester, New York, won a Tony award for his choreography of the Broadway hit, *The Lion King*.

Between 1962 and the present, the creative dance movement has had a profound influence on the society. The Jamaica Cultural Development Commission (JCDC) has sustained dance activity by holding workshops related to the Annual Festival Competition and compiling a dance syllabus that has helped document dance forms. The Festival contributes to conservation by encouraging competitors of all ages from all over Jamaica: it is often older dancers who present previously unknown dances. The NDTC has helped enormously by including traditional dance in its repertoire. The School of Dance offers programs leading to certification. The annual pantomime employs dancers and provides choreographers with opportunities for experiment. Above all, dance is no longer the preserve of any 'class,' and the *idea* of dance is a Jamaican one, for the exploration of Jamaican metaphors in a Jamaican dance idiom.

In the Christmas riots of 1840 and 1841, people took to the streets to protest a ban on the traditional Jonkonnu parades. In 1840, the protesters won the day, and no blood was shed. However, on December 27, 1841, the Riot Act was read at 6:45 P.M., and when the crowd of protesters "refused to leave the parade and attacked the police taking prisoners to the barracks . . . [the police] opened fire, killing two men and injuring many more" (Wilmot 1990: 72). If, in the 1840s, Jamaicans laid down their lives to protest their right to freedom of expression including the expression of dance, in 2000 dance has become a medium in which that freedom, dearly bought, is confidently celebrated.

DRAMA

Early Jamaican Theater

The two Jamaican theater traditions—the 'folk' and the 'straight'—became integrated only in the late 1940s, with the 'Jamaicanization' of the annual pantomimes. Before that, the two had been distinct, catering to audiences who, especially in their social outlook, were quite different.

Standard 'straight' theater fare included the English school of Shakespeare, Dryden, Sheridan, and Goldsmith and operettas, pantomimes, and comedies. Plays were intended primarily for the upper crust of Jamaican society. The players were resident amateurs, sometimes joined by army and navy personnel stationed in the island, or touring companies and individuals.[7] Even when Jamaican-written plays began to be presented in the mid-nineteenth century, the target audience remained much the same, and this was reflected in the writing. The actors were fair-skinned, donning blackface when portraying Negroes.

There is evidence of support—not always welcomed by the players—from a wider cross-section of the society. By the early nineteenth century the Kingston Theater was advertising a separate section for people of color because more of them were attending the theater, though these may have been slaves and servants accompanying their owners and employers. In 1812, an ordinance was passed defining appropriate theater-going conduct—audiences sometimes assaulted actors and destroyed scenery and fixtures—and imposing penalties for infractions, to little avail. In 1828 another ordinance with stiffer penalties was passed, penalties for slaves being harsher than for whites and coloreds. These events help to confirm that "by the beginning of the nineteenth century, the Jamaican theater catered to a broad cross section of the public" (Hill 1992: 10).

Meanwhile, black people, urban and peasant, enjoyed and supported their own entertainments, such as ring games, which sometimes involved singing, acting, and dancing; dances often involved role-playing. The stylish tea meetings, which were concerts-cum-auctions to raise funds for the host (individual or organization), were perhaps closest to a 'stage' presentation, and deliberately so. The audience was expected to dress in their finest clothes, to the point of parody—top hat and tails, gowns, gloves—of the people who attended the Theater Royal. 'Speechifying,' declamatory set pieces, and songs would be bid, for and against, by the audience, as would the Queen, a veiled local beauty with finery and retinue, as to whether she should unveil. Real tea meetings are hardly held now, but fund raisers for schools and churches contain some of the same elements.

Rituals like 'dinky minnies,' 'nine nights,' and 'set ups' would take place on special occasions, when 'playing' of all types would be appropriate. Jonkonnu both integrated the theater arts and married the traditions. Storytelling, elaborated from the rich heritage of African lore, especially tales revolving around Anansi, the Akan God-spider who empowered the helpless in the constant struggle against the powerful, remained a popular pastime until the advent of television. Whatever its purpose, intimate or public, storytelling always had an element of performance, with singing, mime, and dance.

The peasantry were not the only storytellers. In 1858, Jamaican Raphael de Cordova, an emigré to the United States, had commenced an illustrious career of writing humorous stories and telling them all across the United States. In 1869, Henry G. Murray, a black Jamaican, began telling humorous stories based on Jamaican manners and customs. When he died in 1877, his sons Andrew and William carried on with storytelling.

By the end of the nineteenth century, the two traditions, while still far apart, were beginning to come together. Jamaican playwrights had produced a body of dramatic writing in a variety of forms. Writing blank verse and prose, they skillfully employed both English and Jamaican Creole to suit their dramatic purposes. With the Murrays, the folk form of storytelling, which used the Creole and belonged not to European theater but to West African Anansi tales, had entered the arena of performance.

The Twentieth Century

Accounts of Jamaican theater in the twentieth century often begin with British playwright George Bernard Shaw's visit in 1911. Concerning theater, he had this advice to offer: "all the ordinary travelling companies from England and America [should be] sternly kept out of it, for unless you do your own acting and write your own plays, your theater will be no use; it will, in fact, vulgarise and degrade you" (Hill 1992: 3).

Jamaicans did not immediately heed Shaw's advice. Up to the 1930s, touring companies continued to visit, focusing on Shakespeare and modern pieces, including Shaw. Many amateur groups as well as the schools emulated theater of this kind. However, the impulse to create local theater had reached some schools: in the last decade of the nineteenth century, two high schools, Villa Maria and the Alpha Cottage, had mounted original works.

By the second decade, things were beginning to change. At the newly built Ward Theater, Marcus Garvey, the first Caribbean person to present "the black man on stage as a dignified, intelligent human being determined to chart his own future" (Hill 1972: 39), staged an "Elocution and Literary Concert" in 1913. He also used the theater for his lectures and for international UNIA conferences (see Chapter 1).

Garvey went to the United States, from which he was deported in 1927. Two years later, his UNIA established Edelweiss Park in Kingston, which drew huge crowds nightly to witness "follies, vaudevilles, reviews, dances, elocution contests, beauty displays, greasy poles, boxing, an occasional moving picture, and plays" (Hill 1972: 40). Comedians Ernest Cupidon and Ranny Williams emerged at Edelweiss. Also at about this time, two Christmas customs, Grand Market and the Christmas Morning Promenade, engendered a very Jamaican theater event: the Christmas Morning Concert. Musicologist Astley Clerk's friends used to stop at his music shop on Christmas morning to sing, play the piano, and perform on other instruments. This informal 'jam' eventually grew into a concert that attracted so many people it was relocated at the Ward Theater. By then, it included dance and dramatic sketches as well as music.

Eventually the concerts came to be presented by two impresarios, Eric Coverley and Vere Johns.[8] At these events, the first generation of folk performers presented vaudeville and variety items. Minstrels in blackface, imitating the Americans who had come in the previous century, sang and performed skits and farces, using Jamaican Creole for trenchant sociopolitical commentary. The concerts did so well that others sprung up. The Honorable Louise Bennett (affectionately, 'Miss Lou'), Jamaica's most famous theater personality, began her career at Christmas morning concerts where she introduced the Jamaican public to her dialect poems. (She eventually married Eric Coverley.) Traditional middle-class theater-going audiences were slow to warm to these truly Jamaican stage shows.

The 1930s and 1940s were a time of increased political and national awareness, which was reflected in the arts. Garvey wrote and produced several plays "aimed at uplifting his working-class audiences" (Banham, Hill, and Woodyard 1994: 200), and Ernest Cupidon dramatized three of H. G. DeLisser's prose works. With the largely black casts of Cupidon's productions, the color bar in 'straight' theater finally came down. Frank Hill's *Upheaval* in 1939 and Roger Mais's *Hurricane* (1943) also supported the cause of nationalism, and the most significant playwright of the decade, poet Una Marson, wrote plays honestly tackling middle-class problems. *Pocomania* (1938), for example, showed the impact of the puko cult on a conservative middle-class family. Marson wrote two other plays: *At What Price* and *London Calling*.

Still, as the fate of Elsie Benjamin's People's Theater seems to show, neither the middle class nor the working class was necessarily ready to support the same cause. Benjamin eschewed the traditional patronage of the governor when the People's Theater announced its first production, W. G. Ogilvie's *One Sojer Man*, in 1945. Instead, the play was presented "under the kind patronage of the ordinary people of Jamaica" (Hill 1972: 22). They did not come, nor did anyone else. The production folded after one night, and the People's Theater sank into oblivion.

Five years before, the Catholics had had better success, in their 1937 pageant *Jamaica Triumphant*. Jamaican in every respect (except for its director, Father Daniel Lord, an American Jesuit), it was mounted by the Catholic Church to celebrate 100 years of being in the island. With a cast of some 400 enacting Jamaica's history, the pageant ran for 4 nights to a combined audience of 20,000 people. It had several innovative features: it was staged outside, used a follow-spot for the first time, had a stage with several levels on which scenes were simultaneously performed, and drew its cast from Jamaicans of many backgrounds.

Archie Lindo, perhaps the most successful of playwrights in the 1940s, attempted with some success to have theater reflect the real lives of ordinary

Jamaicans. He adapted two Jamaican novels and wrote two plays of his own. His dramatization of H. G. DeLisser's *White Witch of Rosehall* was a milestone. A robust melodrama, it included ordinary Jamaican people as central characters: the evil Annie Palmer's black slaves take charge of their fates and mobilize against her to secure their freedom. Lindo capitalized on the rhythm and power of Jamaican Creole and the visual effects of folk rituals.

The Caribbean Thespians, founded in 1946, contributed significantly to the development of Jamaican theater at that time. The varied background of thespians such as Charles Hyatt and actor-playwrights Easton Lee and Mitzi Townsend confirmed the increasing inclusiveness of theater activity.[9] However, it is the founding of the Little Theater Movement by Greta and Henry Fowler and LTM's mounting of the first pantomime in 1941 that together constituted a watershed in the history of Jamaican theater. By one account,

> The most notable instance of Caribbean integrated theater happened almost by accident. This was the Jamaican pantomime, first introduced [in 1941] . . . in imitation of the English version. Two years later, with an original script . . . *Soliday and the Wicked Bird*, the Jamaican Pantomime began to assert its independence. Then in 1949 under the inspiration of play director Noel Vaz and folklorist Louise Bennett, the pantomime produced *Bluebeard and Brer Anancy*. The experiment of moving to the popular folk character Anancy was so successful that he reappeared in successive productions. . . . [P]antomime has evolved to become identifiably Jamaican in its use of indigenous material including dance, music, song, drama, improvisation, and pithy commentary on the contemporary social and political scene. As a result, the pantomime has become the most popularly supported annual theatrical event in the region. (Hill 1992: 283–284)

The LTM built the Little Theater in 1961, and both are still going, sixty years, sixty pantomimes,[10] and many other productions later. It has provided experience for all the theater occupations, on and off stage. Writers like Trevor Rhone and Dennis Scott have worked on scripts. Miss Lou and Maas Ran (Ranny Williams) have starred and directed, Miss Lou's knowledge of songs, lore, and folkways making her a priceless resource.[11] Ivy Baxter, Rex Nettleford, and Eddy Thomas have been among panto choreographers.

In the 1950s, the annual Schools' and Adults Drama Festivals began. The Schools Festival continues, and has spawned offshoots for French and Spanish plays. The Adult Festival gave way in 1963 to the drama competition of the Jamaica Festival. Both adult and schools competitions contribute enormously to creating the skills and the appetite for theater upon which the (semiprofessional) industry depends.

The 1960s commenced a period of increased theater activity. Many theater groups were formed, including Lloyd Reckord's National Theater Trust, Noel Vaz's New Theater Company, and Yvonne Brewster and Trevor Rhone's Theater 77. A UWI group, including actress-director Jean Small, attempted people's theater in an initiative called Yard Theater. In 1968, the UWI opened the Creative Arts Centre (renamed the Philip Sherlock Centre for the Creative Arts). In addition to providing two performance spaces (available to the wider community), the center has had tutors in drama and music since that time. It is home to an annual UWI drama competition and performances by the UWI Singers and the UWI Dance Group.

The 1960s also saw a series of lavish productions, typified by Sylvia Wynter's *1865: Ballad for a Rebellion*, performed at the Little Theater and also in UWI's Chinese gardens, to celebrate the centenary of the Morant Bay Rebellion. It was a pageant in the Father Lord/Hollywood tradition—a sprawling epic drama in verse and prose, with dance and music and visual effects. Douglas Mack, a Rastafarian, played Paul Bogle, one of the two male leads.

The 1970s saw an explosion of theatrical activity. The decade began resoundingly enough. In addition to the 1970–1971 pantomime *Rockstone Anancy*, there were some fifteen other productions in that year, including two by Trinidadian Douglas Archibald and two by St. Lucian Nobel Laureate Derek Walcott. The Caribbean Thespians, a long-stayer among theater groups, celebrated their twenty-fifth anniversary, and the Barn Theater produced Trevor Rhone's hit, *Smile Orange*.

Jamaica has produced two remarkable theater talents in Trevor Rhone and Dennis Scott. They came to the boards rather differently. Rhone trained as an actor, went to directing then playwrighting, and has scripted three movies—the legendary *The Harder They Come, Smile Orange*, and the prize-winning *Milk and Honey*. He has participated in Robert Redford's Sundance Workshop and has taken several of his plays abroad or had them produced elsewhere. He began by writing school pantos and then bravely decided to write full time. By 1965, when he and Yvonne Brewster converted a garage at Brewster's mother's house into Jamaica's first small theater, the Barn Theater, he had made up his mind that theater would be his living. (This creation of small theater spaces would revolutionize Jamaican theater thereafter.) He has written many plays (several of them published) including an ambitious musical, *Everyman*, and the all-time Caribbean favorite *Old Story Time*, a comedy-drama about roots and dislocation in the traumatic 1970s.

Like Rhone, Dennis Scott started out in teaching. He danced at one point with the National Dance Theater Company, and tried his hand at chore-ography. After a drama-in-education course in England, he worked in sec-ondary schools for a while, and then as head of the Jamaica School of Drama. He teamed up with Rhone, producing *Sleeper* and *Smile Orange*. Eventually he left Jamaica to join the Directing Department at Yale University's School of Drama. While in the United States he worked with the Theater of the Deaf and appeared intermittently as Lester, the father-in-law, on *The Cosby Show*. Between 1976 and 1985, he attended the National Playwriting Con-ference at the Eugene O'Neill Theater Center. He is a prize-winning poet (three collections) and a playwright with a dozen plays to his credit. His death in 1991 left the Caribbean theater community bereft, for his students were intensely loyal and deeply attached to him. Scott's disturbing and deeply moving *An Echo in the Bone*, set during a nine-night ceremony in a series of dreamlike scenes, explores racial memory that echoes 'in the bone.'

Also in the 1970s, the urban folk tradition mated with theater to create a new genre of local plays, mostly utilizing the small theaters. Taking its cue from the farces of early Bim and Bam skits, roots (grassroots) plays were larded with broad humor and crude sexual innuendo. Originally constituting popular theater at its most basic, roots theater has evolved, at least in the hands of skilled playwrights and directors such as Ginger Knight, Balfour Anderson, and Keith Noel, into a medium that embodies "the voice, kinetic orality and social dynamic of the underbelly of the society" (Eugene Williams, personal communication). Roots theater is also commercially successful.

The Jamaican improv tradition, which Miss Lou and others had used in working as drama officers, was reinforced when Sistren Theater Collective was formed in 1977 by Honor Ford Smith and twelve women who were part of the government's street-sweeping program. The idea was to use im-provisation to help Jamaican women identify problems and mobilize to solve them. Sistren originated and produced plays such as *Bellywoman Bangarang, Nana Yah, Muffit in a All a We, Bandaloo Version*, the celebrated *QPH*, and *Domestick*. With Jamaican Creole as the medium and the lives of women as the subject matter, 'theater' and the folk tradition were joined.

Shakespeare persisted into the 1970s. In 1973, LTM presented *The Merry Wives of Windsor*, starring both Louise Bennett and Ranny Williams. It needs to be emphasized that many Jamaican thespians, Miss Lou foremost among them, handle Shakespeare as authoritatively as the comedy of the panto. In a very real sense, it was Miss Lou's person, the lady herself, that reconciled country and town, upper crust and working class, black and white and brown, in Jamaican theater.[12]

A further important development of the 1970s was the handing over (in

1976) of the LTM theater school to the government. It became the School of Drama, part of the Cultural Training Centre (later the Edna Manley School for the Visual and Performing Arts). The school still continues its important work of training not just Jamaicans but Caribbean and international students.

Journalist, writer, commentator, and radio talk show host Barbara Gloudon has been one of the mainstays of LTM since the death of Greta Fowler and Henry's retirement. She has written more pantomimes than any other writer, and in so doing "has demonstrated genuine attempts at crafting a formula for her LTM panto plots . . . to reflect as faithfully as one can the aesthetic energy, form and feeling of some of the primal social and cultural reality of her environment" (Nettleford 1992: 4). The LTM has also formed The Pantomime Company, a permanent, paid group of actors and singers who perform in the pantos and undergo training in interim periods.

Jamaican theater at the beginning of the twenty-first century is a well-established facet of the island's cultural life. Most popular theater, including the pantomime, is commercially based. Pantomimes have for many years enjoyed extended runs, as do many other plays. Smaller theater spaces have increased the number of venues, and the theater audience is enthusiastic. Companies from elsewhere in the region visit from time to time, though George Bernard Shaw would be pleased to know that performances by extraregional groups are extremely rare. Local companies, commercial and amateur, as well as the School of Drama, the UWI, high schools, and some preparatory schools, can be counted on to present year-round indigenous offerings.

Kingston is still the center of production and performance. But many plays, from intimate two-handers to spectacles like the pantomime, make a point of touring to the countryside, where the productions are restaged to fit available space: church halls, school auditoriums, cinemas. They also, especially the comedies, tour abroad to the large Jamaican urban communities in North America and Britain. In that respect, it is no longer 'national' theater, but international.

It has become more international in other respects, too. In the 1970s and 1980s Jamaican playwrights came into their own, exploring their cultural and national roots, mainly through comedy but often, as with Rhone's plays and the productions of Sistren, with a serious undercurrent of personal and societal drama at work. The 1990s saw a new generation of playwrights, such as David Heron and Basil Dawkins, begin to explore more intimate and sensitive themes, such as homosexuality—traditionally the hook for farce, ridicule, or outrage—masculinity, and race in serious, thought-provoking ways. The playwrights are served by a sophisticated audience and an expanding cadre of experienced directors, actors, and backstage staff who have come into their own with material that is 'theirs.'

NOTES

1. Traditional dance can also be classified as religious and secular, or by geographic location or cultural influence, the last two being related.

2. Pukkumina has been more commonly spelt *pocomania*, which is, according to the DCEU, "prob[ably] a Hispano-Anglicized corruption 'poco + mania' of an Afr[ican] term." However, DCEU quotes Alleyne who attributes this 'little madness' interpretation to Europeans' "general demeaning of African culture" and supports Alleyne's alternative: that the word is probably *pukumina*, and related etymologically to *kumina*, another African cult and its associated ritual dance form (Allsopp 1996: 445).

3. Jonkonnu is also rendered Jonkanoo, Junkanoo, John Canoe, John Cannu, John Connu, and and Jankunu. The spelling used in this chapter follows Bettelheim (1976 and 1980).

4. Supposedy a comment on mulatto women, whom the slaves held in contempt for their loose behavior in the great house.

5. These include a Water Mother (better known as Rivermaid or River Mumma, and Cutting Mother—women being prominent among worshippers and eligible to be in charge of a group. There are also Bellringer, Engine Spirit, and Indian Spirit.

6. "The Crossing" is choreographed to the music written by American composer Quincy Jones for the ABC television series *Roots*.

7. By the mid-seventeenth century Spanish Town and Kingston boasted two theaters each. The splendid Theater Royal opened in Kingston in 1840 and, after its destruction in the 1907 earthquake, the even more splendid Ward Theater was built, which still functions.

8. Coverley handled the Christmas morning shows; Johns presented an "Opportunity Hour" during the year.

9. Hyatt would go on to a successful stage-acting and movie career in Britain and Jamaica. Lee and Townsend became TV producer-directors of arts programs that included Jamaican plays, by themselves and others.

10. The Ward has remained the venue for pantomimes.

11. In 1956, Miss Lou became a drama officer for the Jamaica Social Welfare Commission, travelling throughout Jamaica, always imbibing folklore, using group play-making methods to help rural Jamaicans identify their problems and discover solutions.

12. For many years she did much the same thing on a weekly TV program for children called *Ring Ding*.

10

Visual Arts

PAINTING AND SCULPTURE

THE ARTS OF A COUNTRY develop over time, evolving out of belief and ritual, tradition and experiment, criticism and patronage, and the prevailing social, political, and economic circumstances. All have played important roles in Jamaican art, being more or less influential at different times. However, the continuity upon which art depends for consistent development is a fairly recent phenomenon: only in the 1930s did a continuous series of depictions of Jamaican reality by local artists begin. Nonetheless, because the legacy of the past remains a powerful influence, this account of Jamaican art begins with the Taino.

Early Jamaican Art

Sculptures found at different times over the past 200 years, as well as petroglyphs and artifacts, reveal the Taino as people with a strong religious sensibility for whom art was the objective depiction of unseen forces. The creation of *zemis*, three-sided figures representing spiritual beings, was integral to that sensibility.

The Spanish artistic legacy is limited to a few stone friezes carved for a church in New Seville that was never completed. Delicately executed panels of flora and fauna, realistic and fantastical in turn, they seem entirely conventional, and thus, probably carved by Spanish masons and imported. However, close observation reveals figures in some panels who could only be

Taino. Recent research strongly suggests that the friezes were done by Taino carvers who, though building at their conquerors' behest, took advantage of the chance to make their mark.

The almost total interdiction against the display or reproduction of things African that existed for most of the slavery period effectively negated African survivals in objective form. Indeed the proscription was so severe that, even for the period after Emancipation, hardly anything of consequence survives, except in some architectural embellishments. Nevertheless, artists emerging in the twentieth century could not have simply sprung up overnight. We must therefore presuppose artistic retentions at some level—an underground 'tradition' strong enough to revive when the time was ripe.

Until the 1920s 'public' Jamaican art was generally the product of visiting painters—a few of whom never went home—and one or two local painters. In the heyday of sugar, itinerant or long-stay visitors came to paint landscapes, and portray planters and their families, on commission, in the manner of the European gentry. Notable among the visiting artists were Kidd, who produced the important series, *Fifty Spectacular Views of Jamaica*, and Hakewill, who came to the island in 1820 and painted a number of fine watercolors (1825).

Recent research suggests that Issac Belisario, a nineteenth-century artist, was born in Jamaica. He traveled, returned, and settled in the island, setting up a studio in Kingston in 1835. There he painted portraits of prominent citizens and rendered aspects of Jamaican life. He is famous for his sketches of John Canoe dancers and Set Girls published in 1837 (See Chapter 9).

The decline of sugar in the first half of the nineteenth century impacted artistic production, pretty much limiting it to the itinerant artists, some of them American. Frederic Church of the Hudson River School "produced some spectacular Jamaican views in the late 1860s, while another American painter, Ralph Blakelock, is known to have painted a superb landscape of the coast east of Kingston during his visit in 1875" (Boxer 1998: 13).

Since wealthy patrons had pretty much vanished near the end of the nineteenth century, the task of making a visual record of the island fell to talented amateurs, one of whom produced a noteworthy series of orchids with landscapes as background. Significantly, it was a woman, named Charlotte Hall, who earned her living as a portrait painter. Though the question of discrimination against women still attaches to many vocations, there was never a prejudice against Jamaican women artists—no great encouragement, perhaps, but no active disapproval either.

The Early Intuitives

Primitive and naive are terms often used to describe self-taught artists (for example, Grandma Moses is referred to as an 'American Primitive' painter) but they are inappropriate for describing the Jamaican intuitives. 'Primitive' is widely used to mean historically early or else to refer to the traditional tribal arts of Africa, Australia and pre-Columbian America, while 'naive' suggests 'unsophisticated' or 'simple.' None of these characteristics applies to the Jamaican intuitive artist. Both terms also have unfortunate negative connotations. In fact, even 'self-taught' is problematic as a label since some self-taught artists teach themselves "in an essentially academic fashion" (Boxer 1980: 17).

Above all, these terms fail to describe the paintings, sculptures, and carvings of generations of Jamaican artists who, though untutored, bring to their work complex insights about human nature, history, philosophy, religion, and the natural and man-made environments. 'Intuitive' best describes the honest, penetrating, underived quality characterizing these works in both their conception and their execution.

It is interesting to suppose—since no one knows—that the tentatively emerging Jamaican art scene was propelled into clearer definition by the welling-up of the underground African 'little tradition' in the early twentieth century. What is truly fascinating, however, is evidence, in a formal portait-type painting, of the existence of the intuitive eye as early as the 1730s. This evidence links, from the beginning, literature and the arts, and the intuitive and mainstream arts. It exists in the form of the portrait of Francis Williams, the free Negro poet, with whom many accounts of Jamaican literature begin. It has been suggested that the painting was executed by a local who was untrained. Even an untutored eye can see that the work resembles that of the intuitive artists who emerge two centuries later.

Three artists are important to the first coming-to-light of the intuitives: David Miller, Sr.; his son, David Miller, Jr.; and John Dunkley. Miller, Sr., originally a maker of curios, eventually began carving and then taught his son. The Millers plied their trade largely unnoticed until the 1940s. They worked together, trying to merge styles so the carvings would seem to come from a single hand. Though the carvings of both Millers recall African traditions, they did not succeed in their purpose: the surreal figures and carved animals made by Miller, Sr., a complex personality familiar with various cultural mythologies that influenced his work, are easily distinguished from the son's smaller animal figures and his superb Negro heads.

John Dunkley was born in 1891, left school at age 14, and soon travelled to Panama. He journeyed throughout Central America, by his daughter's report, enduring great hardships and deprivation. He then became a sailor and visited Britain and North and South America before returning to Panama where he took up barbering—and began to paint. Returning home in the late 1920s, he set up as a barber in Kingston. (He apparently left several paintings in Panama, as gifts to friends.) It was the decorations in his barbershop, a social center of working-class life now as then, that first attracted attention.

The first recognized Jamaican intuitive, Dunkley is still the finest. His work has been compared to Henri Rousseau's, and there are those who believe, of the two, he is the finer painter. His astonishing paintings are unlike anything on the local or international art scene. They are dark surreal landscapes that draw the viewer in. Peopled by strange creatures (jerboas, spiders, crabs, birds) and lush flora and fauna, they reveal an underived sensibility. He hardly showed them except to the community in which he worked, and gently declined to become a part of the art groups and training programs of the late 1930s, though a painting of his was exhibited at the New York World's Fair in 1939.

Of the artists who came to Jamaica, it is primarily a woman, English-born Edna Manley, and, in lesser measure, Armenian-born Koren der Harootian, who arrived in the 1920s and helped to catalyze artistic activity. By the end of the decade, Manley's influence had touched Harootian's work and spread to a few others, including a young sculptor, Alvin Mariott, whom Marcus Garvey was to describe as the 'Michelangelo of Jamaican art.' This aspect of cross-fertilization, present at the 'birth' of Jamaica's mainstream artistic tradition, has persisted throughout its development.

Edna Manley graduated as a sculptor in 1921 in London and came to Jamaica for the first time in 1922, having married her Jamaican cousin, Norman. Working alone, like Dunkley, the Millers, and Alvin Marriott, whom she gradually got to know, Edna's original experience of Jamaica transformed her style and content. An early interest in African sculpture found its ideal subject matter in Jamaican working women, and resulted in a series of cubist-influenced works that were completely different from the academic animal studies that had been her hallmark as a student.

As we have said elsewhere, in early-twentieth-century Jamaica, there was a growing frustration caused by post-Emancipation disillusionment with a class-and color-bound socioeconomic and political milieu that excluded black people from their just place in society. Garvey voiced this frustration. His speeches and writings, and the activities of the UNIA, fertilized a ripening black subconscious. This is reflected tellingly in the art of the period immediately following Garvey's most active years in the island, and his influence on subsequent generations of artists continues undiminished.

Little in the arts—or politics—at the end of the 1920s reflected black Jamaicans, visually or spiritually. Institutionally, there wasn't much to offer hope either. The Institute of Jamaica, which had started to collect the literary and documentational material that would eventually become a widely re-garded reference library, had been unable to organize proper art training, largely because of the lack of teachers. When classes were available, the cost of tutoring and supplies excluded all but the elite from participating.

By the end of the 1930s, under the leadership of two Jamaicans—Philip Sherlock, a poet and historian, and Robert Verity, an art lover and humanist who ran the Institute's Junior Center—the Institute began an activist phase in the arts. Art classes for children and adults were organized, and these were more accessible to the broad mass of interested persons. They were taught by Edna Manley among others. The Institute began exhibiting and buying the work of living artists, forming the nucleus of the national collection (now housed at a National Gallery building constructed in 1974 for that purpose). The juried Annual Exhibitions, which still continue, have showcased artists from all 'schools' and walks of life.

Edna Manley did not hold her first solo exhibition in Jamaica until 1937. By that time a small cadre of Jamaican-born artists were known to be working and exhibiting. In addition to Marriott, Dunkley, and the two Millers, there were David Pottinger (born in 1911), whose long life has been lived in a working-class district of Kingston, which is his main subject matter; Carl Abrahams (born in 1913), slightly Pottinger's junior; and the even younger Albert Huie (born in 1920), who went on to train in Canada and England. Cecil Baugh (born in 1908), a master potter of international stature, also belongs to this group of pioneers. His work is discussed in the section on ceramics.

All these artists, trained or self-taught, took as their theme the Jamaican landscape and people, reflecting their immediate world in the strong forms, colors, and styles emanating from deeply felt, personal responses. It was a movement away from the genteel landscapes and flattering portraits that had been the norm. It was also a conscious response to the nationalist passions that were stirring in the society and were reflected in the literature being created at this time. To a considerable extent, both movements centered around Edna Manley and the Manley household.

John Dunkley died in 1947—a relatively young man at age 56. However, many of the artists of the 1930s founding era continued to produce, exhibit, and eventually teach, into the 1960s and the 1970s. Some were still working in the 1980s and a few have worked through the 1990s and into the twenty-first century. This factor of continuity, and of the physical and psychic intimacy that a small country enforces, is another important influence in Jamaican art.

The 1940s and 1950s

The Institute of Jamaica now offered formal art classes, one rallying point for budding talent. The other was the Manleys' home, where a small group of artists including Huie, Pottinger, Henry Daley (born in 1919), and Ralph Campbell (born in 1921) gathered. Huie painted portraits and everyday country life; Campbell and, in a special way, Pottinger concentrated on the Kingston streets. Daley, who died tragically, probably of starvation, at age 32, did self-portraits or painted trees. Although they adopted European post-impressionistic styles, "these artists together laid the foundation for an indigenous iconography: Jamaican life, Jamaican landscape, Jamaican faces became the means to convey the nationalist sentiments that the group strongly felt" (Boxer 1998: 18).

Roger Mais, born in 1905, was well known as a writer committed to the cause (see Chapter 7). He began painting relatively late—towards the end of the 1940s—and his passionate support for nationalism (see Chapter 2) influenced his painting as well as his writing. On occasion, the two arts served each other: his novel, *Brother Man*, was illustrated with drawings by the author. An early death cut his careers short: he died in 1955, a mere fifty years old. Some of his later paintings hint at a developing expressionism.

Leslie Clerk is another artist who began late in life and, like Mais, came into his own in the 1950s. A piano-tuner from a family with paranormal gifts, Clerk was born in 1895 and was a lifetime friend of Norman Manley's. Largely self-taught, though not an intuitive, he started painting in his fifties. He turned eventually to sculpture, becoming in Edna Manley's words, "one of our finest carvers" (Manley 1989: 151). A solidity, deliberateness, and deep calm pervade the generous rounded forms in his works. He died in 1973.

There were other artists developing outside the orbits of either the Institute or "Drumblair," the Manley's home. Among these were Carl Abrahams, who started as a cartoonist—which perhaps explains his occasionally irreverent portrayals, even of sacred subjects. He came by his idiosyncratic style under his own tutoring and the influence of Augustus John, the English artist, whom he met in Jamaica in 1937. Having taken correspondence courses and copied the masters, by the 1950s Abrahams had come into his own. Further contributing to cross-fertilization was Polish-born Michael Lester. He came to the island in 1950 and stayed till he died in 1975. He settled in Montego Bay and, influenced by the island circumstance, produced canvases soaked with tropical color.

By this time, a second woman who was to stay the course (she still paints) had joined the growing artistic colony. Born in 1923 in rural Jamaica, Gloria Escoffery was educated locally, in Canada, and in London. A poet, art critic, and schoolteacher as well as painter, Escoffery has lived much of her life in the country, and her compositions reflect that presence. Real and abstract, small-scale or grand, at once feeding her poetry and feeding off it, Escoffery's art, like her verse, employs multiple metaphors. She derives her motifs from landscape, heritage, rural life, religion, wide reading, and personal idiosyncracy.

Not all artists stayed. Namba Roy and Ronald Moody, both born in 1910, are examples of Jamaican artists who went abroad and never came back, and produced oeuvres that nonetheless drew deeply from the island source. Roy was distinguished as a painter and novelist, as well as carver. Having served in the British army in World War II, he settled in England, married, and began to paint and carve. He traced his Maroon ancestry to a line of Congolese carvers, and himself learned the skill from his father. Eschewing wood for the more expensive medium of ivory, he produced carvings that, like Dunkley's paintings, are unique. In them he brilliantly explores his medium as, with a sure lyrical hand, he celebrates African features and forms.

The 1960s

The job of providing continuity to the art scene fell at first to Edna Manley and the small founding cadre of artists who continued to produce. Her role as a leading politician's wife severely curtailed her artistic activity, but she continued to mentor younger artists. After Norman Manley's death in 1969, she resumed art, working through her grief in a set of mourning carvings, then proceeding to explore the 'final age of man' as part of her treatment of the 'ages of man' theme.

The artistic community profited from a new infusion of blood after Independence in 1962. It came from the work of three Jamaican artists, all of whom had lived and studied abroad: Barrington Watson, Eugene Hyde, and Karl Parboosingh. Having studied in several European capitals, Watson returned to paint massive realistic studies of history and 'ordinary' life in a style that observed European classical criteria. It could be argued that, in terms of subject matter and approach, he emboldened the body of work that existed, but it was Hyde and Parboosingh, and, indeed, Parboosingh's second wife, Seya, who pushed things in a different direction.

Hyde trained in California where he tackled the ravages of colonialism on a scale as grand as Watson's but in an entirely different style. An abstract expressionist, he produced black and white etchings and enormous canvases, which confounded the local audience. He is perhaps best known for three series of Jamaican flora: "Sunflowers," "Spathodias," and "Crotons." Sadly, in his fiftieth year, he lost his life while rescuing his sons from drowning.

Karl Parboosingh studied in New York, Paris, and Mexico. He had exhibited in all three places before returning to Jamaica to spend his life exploring various kinds of expressionist influences. Parboosingh was at his best when he tackled traditional Jamaican subject matter: attracted to Rastafarianism near the end of his life, he painted a striking series depicting Rastas using ganja for worship.

Karl's second wife, Seya, a Lebanese woman whom he had married in New York, returned with him to Jamaica. Tutored by him, she began to paint. She developed rapidly and had already exhibited with him by the end of the 1960s. She brought a highly idiosyncratic approach to exploring autobiographical subjects, often from her childhood. She stayed after Parboosingh's death in 1975, adding one more woman and a whimsical, feminine dimension to the mainstream of Jamaican painting.

There were other returnees in the 1960s, and some adoptions who would, together, begin a push towards surrealism—an element present in Dunkley's work at the beginning, for one could argue that his oeuvre combined many of the elements of Jamaican art, even before there *was* Jamaican art.

The most important Jamaican-born surrealist to come to light in the 1960s was Osmond Watson. He grew up in the tradition, taking classes at the Junior Center, graduating from the Jamaica School of Art (hereafter, JSA), and exhibiting locally, before going to the United Kingdom for further study. His odyssey came full circle when he returned to teach art and carve, sculpt, and paint. Deriving his metaphors from religious rituals, African masks, and Taino symbols and applying a Picassoesque cubism for his own ends, Osmond Watson imbues his profoundly Jamaican subject matter with a special numinousness and power. By his interest in Africana, he nudges the tradition in the direction of the intuitives.

Colin Garland came to Jamaica from Australia in 1962, the year of Jamaica's Independence. Trained in Australia and the United Kingdom, his unmistakable artistic signature is written on (often enormous) canvases that depict fastidiously rendered objects and people in dreamscapes that are always strange, often whimsical, sometimes bizarre. An admirer of Haitian art, he employs every variety of land and sea creature, flower, bird, insect, landscape, and person as it exists or as he recreates it, in these mysterious moody confabulations.

Other artists who emerged at this time were Susan Alexander, Karl Gerry Craig, and George Rodney. Craig and Rodney are Jamaican born. Confirming the tendency of 'exodus for education,' Craig studied in London and the United States, and Rodney went to New York after attending the JSA. Alexander was born in the United States. She studied in New York and in Switzerland, married a Jamaican, and began to exhibit in the 1960s—adding another woman to the community of artists.

The 1970s

The unprecedented political turmoil and violence of the 1970s seemed to fuel an outpouring of art. The upheaval "brought a new urgency to the work of many artists, especially Edna Manley, Roy Reid, Carl Abrahams, David Boxer, and Eugene Hyde who produced emotionally gripping works in response" (Poupeye, in Boxer and Poupeye 1998: 30).

While thousands of Jamaicans emigrated in the 1970s, there were artists who returned home, bringing with them new interests and new techniques. One of the 1970s returnees (from the United States, where he had studied art history) was David Boxer. A virtually self-taught practitioner in sculpture and mixed media, he employed both to produce disturbing installations that were radically different from anything in the local tradition. He is an early example of the dialectic of universalist versus personal/local concerns. Initially he was preoccupied with broad existential questions—the ravages of oppression, war, genocide. Those musings eventually found local foci: the annihilation of the Taino and colonial conflict are among his later themes. His twenty-five-year association with the National Gallery as director has contributed enormously to creating a stable environment in which Jamaican artists could exhibit and answer the challenge of an audience. His writings on Jamaican art, in particular its history and development, are invaluable contributions.

Winston Patrick, perhaps Jamaica's most important modernist sculptor, also returned in the early 1970s, having trained in New York. He worked through a series of imported influences, beginning with Pop/Op, and eventually arrived at his own illusionist style. Painter Ricardo Wilkins and sculptor Christopher Gonzales also returned. Both had ventured far, to Africa and Scandinavia, respectively. Wilkins's felt tie to Africa prompted him to change his name to Kofi Kayiga. Borrowing his technique from the abstract impressionists and his symbolism from African ritual and lore, he uses vivid colors and primitive rhythms to explore his subject matter. Gonzalez started out an abstractionist, a tendency that may explain some of the caprice in his startling images. He abandoned abstraction early on for a symbolism inspired by Edna Manley. With Osmond Watson and Kayiga, among others, he shares an interest in Africana.

One thing that has contributed continuity and helped to build Jamaica's artistic tradition is the fact that, beginning with David Miller, Sr., and Edna Manley, artists have taught other artists. Many have taught at the JSA at various points in their careers. These include Christopher Gonzalez, Colin Garland, Osmond Watson, Kofi Kayiga, Karl Craig, and Hope Brooks. Brooks, who is still associated with the school, was trained in Scotland. Her paintings are quiet, painstaking explorations of differing aspects in natural objects or nature itself, or the occasional manmade thing. They are often enriched by the use of textures. Despite the vibrant tropical surround, her preference is for subdued monochromatic tones.

Another important artist who began work in the 1960s and emerged in the 1970s was Milton George. He is virtually untrained—by choice, not lack of opportunity. After attending some classes at JSA, he rejected all artistic prescriptions, preferring to forge his own style. An expressionist influenced by Parboosingh and Kayiga, locally, and perhaps Henri Matisse and The Fauves, his work boasts a highly distinctive signature. He has been said to employ an "unerring colour sense . . . highly charged brushstroke, and daring, ironic distortions of the human form" (Boxer 1998: 22).

Contemporary Art: Later Intuitives

It is convenient to speak of the 'early' and 'later' intuitives, though the distinction is deceiving, for after John Dunkley and the Millers, the tradition is virtually unbroken. One striking instance of this is that, in 1947, precisely the year Dunkley died, Mallica Reynolds (better known as 'Kapo'), the most famous of the later intuitives, produced his first important painting.

Jamaica's intiuitives are for the most part self-taught. Boxer portrays the mainstream of Jamaican art, from Edna Manley through to today's trained and skilled practitioners, as the 'nervous system' of the artistic body, wherein the intuitives are the 'bloodstream.' In the catalogue to a landmark exhibition in 1979 called "The Intuitive Eye" (Boxer 1979), the commentator describes the intuitives' artistic visions as unmediated expressions of their relationships to the world around them and to their inner world.

Without doubt, the most important of the later intuitives is Kapo—born Mallica Reynolds in 1911. It is not surprising that Kapo's first significant painting was of a black Christ, for that subject configures two crucial elements in the intuitive oeuvre: a world view that is African-based, and one in which the religious/spiritual dimension is paramount. Himself a Revival 'shepherd' (leader—see Chapter 2), Kapo abandoned painting soon after his black Christ, turning to sculpture instead. Inspired by Revivalism (see Chapter 2), he produced an extraordinary body of work between 1947 and 1960. He resumed painting after that, recording religious subjects, everyday life, and remarkable landscapes: hillsides covered by rhythmic lines of trees, or by a single tree laden with cashews, or by a group of trees completely covered with plump bunches of flowers or leaves. By the 1960s his work was acclaimed both locally and abroad.

Though he was older than Kapo by sixteen years, Sydney McLaren (born in 1895) belongs with the 'later intuitives' because, like the American primitive artist Grandma Moses, he only started to paint after his sixtieth birthday. A realist devoted to careful depiction of scenes of everyday life, he achieves 'virtual' perspectives in city streets, which draw the viewer in—up toward the Blue Mountains in *Parade*, round a curve and into a dense grove of tropical trees in *Hope Gardens, 1976*. He receives many of his designs in visions.

While Kapo was still carving, another intuitive, Gaston Tabois, had also achieved considerable success for paintings whose vibrant colors proclaimed the *joie de vivre* of island life. As early as 1955, Tabois was receiving glowing reviews in the press, and in 1956 and 1957 he exhibited in the United States with great success. It has been suggested that McLaren and Tabois "are far more closely oriented to the folk painting tradition evident in most societies" and thus might be better considered "naive" since their work communicates no great truth but simply records everyday life (Archer-Straw and Robinson 1990: 127).

Also in this generation are two sculptors—John 'Doc' Williamson (born in 1911) and William 'Woody' Joseph (born in 1919)—and a Rastafarian painter and sculptor, Everald Brown (born in 1917). 'Doc' Williamson and fellow sculptor Lester Hoilett have been characterized as "elemental carvers utilizing basic reductionist methods and a convincing sense of characterization" (Boxer 1998: 25). Williamson was one of the first sculptors to use alabaster, and he creates most of his works in this medium. Woody Joseph may be the intuitive with the nearest connection to the roots that tie Jamaican intuitive art to Africa. A deeply felt desire impelled him to carve. Outside of 'race memory' and the 'collective unconscious,' it is hard to explain his un-mistakably African figures, for he lives a hermitic life, is not bookish, and is entirely self-taught.

One art critic has said, "in some of his works, [Everald] Brown adopts a style not so far from the descriptive/symbolic medium of Kapo" (Escoffery 1987–1988: 14), thus placing Brown firmly in the tradition beginning with the Millers. Brown's work spans three decades, however, so some of it "steps across the threshold of description into abstract meanings inherent in nature" (Escoffery 1987–1988: 18)—a link in purpose, if not in style, with main-stream artist Hope Brooks. Brown is also famous for producing a highly decorated combo instrument that combines harp, drum, guitar, and rhumba box.

Brown and fellow Rastafarian Albert Artwell (born in 1943) use vivid colors, especially the Rastafarian red, green, and gold, to explore subjects that are often religious. Applying a keen sense of design, they fill the creative space with dense, carefully observed and executed images, rich in symbolism. Allan Zion Johnson (born in 1930) also paints in this vein; though his approach is more stylized, his subject matter is also essentially religious.

Two other artists in this second generation of intuitives are 'wild men,' Leonard Daley (born in 1930) and Roy Reid (born in 1937). Their paintings are bizarre in different ways. Daley uses dark, intense tones to record strange dream-trails peopled by troubling images; Reid is mainly concerned with city life, upon which he offers trenchant social comment through idiosyncratic, sometimes shocking imagery.

The African tradition survived slavery by going underground, and it thrives there still (see Chapters 1 and 9). Sculptor Errol MacKenzie (born in 1954) whose biomorphisms express highly personal metaphors, is one of the most recent intuitives. Others are painters William Rhule (born in 1956) and Eli Jah and sculptor Dennis Minott (born in 1954), all of whom explore religious subjects. It is only prudent to be aware that the intuitives whom we know are not the entire artistic corps. Some newcomers, like Paul Perkins, happily join the art scene. Others appear and disappear. One of these is Dennis Minott. Discovered in 1989, he produced a few pieces, then vanished. Whether his absence is by choice or by mischance, we wait to know—in the same way that we wait to discover other self-taught talents.

An interesting detail concerning Eli Jah's work points in an entirely dif-ferent direction and also conjoins developments in intuitive and mainstream art, and local and universal interests. Jah, a church leader from downtown Kingston and "one of very few female intuitives to work without a male partner" (Poupeye 1998: 35) had been exhibiting in Switzerland for several years before she came to the attention of the local art community. This could be seen as remarkable, or not, given the artistic tidal drift.

Contemporary Art: Mainstream Artists

This account of the 1970s ends with Milton George because his approach, determinedly individualistic, perhaps can be seen as presaging the 'inventions' that were to take place in the next decade. In the early 1980s, the Smithsonian Institution Traveling Exhibition Service (SITES) and the National Gallery of Jamaica mounted the *Jamaican Art 1922–82* exhibition. Regarding the new directions in Jamaican art since then, "a new generation of Jamaican artists has appeared whose inquiries are more diverse and open-ended than their predecessors" (Poupeye 1998: 29). By the mid-1980s, most Jamaican artists had, at some point, been abroad for training, and so, inevitably, more and more 'foreign' ideas, techniques, and approaches were being adopted or experimented with.

If Milton George's work pointed to the 1980s innovations, Laura Facey, Eric Cadien, Petrona Morrison (all three born in 1954), and Margaret Chen (born in 1951) represent the crossover generation. All but Morrison had studied at the JSA, been to the United States for further study, and, returned. Each had exhibited in the 1970s. However, they came into their own in the 1980s, and the visions they began to explore at that time belong to the post-1982 generation. In addition, Brooks, Chen, Facey, Morrison, and Marguerite Stanigar (born in 1952) helped to enlarge the early trickle of women artists into a sturdy stream.

Laura Facey is a sculptor, painter, and illustrator who, like David Boxer, employs her multiple skills in installations. In these, she creates, with a sure poetic hand, surreal worlds of uneasy stillness, which recall the paintings of Hope Brooks and the graceful resonant sculptures of Winston Patrick. Both were her tutors. Eric Cadien links 1980s expressionists (like Omari Ra and Stanford Watson) to their 1970s predecessors (Osmond Watson, Kayiga, and Parboosingh). Trained as a sculptor and therefore very conscious of formal elements, Cadien's 'coolly expressionist' paintings (the term is David Boxer's) seem to avoid social comment. That appearance may be deceptive. Given the poor state of public transportation in Jamaica, *Family with Bicycle*, in which one person 'steers' the chassis of a bicycle while two 'passengers' sit behind him, could be seen as wry but trenchant comment.

As in the beginning, art has continued to reflect political thought and aspiration. Stanford Watson and Omari Ra were part of a group of artists who came of age in the 1970s and whose work in the 1980s reflects the turmoil and political upheaval of the earlier decade, especially as it impacted urban life. The group, painting in the manner of the local expressionists, produced social comment from a black nationalist perspective.

Jamaica's artistic community has always attracted artists from abroad, many of whom visit regularly, some of whom (like Colin Garland) remained. Rex Dixon (born in 1939) is perhaps the most distinguished of Jamaica's recent artist-immigrants. He came in 1985 to a Jamaica in the throes of sociopolitical change, from a Belfast in much the same state, so that the dynamics in the 'artistic surround' did not alter much. His transition into local subject matter was, therefore, natural, not engineered.

Like Ronald Moody and Namba Roy, many Jamaican artists who have since ventured abroad (most often to study) have remained there. Among Jamaicans who are currently living and working in the United States are Keith Morrison (born in 1942), a painter, educator, writer, and curator; Albert Chong (born in 1958), a photographer and installation artist; Peter Wayne Lewis (born in 1953), a painter who creates enormous abstract and semiabstract works; and Nari Ward (born in 1963), who constructs installations in Harlem. Not surprisingly, they often turn to exploring issues of identity and cultural heritage, and the disjunctures, personal and social, that are the consequence of migration.

In an interesting parallel development, younger Jamaican artists appear, more recently, to be turning from social and political comment to more spiritual concerns: issues of personal identity, the environment, the nature of things. Petrona Morrison and Margaret Chen, both trained in Canada, each explore heritage, albeit in different ways. Chen went to Canada after attending the JSA, while Morrison trained in Canada first, then did postgraduate work in the United States. Morrison also spent time in Kenya, which, with her Howard University experience, influenced her work strongly. Both began exhibiting in Jamaica in the 1980s. The monumental size as well as the character of their assemblages and installations shook up a largely conservative sculpture tradition—always excepting the work of Facey, Boxer, Patrick, and Gonzalez.

Chen began (in Canada) with the gigantic *Steppe Series*, which records a journey back, through the minds of her Chinese ancestors, into the "vague shadows" and "nebulous shapes" of what remained of their lives, layered beneath the Asian steppes. Her more recent *Passage Series*, also of large proportions, considers the fugitive nature of time and the evanescence of human experience. Morrison, who paints as well as sculpts, began small, using *objets trouvés* (found objects) in soberly toned assemblages that betray her interest in African art. A strong spiritual quality pervades this earlier work, meant to signify transformation and healing. Over time the works grew, eventually becoming highly abstract, totem-like structures, with statue- or altar-like qualities signalling her concern with ritual and ceremony.

Some other artists who have recently returned to Jamaica, and whose work is preoccupied with issues of self, personal history, and identity are Roberta Stoddart (born in 1963), Nicholas Morris (born in 1967), and Charles Campbell (born in 1970). All are painters. It is interesting that, of the three, it is the youngest, Campbell, whose concern with social and historical issues most connects him with the artists of the 1980s.

The work of Anna Henriques (born in 1967) provides a fitting conclusion. She trained abroad, both in Europe and the United States. She writes, incorporating writing into her art; and she works across media (paintings, assemblages, installations, video pieces). Her oeuvre calls on personal history and heritage but addresses the universal. The remarkable *Book of Mechtilde*, in which she commemorates the death of her Chinese-Jamaican mother, joins many threads of island story. Meant "just as a memorial to my mother" and published by Knopf in 1997, it recounts the story of Sheila Henriques's death towards the end of the turbulent 1970s, signifying on Jamaican cultural elements: Taino, African, Chinese, and Jewish (her father's heritage) (Henriques 1997).

At the end of the first eighty years of Jamaican art, then, there is a core art community represented in three generations of artists that continues to be enriched by encroaching foreigners and out-venturing homies. To use David Boxer's metaphors: the 'nervous system' of mainstream artists continues to grow while the 'bloodstream' of self-taught artists pulses slow and steady. The body of Jamaican art, engined by these two systems, develops according to its own rhythms, with intuitive insight invading mainstream consciousness perhaps more than is at first recognized.

CERAMICS

Ceramics, or pottery making, is the Jamaican artistic activity with the longest and most consistent history. It began with the Taino who used the island's red clay to make various kinds of earthenware, including cooking vessels. The slaves, introduced by the Spanish in 1517, brought West African methods, and there were inevitably influences coming from the Europeans.

Jamaica's most distinguished ceramist,[1] Cecil Baugh, explains that there are two traditional methods of making pots: the West African method from Spanish Town, practiced by potters like the late Lucy 'Ma Lou' Jones and her daughter, and a method used in Kingston that (Baugh thinks) reflects

European influences. In the Spanish Town method, clay is placed on a *keke*, a broken piece of pottery resting on the ground. The *keke* turns, functioning much like a potter's wheel. Women make smaller pots using the *keke*; men make larger pots using the *walkaround* technique. In walkaround, the clay rests on a sand-covered batt on top of a barrel, which the potter walks around as he molds the pot. Very big pots are made this way, such as Spanish jars and monkey jars. In the Kingston method, clay is molded on a table where it has previously been wedged. After this, women potters wet the table, thus allowing the pot to move freely without the assistance of wheel or *keke*. Kingston pots are also glazed with lead and fired in kilns—other influences Baugh thinks are European.

Pottery is indigenous in the sense that all the necessary materials are local. There are deposits of red as well as white stoneware clay. There is wood, which was originally used for firing the pots and was the fuel Baugh used in the first brick kiln he built. (He still prefers manually fired kilns because they require the potter to be in control of the firing.) There are also many local substances useful for developing glazes: an early and favorite invention of Baugh's is his 'Egyptian blue' glaze.

Baugh is an embodiment of almost all the characterizing factors discussed in the section on art and sculpture. Born in rural Jamaica in 1908, he 'intuited' his earliest works, carving small objects and abstract shapes from stones when he was about nine. He learned potting the traditional way, apprenticed to two ladies from Spanish Town. He enlisted to fight in World War II, motivated by the hope of learning something about ceramics in postwar England. Posted in Aden, he took time off to go to art school. After the war he returned to Jamaica, but he was anxious to get back to England. Too impatient to wait for a British Council scholarship, he paid his way there in 1948, determined to meet and train with Bernard Leach, which he eventually did. Later in life, he would travel extensively, always bringing something new to workshops and exhibits, as a principle. If any art is at once hybrid and indigenously personal, it is his.

Thus, his ceramics embrace and engage multiple influences; he can 'walkaround' to make a monkey jar or 'throw' a pot on a wheel with equally consummate skill. Convinced that a potter is 'half-artist, half-scientist,' he digs clay as comfortably as he operates the physics of glazes and tirelessly searches for local materials to use in glazes. Highly creative and an experimenter, Baugh builds pots that are often whimsical or downright humorous. He is renowned for his glazes and his decorative effects, many of which are bas relief. As capable of understatement as he is of rich oriental-type ornament or bold contemporary effects, his ceramics are an expression of the

Jamaican environment: Jamaican jokes, Jamaican characters, Jamaican materials, an undeniably Jamaican sensibility.

Baugh is also a teacher of ceramists. In 1950, Mrs. Manley asked him to join herself, Huie, Lyndon Leslie, and Gerry Isaacs in setting up a school of arts and crafts. When it was eventually succeeded by the full-time Jamaica School of Art in 1964, he was the only founding tutor still there. He retired in 1974, having single-handedly coaxed local pottery into a fine art. It was he who highlighted the importance of traditional methods of making pottery, and introduced into the island stoneware and the art of firing pots under reducing atmosphere, both learned from Bernard Leach.

The first of Baugh's students to become a full-time potter was his niece, Madge Spencer, now a ceramist in the United Kingdom. Others following in Madge's wake include Norma Harrack and Gene Pearson, both professional potters distinguished in their field. Pearson is famous for his heads, sculpted in terra cotta. Harrack's signature is also distinctive: utilitarian or purely aesthetic, her pieces are often experimental with their semiabstract and abstract designs, raised decoration, and innovative shapes. Her ceramic relief "Portrait of My Land" is a formidable piece.

ARCHITECTURE AND STYLE

Many features of Jamaican architecture are a result of the devastating earthquake and fire that destroyed much of Kingston and the surrounding areas in 1907. Building regulations were rewritten to enforce more solid foundations against earthquake, but also encouraging the use of Jamaican hardwoods, which peasants and planters had been using for generations in bungalows and great houses.

As with so many of its cultural expressions and artifacts, the origins of Jamaican architectural style are to be found in the interaction of English tradition and African interpretation, in this case tempered by the physical environment—topography, materials, and climate.[2]

The English first built for defense and shelter, not, initially, for grace or style. "It was not unusual," said a mid-eighteenth-century writer, "to see a plantation adorned with a very expensive set of works, of brick and stone, well executed, and the owner residing in a miserable thatched hovel, hastily put together with wattles and plaster, damp, unwholesome, and infested with every species of vermin" (Long 1774). One can imagine from that the condition in which his staff and slaves lived!

These make-shifts, as they were called, gradually gave way to more graceful buildings, statements of assurance based on a burgeoning economic and political confidence. The emergence of the Georgian style in England in the eighteenth century, coinciding as it did with the golden age of Caribbean sugar, permitted the planters in the countryside, and the officials and merchants in the towns that were being built, chief among them Spanish Town, to indulge their pretensions at tropical grandeur. The town center of old Falmouth on the northwest coast and the civic center of old Spanish Town,[3] despite the obvious depredations of time and modern development, remain today as impressive and haunting reminders of those pretensions. The buildings were made from drawings sent from England, interpreted by African masons, carpenters, coopers, and other craftsmen who were the most highly prized of all slave labor.

Several of the great houses built between 1750 and Emancipation still survive and are in use, even if the plantations that supported them have passed. Good Hope in Trelawny and Marlborough Great House in Manchester are particularly fine examples. The wealthy built splendid town houses as well. Headquarters House in Kingston, which did not entirely escape the earthquake but was lovingly rebuilt, was the seat of legislative government before Gordon House was built for Independence. It is now, appropriately, the office of the Jamaica National Heritage Trust Commission, the agency charged with nurturing the island's architectural heritage.

Structures built before the earthquake, as one writer put it, "touched the earth lightly" (Voorthuis 1998). None more so than small settler cottages in the rural areas, constructed in a style that architects now call the Jamaican Vernacular. These small graceful houses, mostly of wood, were cool and resilient. A stylish characteristic was fretwork fringing the roof eaves and barge boards, and the fanlight over interior doorways. The style spread to middle-class houses and even to large public buildings like hotels, Titchfield Hotel in Port Antonio—once owned by film star Errol Flynn, now a secondary school—being just one example.

After 1907, however, public buildings became monumental and imposing. Coolness was retained not, as before, by carefully placed louvered windows that took advantage of the prevailing winds, but by ceiling and standing fans, making the buildings easily adaptable to air conditioning, which caught on after World War II.

The post-1907 rebuilding also accelerated the process of 'suburbanization' in Kingston. The boundaries of the old city extended across the Liguanea Plain and toward the hills. Various towns—Vineyard Town, Rae Town, Franklin Town—developed as unplanned but fairly cohesive socioeconomic groupings. These still retain their individual architectural styles—urban Jamaican Vernacular—and names, but their status has, inevitably, slipped.

At the beginning of the 1950s, just after yet another destructive hurricane, a cement factory was established on the edge of Kingston. Making use of the considerable deposits of limestone in the hillsides behind it, the plant's production transformed building styles and construction methods across the island. Block-and-steel (cement blocks reinforced with steel rods) construction imposed a necessary similarity in house design but also facilitated mass construction of housing. The first large-scale schemes at the end of the decade, Mona Heights and Hope Pastures in Kingston, were for middle-class purchasers, many of whom still live in the same houses forty-five years later.

With the refining of prefabrication technologies, the creation of complete towns became possible, and in the years since Independence they have grown from bush and farmland on the plain west of Kingston and across the island. Like the suburbs of earlier times, these developments are of fairly cohesive socio-economic groupings. The architecture, however, which could most generously be called urban concrete slab, does not often delight the eye, even of their owners, who compete to transform them by adding 'improvements.'

For the middle and upper socioeconomic groups, the picture is more varied. In rural areas there is still space for single-family dwellings on land space of a size that would be unthinkable in the cities and towns. Of late, Jamaicans returning from 'foreign,' and neighborhood 'dons' who may or may not be involved in unlisted agricultural exports, have invested in a style of house colloquially called 'deportee': concrete castles that put all but the largest great houses of the past to shame, in size if not in grace.

In Kingston, the age of grandiloquent individual houses has all but passed. There are a few still being built on the hillsides, but townhouse and low-rise condominium complexes are the most popular among middle-class homeowners and renters, for a variety of reasons. Population pressures, escalating building costs and mortgage rates, and a nonfunctional public transportation system encourage intensive use of valuable land space. Concerns about personal security, particularly prevalent in Kingston, are more easily addressed by clustered housing; the number of gated communities, some with detached houses, is rising.

Architecturally, modern Jamaican housing is less influenced by the Jamaican Vernacular of yore than by the modern styles of North America: from ranch-style bungalows to concrete-block rectangular towers (though not as high as those found in most cities to the north). The same is true of public buildings, many of which would fit easily into a small U.S. or Canadian city.

Housing, of whatever style or for whatever class or income group, remains a charged issue in Jamaica. Atop the universal preoccupation about location and status are heaped issues of security and relentlessly rising costs. And for those at the bottom of the socioeconomic scale, the chance for affordable housing is a remote one. Squatting—erecting living quarters on property without permission from the owner—has a long history in Jamaica, going back to the beginning of English settlement more than three centuries ago. Every government of modern times, predating Independence, has had a land settlement program involving both ownership and shelter; the need remains. Urban squatting, also, appears to be insoluble: Jamaican towns and cities seem destined to include particularly 'vernacular' versions of the Jamaican style for some time to come.

Notes

1. Among many other awards, Baugh has received the Institute of Jamaica's Silver (1964) and Gold Musgrave medals (1980), the Order of Distinction (1975), the Norman Manley Award for Excellence (1977), and the Centenary Medal of the Institute of Jamaica (1980). He is also internationally known.

2. But for the friezes described in this chapter, little by way of architecture remains above ground of the Taino and Spanish periods, though re-creations exist at museums.

3. The civic center is still partially in use: the old House of Assembly is the headquarters of St. Catherine Parish Council, and the coach house of the old King's House, the governor's dwelling, houses the Folk Museum.

Bibliography

CHAPTER 1: CONTEXT

Aaron, John A. "W. Adolphe Roberts and the Movement for Self-Government." *Jamaica Journal* 16, no. 4 (1983).

Allsopp, Richard. *Dictionary of Caribbean English Usage*. Oxford: Oxford University Press, 1996.

Beckford, George. *Persistent Poverty: Underdevelopment in Plantation Economies of the Third World*. Kingston: The Press, University of the West Indies, 1998.

Beckles, Hilary, ed. *Inside Slavery: Process and Legacy in the Caribbean Experience*. Kingston: Canoe Press, 1996.

Black, Clinton V. *History of Jamaica*. Burnt Mill: Longman, 1983.

Boxhill, Ian. "Revisiting the Seventies." *The Daily Gleaner*, September 1, 1998, 40.

Brathwaite, Kamau. *The Development of Creole Society in Jamaica 1820–1870*. (Reprint.) Kingston: Ian Randle Publishers, 2000.

Brereton, Bridget, and Kevin Yelvington, eds. *The Colonial Caribbean in Transition: Essays on Postemancipation Social and Cultural History*. Gainesville: University Press of Florida, 1999.

Bryan, Patrick. *The Jamaican People 1880–1902: Race, Class and Social Control*. London: Macmillan Caribbean, 1991.

Bustamante, Gladys. *Lady Bustamante's Memoirs*. Kingston: Kingston Publishers, 1997.

Clarke, John Henrik. "Marcus Garvey: The Harlem Years." *Jamaica Journal* 8, no. 1 (1974).

Curtin, Philip. *The Two Jamaicas: The Role of Ideas in a Tropical Colony, 1830–1865*. (Reprint.) Princeton: Markus Wiener Publishers, 1998.

Dayfoot, Arthur Charles. *The Shaping of the West Indian Church 1492–1962*. Gainesville: University of Florida Press, 1999.

Fincham, Alan. *Jamaica Underground: The Caves, Sinkholes and Underground Rivers of the Island*. Kingston: The Press, University of the West Indies, 1998.

Girvan, D.T.M. *Working Together for Development*. Kingston: Institute of Jamaica Publications, 1993.

Gordon, Shirley C. *Caribbean Generations*. London: Longman's Group, 1983.

————. *Our Cause for His Glory: Christianization and Emancipation in Jamaica*. Kingston: The Press, University of the West Indies, 1998.

Hall, Douglas. *Free Jamaica*. New Haven: Yale University Press, 1959.

————. *In Miserable Slavery: Thomas Thistlewood in Jamaica 1750–1786*. Kingston: The Press, University of the West Indies, 1999.

Hart, Richard. *From Occupation to Independence: A Short History of the Peoples of the English-Speaking Caribbean Region*. Kingston: Canoe Press, 1998.

————. *Towards Decolonization: Political, Labour and Economic Development in Jamaica 1938–1945*. Kingston: Canoe Press, 1998.

Heuman, Gad J. *Between Black and White: Race Politics and the Free Coloreds in Jamaica, 1792–1865*. Westport: Greenwood Press, 1981.

Higman, Barry. *Montpelier, Jamaica: A Plantation Community in Slavery and Freedom 1739–1912*. Kingston: The Press, University of the West Indies, 1998.

————. *Slave Population and Economy in Jamaica 1807–1834*. Kingston: The Press, University of the West Indies, 1995.

Hill, Frank. *Bustamante and His Letters*. Kingston: Kingston Publishers, 1976.

Johnson, Howard, and Karl Watson, eds. *The White Minority in the Caribbean*. Princeton: Markus Wiener Publishers, 1998.

Knight, Franklin W. *The Caribbean: The Genesis of a Fragmented Nationalism*. 2nd ed. New York: Oxford University Press, 1990.

Le Franc, Elsie, ed. *Consequences of Structural Adjustment: A Review of the Jamaican Experience*. Kingston: Canoe Press, 1994.

Lewis, Rupert. *Marcus Garvey, Anti-Colonial Champion*. Trenton: Africa World Press, 1988.

Lewis, W. Arthur. "The 1930s Social Revolution." In Hilary Beckles and Verene Shepherd, eds., *Caribbean Freedom: Economy and Society from Emancipation to the Present*. Princeton: Markus Wiener Publishers, 1991.

Look Lai. *The Chinese in the West Indies 1806–1995: A Documentary History*. Kingston: The Press, University of the West Indies, 1998.

Manley, Michael. *The Politics of Change, a Jamaican Testament*. London: Andre Deutsch, 1974.

Mansingh, Laxmi, and Ajai Mansingh. *Home Away from Home: 150 Years of Indian Presence in Jamaica 1845–1995*. Kingston: Ian Randle Publishers, 1999.

Mars, Pairadeau. *Ideology and Change: The Transformation of the Caribbean Left*. Detroit: Wayne State University Press, 1998.

Meeks, Brian. *Radical Caribbean: From Black Power to Abu Bakr*. Kingston: The Press, University of the West Indies, 1996.

Mordecai, John S. *The West Indies: The Federal Negotiations*. London: George Allen and Unwin, 1969.

Munroe, Trevor. *The Cold War & the Jamaican Left 1950–55*. Kingston: Kingston Publishers, 1992.

———. *Renewing Democracy into the Millenium: The Jamaican Experience in Perspective*. Kingston: The Press, University of the West Indies, 1999.

Nettleford, Rex, ed. *Jamaica in Independence: Essays on the Early Years*. London: James Curry, 1989.

Porter, Anthony. *Jamaica: A Geological Portrait*. Kingston: Institute of Jamaica Publications, 1990.

Ranston, Jackie. *Lawyer Manley, Vol. 1: First Time Up*. Kingston: The Press, University of the West Indies, 1999.

Schuler, Monica. "Akan Slave Rebellions." In Hilary Beckles and Verene Shepherd, eds., *Caribbean Slave Society and Economy: A Student Reader*. Princeton: Markus Wiener Publishers, 1991.

Shepherd, Verene, ed. *Women in Caribbean History*. Princeton: Markus Wiener Publishers, 1999.

Shepherd, Verene, and Hilary Beckles, eds. *Caribbean Freedom: Economy and Society from Emancipation to the Present*. Princeton: Markus Wiener Publishers, 1993.

———. *Caribbean Slavery in the Atlantic World*. Princeton: Markus Wiener Publishers, 1999.

Sherlock, Philip, and Hazel Bennett. *The Story of the Jamaican People*. Princeton: Markus Wiener Publishers, 1998.

Stone, Carl. "Political Trends Since Independence." *Jamaica Journal* no. 46 (1982).

Turner, Mary. *Slaves and Missionaries: The Disintegration of Jamaican Slave Society, 1787–1834*. Kingston: The Press, University of the West Indies, 1998.

CHAPTER 2: RELIGION

Allsopp, Richard. *Dictionary of Caribbean English Usage*. Oxford: Oxford University Press, 1996.

Bisnauth, Dale A. *A History of Religions in the Caribbean*. Kingston: Kingston Publishers, 1989.

Brathwaite, Kamau. "Kumina—The Spirit of African Survival." *Jamaica Journal*. no. 42 (1978).

Chevannes, Barry. "Towards Afro-Caribbean Theology." *Caribbean Quarterly* 37, no. 1 (March 1991).

Chevannes, Barry, ed. *Rastafari: Roots and Ideology*. Syracuse, NY: Syracuse University Press, 1994.

———. *Rastafari and Other African-Caribbean Worldviews*. New Brunswick: Rutgers University Press, 1998.

Curtin, Philip. *The Two Jamaicas: The Role of Ideas in a Tropical Colony, 1830–1865*. (Reprint.) Princeton: Markus Wiener Publishers, 1998.

Dayfoot, Arthur Charles. *The Shaping of the West Indian Church 1492–1962*. Gainesville: University Press of Florida, 1999.

Owens, Joseph. *Dread*. Kingston: Sangster's Bookstores, 1976.

Pocketbook of Statistics Jamaica 1998. Kingston: Statistical Institute of Jamaica, 1999.

Pradel, Lucie. "African Sacredness and Caribbean Cultural Forms." In Verene Shepherd and Glen Richards, eds. *The Creole Society Model Revisited* (a special double edition of *Caribbean Quarterly*). *Caribbean Quarterly* 44, nos. 1–2, (March–June 1998).

Roper, Garnett. "The Impact of Evangelical and Pentecostal Religion." *Caribbean Quarterly* 37, no. 1 (March 1991).

Schuler, Monica. "Myalism and the African Religious Tradition in Jamaica." In Margaret E. Crahan and Franklin W. Knight, eds., *Africa and the Caribbean: The Legacies of a Link*. Baltimore: Johns Hopkins University Press, 1979.

Seaga, Edward. "Revival Cults in Jamaica: Notes towards a Sociology of Religion." *Jamaica Journal* 3, no. 2 (June 1969): 3–13.

Smith, Ashley. "Pentecostalism in Jamaica." *Jamaica Journal*, no. 42 (September 1978).

Wint, Eleanor. "Who is Haile Selassie? His Imperial Majesty in Rasta Voices." In Nathaniel Samuel Murrell, William David Spencer, and Anthony Adrian McFarlane, eds., *Chanting Down Babylon: The Rastafari Reader*. Philadelphia: Temple University Press, 1998.

CHAPTER 3: EDUCATION

"Banishing Illiteracy." Editorial. *Gleaner Online*, June 9, 1998.

Boxill, Ian. "The Illiteracy Problem." *Gleaner Online*, September 23, 1997.

Bryan, Patrick. *The Jamaican People 1880–1902: Race, Class and Social Control*. London: Macmillan Caribbean, 1991.

Craig, Dennis, ed. *Education in the West Indies: Developments and Perspectives, 1948–1988*. Kingston: Institute of Social and Economic Research, 1996.

Davies, Rose. "Striving for Quality in Early Childhood Development Programmes: The Caribbean Experience." In Ruby King, ed., *Institute of Education Annual*, pp. 61–77. Kingston: Institute of Education, University of the West Indies, 1998.

Gordon, Derek. "Access to High School Education in Postwar Jamaica." In Errol Miller, ed., *Education and Society in the Commonwealth Caribbean*, pp. 181–206. Kingston: Institute of Social and Economic Research, 1991.

Goulbourne, Harold D. "Elementary School Teachers and Politics in Colonial Jamaica: The Formation of the Jamaica Union of Teachers." *Caribbean Quarterly* 31, nos. 3–4 (1985): 16–30.

Hamilton, Marlene. "A Review of Educational Research in Jamaica." In Errol Miller, ed., *Education and Society in the Commonwealth Caribbean*, pp. 105–142. Kingston: Institute of Social and Economic Research, 1991.

King, Ruby. "Educational Inequality in Jamaica: The Need for Reform." In Ruby King, ed., *Institute of Education Annual*, pp. 43–58. Kingston: Institute of Education, University of the West Indies, 1998.

Knight, Franklin W. *The Caribbean: The Genesis of a Fragmented Nationalism*. 2nd ed. New York: Oxford University Press, 1990.

Learn, Stretch, Reach. Kingston: University of the West Indies/Bernard Van Leer Foundation North Coast Project for training basic school teachers in Jamaica, 1993.

Lowenthal, David, and Lambert Comitas. *Consequences of Class and Colour: West Indian Perspectives*. New York: Anchor Books, 1973.

Miller, Errol. "Educational Development in Independent Jamaica." In Rex Nettleford, ed., *Jamaica in Independence*, pp. 205–227. Kingston: Heinemann (Caribbean) Ltd., 1989.

———. *Jamaican Society and High Schooling*. Kingston: Institute of Social and Economic Research, 1990.

Miller, Errol, ed. *Education and Society in the Commonwealth Caribbean*. Kingston: Institute of Social and Economic Research, 1991.

Nettleford, Rex, ed. *Jamaica in Independence: Essays on the Early Years*. London: James Curry, 1989.

Nunes, Fred. "The 70/30 Education Regulation: Policy-Making, Reactions and Consequences." *Caribbean Journal of Education* 3, no. 3 (1976): 185–218.

Pocketbook of Statistics. Kingston: The Statistical Institute of Jamaica, 1988.

Sherlock, Philip, and Hazel Bennett. *The Story of the Jamaican People*. Kingston: Ian Randle Publications; Princeton: Marcus Weiner Publishers, 1998.

Wint, Carl. "NAP—A Good Replacement for CEE?" *Gleaner Online*, February 3, 1998.

CHAPTER 4: LANGUAGE

Alleyne, Mervyn. *Comparative Afro-American: An Historical-Comparative Study of Some Afro-American Dialects in the New World*. Ann Arbor, MI: Karoma, 1980.

———. "The Epistemological Foundations of Caribbean Speech Behaviour." *Caribbean Journal of Education* 10, no. 1 (1983): 1–17.

———. *Roots of Jamaican Culture*. London: Pluto Press, 1988.

Allsopp, Richard. *Dictionary of Caribbean English Usage*. Oxford: Oxford University Press, 1996.

Bailey, Beryl. *Jamaican Creole Syntax: A Transformational Approach*. Cambridge: Cambridge University Press, 1966.

Bickerton, Derek. *Roots of Language*. Ann Arbor, MI: Karoma, 1981.

Carrington, Lawrence D., et al., eds. *Studies in Caribbean Language*. St. Augustine, Trinidad: Society for Caribbean Linguistics, 1983.

Cassidy, Frederic. *Jamaica Talk*. Basingstoke and London: Macmillan Education Ltd., 1961.

Chevannes, Barry. *Rastafari Roots and Ideology*. Syracuse, NY: Syracuse University Press, 1995.

Christie, Pauline, ed. *Caribbean Language Issues Old and New*. Barbados, Jamaica, Trinidad and Tobago: The Press, University of the West Indies, 1996.

Craig, Dennis. "Developmental and Social-Class Differences in Language." *Caribbean Journal of Education* 1, no. 2 (1974): 5–23.

DaCosta, Jean, and Barbara Lalla. *Voices in Exile*. Tuscaloosa: University of Alabama Press, 1989.

Devonish, Hubert. Review of Derek Bickerton, *Roots of Language* (Ann Arbor, MI: Karoma, 1981). *Caribbean Journal of Education* 10, no. 1 (1983).

———. "Vernacular Languages and Writing Technology Transfer: The Jamaican Case." In Pauline Christie, ed., *Caribbean Language Issues Old and New*, pp. 101–111. Barbados, Jamaica, Trinidad and Tobago: The Press, University of the West Indies, 1996.

Jourdan, C. "Pidgins and Creoles: The Blurring of Categories." *Annual Review of Anthropology* 20 (1991): 187–209.

Lalla, Barbara, and Jean DaCosta. *Language in Exile*. Tuscaloosa: University of Alabama Press, 1990.

McArthur, John, ed. *The Oxford Companion to the English Language*. Oxford: Oxford University Press, 1992.

Mordecai, Pamela. *de Man*. Toronto: Sister Vision Press, 1995.

Mufwene, Salikoko. "Creole Genesis: A Population Genetics Perspective." In Pauline Christie, ed., *Caribbean Language Issues Old and New*. Barbados, Jamaica, Trinidad and Tobago: The Press, University of the West Indies, 1996.

Nugent, Lady Maria. *Lady Maria Nugent's Journal of Her Residence in Jamaica from 1801 to 1805*, revision edited by Philip Wright. Kingston: Institute of Jamaica, 1966.

Owens, Joseph. *Dread*. Kingston: Sangster's Bookstores, 1976.

Pollard, Velma. *Dread Talk: The Language of Rastafari*. Kingston: Canoe Press, 1994.

Thomason, Sarah Grey, and Terence Kaufman. *Language Contact, Creolization and Genetic Linguistics*. Berkeley: University of California Press, 1988.

CHAPTER 5: SOCIAL CUSTOMS

Beckles, Hilary McD. *The Development of West Indies Cricket, Vol. 1: The Age of Nationalism*. Kingston: The Press, University of the West Indies, 1998.

———. *The Development of West Indies Cricket, Vol. 2: The Age of Globalization*. Kingston: The Press, University of the West Indies, 1998.

Beckles, Hilary, ed. *A Spirit of Dominance: Cricket and Nationalism in the West Indies*. Kingston: Canoe Press, 1998.

Campbell, Marjorie Pringle. *A Collection of 19th Century Jamaican Cookery and Herbal Recipes*. Kingston: The Mill Press, 1990.

Carnegie, James. *Great Jamaican Olympians*. Kingston: Kingston Publishers, 1997.

Donaldson, Enid. *The Real Taste of Jamaica*. Kingston: Ian Randle Publishers, 1993.

Grant, Rosamund. *Caribbean and African Cookery*. Kingston: Ian Randle Publishers, 1992.

James, C.L.R. *Beyond a Boundary*. Kingston: Sangster's, 1963. (Reprint.) New York: Pantheon Books, 1994.

Mackie, Cristine. *Life and Food in the Caribbean*. Kingston: Ian Randle Publishers, 1995.

CHAPTER 6: MEDIA AND CINEMA

Black, Clinton V. *History of Jamaica*. Burnt Mill: Longman, 1983.

Dunn, Hopeton S., ed. *Globalization, Communications and Caribbean Identity*. New York: St. Martin's Press, 1995.

Ministry Paper No. 5. "Broadcasting Proposals for Establishment of a Public Broadcasting Corporation and for the Extension of a Licence Held by the Jamaica Broadcasting Company, Limited." January 31, 1958.

CHAPTER 7: LITERATURE

Baugh, Edward. *Critics on Caribbean Literature*. London: George Allen and Unwin, 1978.

———. *A Tale from the Rainforest*. Kingston: Sandberry Press, 1988.

———. "Poem, Reading, Performance." In Lowell Fiet, ed., *Caribbean 2000: Regional and/or National Definitions, Identities and Cultures. A Gathering of Players and Poets: Voice and Performance in Caribbean Culture(s)*, pp. 38–46. Rio Piedras, Puerto Rico: *Caribe 2000*—Facultad de Humanidades, 1999.

———. "Poetry (The Caribbean)." In Eugene Benson and Leonard W. Conolly, eds., *The Routledge Encyclopaedia of Post Colonial Literature*, pp. 1241–1244. London, New York: Routledge, 1994.

———. "The Sixties and Seventies." In Bruce King, ed., *West Indian Literature*, 2nd ed., pp. 64–75. London, Basingstoke: Macmillan Press Ltd., 1995.

Bennett, Louise. *Jamaica Labrish*, Rex Nettleford, ed. Kingston: Sangster's Bookstores Ltd., 1972, 1975.

———. *Selected Poems*. Mervyn Morris, ed. Kingston: Sangster's Bookstores Ltd., 1982.

Benson, Eugene, and Leonard W. Conolly, eds. *The Routledge Encyclopaedia of Post Colonial Literature*. London, New York: Routledge, 1994.

Bloom, Harold, ed. *Caribbean Women Writers*. Philadelphia: Chelsea House Publishers, 1997.

Brathwaite, Kamau. "Creative Literature of the British West Indies during the Period of Slavery." In *Savacou* 1, pp. 46–73. Kingston and London: Caribbean Artist Movement, 1970.

Breiner, Laurence A. "The Eighties." In Bruce King, ed., *West Indian Literature*, pp. 76–87. London, Basingstoke: Macmillan Press Ltd., 1995.

Brodber, Erna. *Jane and Louisa Will Soon Come Home*. London, Port of Spain: New Beacon, 1980.

Burnett, Paula, ed. *The Penguin Book of Caribbean Verse in English*. Harmondsworth: Penguin Books, 1986.

Campbell, George. *First Poems*. Kingston: City Printery, 1945. (Reprint.) New Haven: Yale University Afro-American Studies, 1982.

Chamberlin, J. Edward. *Come Back to Me, My Language*. Toronto: McClelland & Stewart, 1993.

Cobham, Rhonda. "The Literary Side of H. G. de Lisser (1878–1944)." *Jamaica Journal* 17, no. 4 (1984–1985): 2–9.

Cooke, Michael. "The Strains of Apocalypse: Lamming's Castle and Brodber's Jane and Louisa." *Journal of West Indian Literature* 4, no. 1 (1990): 28–40.

Cumber Dance, Daryl. *New World Adams—Conversations with Contemporary West Indian Writers*. Leeds, UK: Peepal Tree Press, 1992.

Cumber Dance, Daryl, ed. *Fifty Caribbean Writers: A Bio-bibliographical Critical Source Book*. Westport, CT: Greenwood Press, 1986.

Dawes, Kwame. *Wheel and Come Again: An Anthology of Reggae Poetry*. Fredericton, New Brunswick: Goose Lane, 1998.

Donnell, Alison, and Sarah Lawson Welsh, eds. *Routledge Reader in Caribbean Literature*. London and New York: Routledge, 1996.

Goodison, Lorna. *Selected Poems*. Ann Arbor: University of Michigan Press, 1992.

———. *To Us, All Flowers Are Roses*. Chicago: University of Illinois Press, 1995.

———. *Turn Thanks*. Chicago: University of Illinois Press, 1999.

Juneja, Renu. "Contemporary Women Writers." In Bruce King, ed., *West Indian Literature*, 2nd ed., pp. 89–101. London and Basingstoke: Macmillan Press Ltd., 1995.

King, Bruce, ed. *West Indian Literature*. 2nd ed. London, Basingstoke: Macmillan Press Ltd., 1995.

Lalla, Barbara. *Defining Jamaican Fiction: Marronage and the Discourse of Survival*. Tuscaloosa and London: University of Alabama Press, 1996.

Lamming, George. "The Peasant Roots of the West Indian Novel." In Edward Baugh, ed., *Critics on Caribbean Literature*, pp. 24–26. London: George Allen and Unwin, 1978.

MacDermot, Thomas Henry. *Becka's Buckra Baby*, with Foreword. Kingston: The All Jamaica Library, 1903.

Mais, Roger. *The Hills Were Joyful Together*, with an Introduction by Daphne Morris. London, Kingston, Port of Spain: Heinemann, 1981.

————. *The Three Novels of Roger Mais*, with an Introduction by the Honourable Norman W. Manley, M. M., Q. C. Kingston: Sangster's Bookstores, in association with Jonathan Cape Ltd., 1966, 1970.

Mordecai, Pamela. *From Our Yard*. Kingston: Institute of Jamaica Publications, 1987.

Mordecai, Pamela, and Mervyn Morris. *Jamaica Woman*. London: Heinemann, 1985.

Mordecai, Pamela, and Betty Wilson. *Her True-True Name: An Anthology of Women's Writing from the Caribbean*. London: Heinemann, 1987.

Mordecai, Pamela, and Betty Wilson, eds. *The Literary Review*. Special Issue: Women Poets of the Caribbean. Madison, NJ: Fairleigh Dickinson University, 1992.

Morris, Daphne. "Introduction." In Roger Mais, *The Hills Were Joyful Together*. London, Kingston, Port of Spain: Heinemann, 1981.

Morris, Mervyn. "Contending Values: The Prose Fiction of Claude McKay." *Jamaica Journal* 9, nos. 2–3 (1975): 36–42.

————. *Examination Centre*. London, Port of Spain: New Beacon Press, 1992.

————. "On Reading Louise Bennett, Seriously." *Jamaica Journal* 1, no. 1 (1967): 69–74.

————. Review of *A Quality of Violence* in "Books and Writer." *Jamaica Journal* 25, no. 2 (1994): 61–62.

O'Callaghan, Evelyn. "Rediscovering the Natives of My Person: A Review of Erna Brodber, Jane and Louisa Will Soon Come Home." *Jamaica Journal* 16, no. 3 (1983): 61–63.

————. "Surviving in No-Man's Land: *The Pagoda* by Patricia Powell." In *Ma-Comère* 2, pp. 172–175. Harrisonburg, VA: Association of Caribbean Women Writers and Scholars and James Madison University, 1999.

————. *Woman Version: Theoretical Approaches to West Indian Fiction by Women*. London and Basingstoke: Macmillan Press Ltd., 1993.

Patterson, Richard F. *Caribbean Passages: A Critical Perspective on New Fiction from the West Indies*. Boulder, CO, London: Lynne Rienner Publishers Inc., 1998.

Ramchand, Kenneth, and Cecil Gray. *West Indian Poetry*. London: Longman, 1971.

Reid, Victor Stafford. "Vic Reid in His Own Words: An Interview Conducted by Edward Baugh." *Jamaica Journal* 20, no. 4 (1988): 2–9.

Scott, Dennis. *Dreadwalk*. London, Port of Spain: New Beacon Press, 1982.

————. *Strategies*. Kingston: Sandberry Press, 1989.

Scott, Michael. *Tom Cringle's Log*. (Reprint.) London: J. M. Dent & Sons, 1969.

Smilowitz, Erica. "Una Marson: Woman Before Her Time." *Jamaica Journal* 16, no. 2 (1983): 62–68.

CHAPTER 8: MUSIC

Barrow, Steve, and Peter Dalton. *Reggae: The Rough Guide*. London: Penguin, 1997.

Beckford, George. "Institutional Racism in Jamaica." *Kingston Daily News*, May 8, 1977.

Bilby, Kenneth M. "The Caribbean as a Musical Region." In Sidney W. Mintz and Sally Price, eds., *Caribbean Contours.* Baltimore: Johns Hopkins Press, 1985.

Brathwaite, Kamau. *The Development of Creole Society in Jamaica, 1770–1820.* London: Oxford University Press, 1974. (Reprint.) Kingston: Ian Randle Publications, 2000.

Brodber, Erna. "Black Consciousness and Popular Music in Jamaica in the 1960s and 1970s." *Caribbean Quarterly* 31, no. 2 (June 1985).

Chang, Kevin O'Brien, and Wayne Chen. *Reggae Routes: The Story of Jamaican Music.* Philadelphia: Temple University Press, 1998.

Jahn, Brian, and Tom Weber. *Reggae Island: Jamaican Music in the Digital Age.* Kingston: Kingston Publishers, 1992.

Larkin, Colin. *The Virgin Encyclopedia of Reggae.* London: Virgin Books, 1998.

Lewin, Olive. "Traditional Jamaican Music: Mento." *Jamaica Journal* 26, no. 3 (1998).

———. "Traditional Music in Jamaica." *Caribbean Quarterly* 29, no 1 (March 1983).

O'Gorman, Pam. "An Approach to the Study of Jamaican Popular Music." *Jamaica Journal* 6, no. 7 (1972).

Senior, Olive. *The A–Z of Jamaican Heritage.* Kingston: Heinemann Educational Books (Caribbean) Ltd. and The Gleaner Company Ltd., 1983.

Witmer, Robert. "Kingston's Popular Music Culture—Neo-colonialism to Nationalism." *Jamaica Journal* 22, no. 1 (February–April 1989).

CHAPTER 9: PERFORMING ARTS

Allsopp, Richard. *Dictionary of Caribbean English Usage.* Oxford: Oxford University Press, 1996.

Banham, Martin, Errol Hill, and George Woodyard, eds. *The Cambridge Guide to African and Caribbean Theatre.* Cambridge: Cambridge University Press, 1994.

Barnett, Sheila. "Jonkonnu—Pitch Patch." *Jamaica Journal* no. 43 (1979): 19–39.

Baxter, Ivy. *The Arts of an Island.* Metuchen, NJ: The Scarecrow Press, 1970.

Bennett, Louise. Interview with Dennis Scott. *Caribbean Quarterly* 14, nos. 2–3. (1968).

Bennett, Wycliffe. "The Jamaican Theatre." *Jamaica Journal* 8, nos. 2–3 (1974): 3–9.

Bettelheim, Judith. "Jamaican Jonkonnu and Related Caribbean Festivals." In M. Graham and Franklin Knight, eds., *Africa and the Caribbean*, pp. 80–100. Baltimore: Johns Hopkins University Press, 1980.

———. "The Jonkonnu Festival." *Jamaica Journal*, 10 no. 2 (1976): 20–27.

Brathwaite, Kamau. "Ala(r)ms of God—Konnu and Carnival in the Caribbean." *Caribbean Quarterly* 36, nos. 3–4 (1990): 77–107.

Ford Smith, Honor. "Sistren: Exploring Women's Problems Through Drama." *Jamaica Journal*, 19, no. 1 (1986): 2–11.

Fowler, Henry. "A History of Theatre in Jamaica." *Jamaica Journal* 2, no. 1 (1968): 53–59.

Gloudon, Barbara. "The Hon. Louise Bennett, O.J.: Fifty Years of Laughter." *Jamaica Journal* 19, no. 3 (1986): 2–10.

———. "A Survey of the Performing Arts." *Jamaica Journal* 6, no. 7 (1972): 55–56.

Graham, M., and Franklin Knight, eds. *Africa and the Caribbean.* Baltimore: Johns Hopkins University Press, 1980.

Hill, Errol. "The Emergence of a National Drama in the West Indies." *Caribbean Quarterly* 18, no. 4 (1972): 9–40.

———. *The Jamaican Stage 1655–1900: Profile of a Colonial Theatre.* Amherst: The University of Massachussetts Press, 1992.

Lewin, Olive. "Folk Music of Jamaica: An Outline for Classification." *Jamaica Journal* 4, no. 2 (1970): 68–72.

Long, Richard. "Rex Nettleford and the National Dance Theatre Company." *Caribbean Quarterly* 43, no. 2 (1997): 69–73.

Milner, Harry. "The Theatrical Year." *Pepperpot Annual* (1952): 20. Cited in Ivy Baxter, ed., *The Arts of an Island.* Metuchen, NJ: The Scarecrow Press, 1970.

Nettleford, Rex. " 'The Crossing'—The Editor Interviews Rex Nettleford." *Jamaica Journal* no. 43 (1979): 2–11

———. *Dance Jamaica: Cultural Definition and Artistic Discovery: The National Dance Theatre Company of Jamaica. 1962–1983.* New York: Grove Press, 1985.

———. "Fifty Years of the Jamaican Pantomime." *Jamaica Journal* 24, no. 3 (1992): 2–9.

———. "The Jamaica National Dance Company." *Jamaica Journal* 2, no. 3 (1968): 31–37.

———. "Pocomania in Dance-Theatre." *Jamaica Journal* 3, no. 2 (1969): 21–24.

———. "Rex Nettleford Talks to Shirley Maynair Burke About Islands." *Jamaica Journal* 19, no. 3 (1986): 13–19.

Omotoso, Kole. *The Theatrical into Theatre: A Study of the Drama and Theatre of the English-Speaking Caribbean.* London, Port of Spain: New Beacon Books, 1982.

Rhyman, Cheryl. "The Jamaica Heritage in Dance: Developing a Traditional Typology." *Jamaica Journal* 44 (1980): 3–14.

———. "Jonkonnu, a Neo-African Form." *Jamaica Journal* 17, no. 1 (1984): 24–25.

Seaga, Edward. "Revival Cults in Jamaica: Notes toward a Sociology of Religion." *Jamaica Journal* 3, no. 2 (June 1969): 3–13.

Wilmot, Swithin. "The Politics of Protest in Free Jamaica—The John Canoe Christmas Riots, 1840 and 1841." *Caribbean Quarterly* 36, nos. 3–4 (1990): 65–75.

Wright, Richardson. *Revels in Jamaica 1682–1838*. Kingston: Bolivar Press, 1986.

Wynter, Sylvia. "Jonkonnu in Jamaica: Towards the Interpretation of Folk Dance as Cultural Process." *Jamaica Journal* 4, no. 2 (1970): 34–48.

CHAPTER 10: VISUAL ARTS

Anderson, Kay. "John Dunkley: An Analysis of Three Paintings." *Jamaica Journal* 24, no. 2 (1991): 20–23.

Archer-Straw, Petrine, and Kim Robinson. *Jamaican Art: An Overview—with a Focus on Fifty Artists*. Kingston: Kingston Publisher Ltd., 1990.

Baugh, Cecil, and Laura Tanna. *Baugh: Jamaica's Master Potter*. Kingston: Selectco Publications Ltd., 1986.

Beshoff, Pamela. "Namba Roy: Maroon Artist and Writer." *Jamaica Journal* 16, no. 3 (1983): 34–38.

Binney, Marcus, John Harris, Kit Martin, and Margaret Curtin. *Jamaica's Heritage, an Untapped Resource*. Kingston: The Mill Press, 1991.

Boxer, David. "Edna Manley: Sculptor." *Jamaica Journal* 18, no. 1 (1985): 25–40.

———. "Jamaican Art 1922–1982." In David Boxer and Veerle Poupeye, eds., *Modern Jamaican Art*, pp. 11–28. Kingston: Ian Randle Publishers, 1998.

Boxer, David (interviewed by Shirley Maynier Burke). "The Intuitive Eye—A Heritage Recalled." *Jamaica Journal* no. 44 (1980): 16–24.

Boxer, David, and Veerle Poupeye, eds. *Modern Jamaican Art*. Kingston: Ian Randle Publishers, 1998.

Dunkley, Cassie. "Life of John Dunkley (1891–1947) (National Gallery Exhibition 1977)." *Jamaica Journal* 11, nos. 1–2 (1977): 82–84.

Escoffery, Gloria. "Acrobats and Artists." *Jamaica Journal* 19, no. 1 (1986): 49–55.

———. "The Impact of Nationhood: The Art World of the Early Sixties." *Jamaica Journal* 19, no. 3 (1986): 43–49.

———. "A Personal Response to 'Fifteen Intuitives' at the National Gallery." *Jamaica Journal* 20, no. 4 (1987–1988): 10–18.

Hendriks, Anna Maria. "On the Eve of a New Era." *Jamaica Journal* 24, no. 1 (1991): 23–31.

Henriques, Anna. *The Book of Mechtilde*. New York: Alfred A. Knopf, 1997.

In Tribute to David Boxer: Twenty Years at the National Gallery of Jamaica: 1975–1995. Kingston: Institute of Jamaica Publications and the National Gallery of Jamaica, 1995.

Long, Edward. *The History of Jamaica*, 3 vols. London, 1774.

Manley, Edna. "Henry Daley, the Artist." *Jamaica Journal* 2, no. 4 (1968): 33–36.

Manley, Rachel, ed. *Edna Manley: The Diaries*. Kingston: Heinemann Publishers (Caribbean) Ltd., 1989.

Poupeye, Veerle. *Caribbean Art*. London: Thames and Hudson, 1998.

———. "Contemporary Jamaican Art." In David Boxer and Veerle Poupeye, eds., *Modern Jamaican Art*, pp. 29–38. Kingston: Ian Randle Publishers, 1998.

———. "Garveyism and Garvey Iconography in the Visual Arts of Jamaica Part 2." *Jamaica Journal* 24, no. 2 (1992): 24–33.

Slesin, Suzanne, et al. *Caribbean Style*. New York: Clarkson Potter Publishers, 1985, 1994.

Smith-McCrea, Rosalie. "Fiction, Personality and Property: A Jamaican Colonial Representation in Miniature." In *In Tribute to David Boxer: Twenty Years at the National Gallery of Jamaica: 1975–1995*. Kingston: Institute of Jamaica Publications and the National Gallery of Jamaica, 1995.

Todd, Edwin. "Abstract Art, the Avant Garde and Jamaica." *Jamaica Journal* 4, no. 4 (1970): 27–34.

———. "Dunkley." *Jamaica Journal* 2, no. 3 (1968): 44–47.

Voorthuis, Jacob. "What Makes Jamaican Architecture So Special?" *The Jamaican* (1998).

Watson, Osmond. "Osmond Watson Talks to Alex Gradussov." *Jamaica Journal* 3, no. 3 (1969): 47–53.

Index

About the Authors

MARTIN MORDECAI, a former Jamaican career diplomat and civil servant, now resides in Toronto and is a freelance writer and photographer, and a businessman.

PAMELA MORDECAI is an independent scholar and poet who has written over a dozen books in language arts for high school students and has edited anthologies of Caribbean literature. She is publisher of Sandberry Press, a small press devoted to Caribbean literary publishing, which operates out of Kingston, Jamaica and Toronto, Canada.

Edwards Brothers Malloy
Thorofare, NJ USA
January 14, 2013